SECRETS
OF THE
MARKETING
MASTERS

SECRETS
OF THE
MARKETING MASTERS

What the Best Marketers Do
—And Why It Works

DICK MARTIN

AMACOM

American Management Association
New York • Atlanta • Brussels • Chicago • Mexico City • San Francisco
Shanghai • Tokyo • Toronto • Washington, D.C.

Special discounts on bulk quantities of AMACOM books are available to corporations, professional associations, and other organizations. For details, contact Special Sales Department, AMACOM, a division of American Management Association, 1601 Broadway, New York, NY 10019.
Tel: 212-903-8316. Fax: 212-903-8083.
E-mail: specialsls@amanet.org
Website: www.amacombooks.org/go/specialsales
To view all AMACOM titles go to: www.amacombooks.org

This publication is designed to provide accurate and authoritative information in regard to the subject matter covered. It is sold with the understanding that the publisher is not engaged in rendering legal, accounting, or other professional service. If legal advice or other expert assistance is required, the services of a competent professional person should be sought.

Library of Congress Cataloging-in-Publication Data

Martin, Dick, 1946–
    Secrets of the marketing masters : what the best marketers do and why it works / Dick Martin.
        p.   cm.
    Includes bibliographical references and index.
    ISBN-13: 978-0-8144-0943-5 (hardcover)
    ISBN-10: 0-8144-0943-1 (hardcover)
    1. Marketing.   2. Success in business.   I. Title.

HF5415.M3246   2009
658.8—dc22

2009004050

Printing number

10 9 8 7 6 5 4 3 2 1

Dedicated to my wife and partner, Ginny,

and to my children, Chris, Liz, and Juli.

Most people want their kids

to do better than they did.

I always wanted my kids to *be* better than me.

The secret to that, I discovered,

is marrying someone better than yourself.

I succeeded on all counts.

Trademarked Terms in *Secrets of the Marketing Masters*

Abercrombie & Fitch
Accenture
Actonel
Activia Light Yogurt
Aeron chair
Air Jordan
Al Fresco
Altoids
Always
Amazon
American Express
American Girl
Anthropologie
Apple
Arm & Hammer
Asacol
AsianAve
AT&T
Aunt Jemima
Avon
Axe deodorant

babyGap
Bacardi
Baileys
Banana Republic
Barbie
Bath & Body Works
Becton, Dickinson (BD)
Belvedere
Best Buy
Betty Crocker
Big Mac
Bisquick Shake 'n' Pour
Biz360
BK Stacker
BL Lime
Black & Decker
BlackBerry
BlackPlanet
BMW
Booz Allen Hamilton
Bristol-Myers Squibb
Budweiser
Burger King
Burton Snowboards
Bushmills
Butterball
BzzAgent

Cabela's
Campbell's
Camry Hybrid
Captain Morgan
Carl's Jr.
Caterpillar
Charmin
Cheerios
Chelsea Milling Company
Chevy Tahoe
Chloé
Chrysler
Circuit City
Ciroc
Cisco Systems
Citigroup
Clairol
Clamato
ClearRx
Clorox
Coca-Cola
Comcast
ConAgra

Constellation Wines
Corona
Courvoisier
CoverGirl
Craigslist
Crayola
Credit Suisse
Crest Whitestrips
Crocs
Crown Royal
CVS

Dacron
DanActive Probiotic Dairy Drinks
Dannon
Dawn
Dell Computer
Del Monte
Delta
DeSoto
DeWalt
Diageo
Digital Equipment
Disney
Dove
Doritos
Double Croissan'wich
Downy Wrinkle Releaser
Dreamweaver
Dunkin' Donuts
DuPont

eBay
Egg Beaters
Enormous Omelet Sandwich

Facebook
FaithBase
Febreze NOTICEables
FedEx
Fiber One Chewy Bars
Fireworks
Fiskars
Flash
Flickr
Folgers
Ford Focus
Four Seasons
FreeHand
Fresh & Easy Smart Box
Frito-Lay

Gain
GapKids
Geek Squad
General Electric
General Mills
General Motors
Ginsu
Gleem
GlobalFluency
Gmail
GO International
Goldfish
Goodwill
Google
Gruma
Guinness

H&M
H&R Block
Harrah's
Harley-Davidson
Hebrew National
Healthy Choice
Heidrick & Struggles
Hearty & Delicious
Herbal Essences
Hewlett-Packard
Hill-Rom
Hilton
Home Depot
Honda
Huggies

IBM
IDEO
IKEA
InnoCentive
Intuit
iPhone
iPod
iTunes

J&B
J.Crew
Jaguar
JCPenney
JetBlue Airways
John Deere
Johnnie Walker
Johnson & Johnson
Jones Soda
Jose Cuervo
Just Ask a Woman

Kelley Blue Book
Kellogg's
Kibbles 'n Bits Brushing Bites
Kimberly-Clark
Kiwi
Kmart
Kraft

Lee One True Fit Jeans
Lego Mindstorm
Levi's Totally Slimming Jeans
Litton Industries
Lycra

M&M's
Mac
Macromedia
Macy's
Maidenform
Marshall Field's
Mattel
McDonald's
Mercedes-Benz
Method
Metro7
Michelin
Microsoft
Miller Chill
Millstone
Motorola
Mr. Clean Magic Eraser
My DNA Fragrance
MySpace

Nabisco
Nescafé
Nestlé
Netflix
Net Promoter
Nice 'n Easy Perfect 10
Nike
NineSigma
Nissan Sentra
Nokia
Nordstrom
Nortel
Nottingham•Spirk

Ogilvy & Mather Worldwide
Oil of Olay
Olay Regenerist
Old Navy
Oldsmobile
Old Spice High Endurance Hair & Body
1–800-FLOWERS
1–800-MATTRES
Oracle
Oreo BK Sundae Shake
Orlon

PAM
Pampers Feel 'n Learn
Pantene
Patagonia
PepsiCo
Pillsbury
Pitney Bowes
Pontiac G6
Porsche
PowerPoint
Pringles
Prius
Proctor & Gamble (P&G)

QuickBooks
Quicken

Range Rover
Reebok
Rolex
Rolodex

SAP
Sara Lee Corporation
Saturn
Schick Quattro
Seagate Technology
Seagram's
Secret
Sheraton
Sherwin-Williams
Simply Shabby Chic
Singapore Airlines
Smirnoff
Snap-on tools
Snausages Breakfast Bites
Soft and Smooth
Sony
Southwest Airlines
Sports Tracker

Staples
Starbucks
Starwood
Studio
Sun Microsystems
Swash
Swiffer

Tampax
Tanqueray
Target
Tesco
The Body Shop
The Gap
The Limited
3Com
3M
3volution
Tide Clean White
Tide Simple Pleasures
Tide Triple Action
Tiffany's
Timberland
Time Warner
TiVo
TMZ
Toyota
Toys"R"Us
Trader Joe's
Tremor
Treo
Trim Flixx
Twist-n-Pour
Twitter
Tylenol

Uncle Ben
Unilever
uPlayMe
Urban Outfitters
USAA

Veg-O-Matic
Verizon
Versace
Victoria's Secret
Vioxx
Virgin
Volkswagen Golf
Volvo

Wachovia
Wal-Mart
Wang
Warner Music Group
Wendy's
Whirlpool
Whole Foods Market
Whopper
Wikipedia
Woolco
Wrigley

Xbox
Xerox

Yahoo!
Yoplait Go-Gurt
YouTube

Zappos
Zara

CONTENTS

SECRETS
OF THE
MARKETING
MASTERS

SECRET SAUCE
OF THE
MARKETING MASTERS

One Part Internal Alignment

One Part External Focus

One Part Customer Connection
(Minimum 70 percent emotional content)

No Artificial Additives

Meets 100 percent Daily Growth Requirements.
Builds strong brands for long-term growth.

Specially formulated for marketing professionals
and the people they serve. Not tested on animals.
Environmentally friendly and recyclable.
Warning: Habit Forming.

SECRETS OF THE MARKETING MASTERS

"The purpose of business is to create and keep a customer.
Only two functions do this: marketing and innovation.
All the rest are costs."

—PETER DRUCKER

WHAT THIS BOOK IS ABOUT

The late business guru Peter Drucker put marketing at the center of a business's purpose, but that center turns out to be peppered with blind alleys and potholes.

What makes some marketers successful while others are the fruit flies of the "C-suite," nuisances who fill the air with buzzing but don't accomplish much in their blessedly short lives? Sadly, in recent years, the fruit flies of marketing have been multiplying.[1] According to executive recruiter Spencer Stuart, chief marketing officers last only about two years. Since it takes almost that long for most marketing campaigns to get off the ground, it seems that the average chief marketing officer has one—maybe two—times at bat. By contrast, the average rookie baseball player can look forward to more than five and half years in uniform.[2]

No one can bat a thousand, but a small number of marketers would be on anyone's All-Star team. I call them the masters of marketing. They sometimes get their names in the paper. If, like some of the people in this book, you work for an industry giant such as Procter & Gamble, Unilever, General Electric, Diageo, Microsoft, Fidelity Investments or American Express, it's hard not to attract the media's attention. But the marketing masters are not necessarily "superstars" whose names bloom brightly in the media before fading away. Some of them work quietly behind the scenes. They all tend to stay in one place longer than average. And they seem to have cracked the code on helping their companies achieve consistent profitable growth. What's their secret? That's the question this book answers in terms that apply to marketers of all stripes, whether "chief" or humble "brave."

WHO ARE THE MARKETING MASTERS?

As far as I know, no one has yet had the nerve to put "marketing master" on his or her business card. And I'd look askance at anyone who claimed the title out loud. If you have to say you're a marketing master, you're probably not. But I know they're out there, and I set out to find some of them.

My first stop was at the door of the top executive recruiters—the headhunters who *created* the title of chief marketing officer. Some cynics say their purpose was merely to inflate the value of their searches; others claim it was to give the head of marketing title parity with other executives in the so-called "C-suite," for example, chief executive officer, chief operating officer, chief financial officer, and the like.[3]

Whatever their motives, the executive recruiters I spoke to made it clear that more than extra feathers come with the designation of chief marketing officer. Jane Stevenson, who leads the marketing practice for the Heidrick & Struggles recruiting firm, says CEOs have different expectations of their top marketers today. "Marketing used to be all about advertising," she says. "In the past, some companies would house the 'creative geniuses' of marketing in padded cells, apart from line leaders. Today, with business heads more stressed than ever, they're looking for business partners. Advertising is a much smaller part of the equation."

Interestingly, the heads of the major advertising associations, who were my next stop, agreed. For example, Bob Liodice, president of the Association of National Advertisers, which bills itself as the voice of the marketing community, says "I'd get rid of 'advertising' in our name if I could, because it creates the connotation of a one-way mono-logue. Marketing is a platform for creating customer connections. It's all about dialogue." As head of the American Association of Advertising Agencies from 1994 until his retirement in 2008, Burtch Drake was Liodice's counterpart in the ad agency world. "Every major ad agency realizes its role is changing," he told me, "but few have figured out what to do about it."

In fact, the ad agency heads I spoke to thought marketing has changed more in the last nine years than in the previous ninety. For example, Shelly Lazarus, chairperson of Ogilvy & Mather Worldwide, thinks that marketing is in its infancy again. "All the old formulas need to be rethought," she says. "New technologies have unleashed changes in people's behavior. They have different habits, whether they're shopping, working, or just hanging out at home."

MARKETING REDEFINED

The academics and consultants I interviewed also describe a function trying to redefine itself. Donovan Neale-May is president of the GlobalFluency communications firm that also operates the nonprofit CMO Council, which he founded. Over the years, he has worked with hundreds of the world's leading marketers and has seen the shift in their responsibilities firsthand. "Successful marketing executives today play a role broader than just leading the marketing organization," he says. "They help drive innovation and provide strategic vision."

At some companies, marketing is the engine of innovation; at others, it provides critical fuel and direction. But everywhere there seems to be a broad consensus that, whereas marketing used to be largely about advertising, now it's expected to influence, if not encompass, the entire product realization cycle, from development to service.[4] Modern marketing is just as central to a business's purpose as Drucker suspected.

"Marketing is all about growing the company by harnessing the elements of the business in a profound way," says Heidrick & Struggles's Stevenson. "In fact, some of the best marketers I know don't even have a marketing background. The CMO of Wachovia came from treasury services, the CMOs of Target, Starbucks, Citigroup, and

Best Buy all have broad management experience that was originally outside of marketing."

THE CANDIDATES

So, two dozen or so interviews in, it was pretty clear I wasn't looking for the secrets of this generation's "Mad Men and Mad Women." The big ad agencies had not only moved off Madison Avenue, they no longer show up as often in corporate boardrooms and executive suites. The intellectual capital of the marketing world seems to have moved to the client side.

With that in mind, I compiled a long list of candidates—people who had attracted the attention of these industry leaders for their marketing savvy. Some were the usual suspects who appeared on nearly everyone's list because of their high profile and record of accomplishment. Others were relatively unknown, doing exceptional work in quiet obscurity, often for companies struggling to recover from reverses on someone else's watch.

I spoke to as many of these individuals as I could, and to people who had worked with them. I read about them and their companies. And in the end, I developed a list of about a dozen people who are clearly masters of marketing. They ranged from the well known—for example, John Hayes at American Express and Beth Comstock at General Electric—to the lower profile—for example, Lauren Flaherty at Nortel and Alessandro Manfredi at Unilever. Some are entrepreneurs—Steve Knox at Tremor and Dan Pelson at uPlayMe and the Warner Music Group—while others have worked at one large company for most of their professional life—Mich Mathews at Microsoft and Michael Francis at Target. Some are technically not chief marketing officers, but CEOs who still cast a large shadow over the function that made their companies so successful—Tony Hsieh at Zappos and Robert Stephens at The Geek Squad. Some are relatively new to the function—Jon Iwata at IBM—while others have spent decades in nearly every marketing discipline—Rob Malcolm at Diageo.

By the time this book is published, some may have moved on. Marketing talent is in such short supply, its masters are in great demand. Some may have jumped to bigger jobs. Some may have been pushed out because they failed to meet heightened expectations. And some may have been reorganized out of a job as their company hunkered down in a declining economy. Others may have simply decided to cash in and pursue other passions. Just as I turned the manuscript for this book over to my editor, Procter & Gamble's Jim Stengel announced that he was retiring at age 53 to devote the balance of his professional life to "promote marketing as a positive force in the world."

Stengel, a twenty-five-year veteran of P&G, with seven years in the top marketing job, was an important player in the company's turnaround of recent years. He also has an almost evangelical belief in marketing's capacity to improve people's lives. At first, the notion that marketing can make people's lives better sounds naively pious at best and a clumsy attempt at misdirection at worst. Veg-O-Matic food processors and Ginsu knives made their marketers' lives better for sure, but their contribution to genuine consumer happiness is arguable. And while erectile dysfunction potions fill an important need, it's probably narrower than its marketing would suggest.

MARKETING ON PURPOSE

But that's precisely Stengel's point—if marketers were to think more deeply about their higher purpose, it would influence what they do, from product conception to promotion. "Think of Pringle's higher purpose as bringing a little unexpected joy into people's lives," he says, "and it affects everything you do from its formulation to its packaging and its promotion." A product's higher purpose isn't necessarily high-minded, but it's deep-rooted. "Every great brand started for a reason," he says. "Purpose-based marketing is about getting back in touch with that idea. When that happens, you see a different level of performance, a more personal commitment to doing things better." He's seen it happen within his own company and elsewhere, as we will see.

But purpose-driven marketing requires a level of customer intimacy that doesn't come naturally to marketers who work from secondhand briefs and shopworn strategies. In a landmark speech to the American Association of Advertising Agencies in 2004, Stengel declared existing marketing models "obsolete" and gave the industry a grade of C−. That restless dissatisfaction with the status quo, combined with keen intellectual curiosity, characterizes all the masters of marketing and is surely among the secrets of their success. For that matter, they're also uniformly intelligent, energetic, and creative. But the secrets revealed in this book aren't hiding in such plain sight. In fact, many of them aren't even obvious to the marketing masters themselves.

WHAT'S SO SECRET?

Spend time with the masters of marketing, and what strikes you first is that they are part of an organizational ecosystem, an institutional process that is tailored to the particular needs and culture of their company. In some cases, they helped shape that process; in others, they inherited it. But in almost every case, they are the source of its momentum and vitality. They keep it rolling and adapting to new situations and new challenges. The scale and scope of their responsibilities may differ, but the fundamental principles they follow can be learned and applied across organizations of every size and type, whether they serve individuals or enterprises.

So what are these secrets? I've organized them into three groups, corresponding to the three parts of this book. The first group of secrets is so fundamental, it suggested the opening section, "Think Inside Out."

Figure Out How You Fit in Your Company's Business Model

Wal-Mart, Target, Microsoft, and General Electric have different marketing disciplines because they have different ways of making money. The masters of marketing know how they fit into their company's business model and, based on that understanding, they develop a personal brand that builds trust with their C-suite colleagues. They treat their colleagues as internal customers, but what they bring to the relationship, in addition to their functional skills, is the voice of their external customer. They're in sync with the company's culture, but they also have the credibility and support to help it evolve to meet changing needs. And they focus on results that matter, sharing their goals, accomplishments, and failures with their colleagues in equal measure.

Which brings us to the group of secrets underlying the second part of this book, "Think Outside In."

Connect to Your CEO's Highest-Order Goal—Profitable Growth

The masters of marketing not only understand how to align themselves with their CEO's expectations, but also how to shape them. Some CEOs want the head of marketing to churn out ads and brochures for the line organizations. Others want the marketing chief to lead the brand police, slapping wrists when the company logo is misused or promotions stray into politically incorrect territory. Some want marketing to create buzz about the company, while the line organizations do the heavy lifting of creating demand. But what all CEOs care about most boils down to one thing—profitable growth. The masters of marketing link everything they do to that goal, translating customer insight into the revenue and profit of business insight.

Finally, the masters of marketing know how to connect with people at an emotional level, circumventing the defense mechanisms that shield them from the onslaught of promotional messages. Indeed, the secrets that inform the final section of this book, "Connect Emotionally," are the exact opposite of trying to drum a message into people's consciousness.

Bring Meaning to the Noisy Confusion of People's Lives

People are increasingly resistant to the ads lobbed at them. According to Yankelovich Partners, 65 percent of consumers feel "constantly bombarded with too much advertising."[5] As one ironic result, little is getting through. Since, by one estimate, the average American is exposed to more than 5,000 commercial messages[6] in the 1,000 minutes he or she is awake every day, that shouldn't be too surprising.

No one can actually read, view, and listen to that many messages—there wouldn't be time for anything else. At best, these messages tend to cancel each other out and, at worse, they create an oppressive, noisy environment. As a result, marketing's reputation is at low ebb, with one agency leader even confessing, "Consumers hate us—the marketers and advertisers who invent new ways to spam them online and offline."[7] The trade press was quick to decry such "self-loathing,"[8] but the man had a point. The masters of marketing get it. They know how to connect with people in meaningful, relevant ways by finding the intersection of their product's higher-level purpose and people's deepest needs, desires, and values.

CHALLENGING TIMES

When Burtch Drake retired as head of the American Association of Advertising Agencies, one friend noted that his career spanned the period from three-martini lunches to multiplatform plays. Burtch himself confessed to me that he could sum up the current state of marketing in one word—confused.

Consider these innovations just leaving the lab. Broadband technologies turn televisions into interactive kiosks and put full-motion video on cell phones. Two-dimensional "QR" codes on supermarket products and in store windows connect cell phones to websites. Radio-frequency identification tags in product packaging cue tailored messages to appear on shopping cart screens when people lift a product from the shelf—"Want jelly with that peanut butter?" Cell phones become electronic "wallets" paying for everything from a bus ride in Helsinki to a Big Mac in Tokyo.

Data mining at point of sale floods corporate offices with a tsunami of customer information. New digital media continue to grow like weeds. And the number of media measurement tools, such as ratings, circulation, and ad recall, jumped from slightly over fifty in the 1970s to more than 400 today, including people meters, engagement, and point-of-purchase data. CPM (cost per thousand) metrics are being supplemented or supplanted by new metrics like CTRs (click-through rates).

Just when marketers master the latest acronyms, a new crop sprouts. Every new development is a double-edged sword. Globalization opens new markets, but also creates new competitors. New technologies feed product innovation, but nothing stays proprietary for very long. Closed markets open, regulations are eased, but instant communication puts every corporation in a glass house and arms their critics with greater influence, if not bricks to throw. Affluence spreads, but pricing pressures mount. Marketers have more ways to reach customers, but customers have greater control over how, when, and even *if* they're reached.

Meanwhile, senior marketing leaders also have to cope with silos within their own companies. Not only do they have trouble winning the cooperation of sales, finance, and operations, they often find themselves arbitrating between shops under their direct control—for example, between market research and communications. Many companies even have competing marketing organizations at headquarters and in business units or regions.

Consulting firm Accenture found that marketing is not held in high regard by a large majority of executives at organizations worldwide. When asked to rate the contribution of eleven corporate functions to their company's success, just 23 percent of executives said marketing makes a "very significant contribution," compared with 61 percent for sales and 43 percent for customer service.

And while marketers cope with all these challenges, their bosses push for more accountability. Department store magnate John Wanamaker might have been willing to accept that half his advertising was worthless, but today's CEO wants to know exactly what he or she is getting for his or her marketing investment. And the CEO wants it in the dollars and cents of sales and profits, not fuzzy brand-speak. In the absence of such data, many CEOs don't know what to do with marketing.

Bill Watkins, CEO of Seagate Technology, told the *Wall Street Journal*, "I watched someone propose a $20 million marketing campaign and we just vomited all over him. Two days later, my CFO and I approved a $950 million research-and-development budget in about 15 minutes. But to spend $20 million on marketing? We just don't know how to do that. It just drives us nuts."[9]

Watkins is not alone. The Fortune 100 companies have a combined 1,200 board members. Only thirteen are marketers. That's about one percent. John Quelch, of the Harvard Business School, estimates that only one-third of boards regularly see even the most basic marketing data.[10] Several executives who serve on prominent Fortune 50 boards told me that they have never been in a meeting where marketing programs were specifically tied to revenue.

"Boards and even CEOs struggle with the connection between marketing and results," one board member told me, "because they don't understand and nobody explains it." Boards, with few exceptions, are reactive to marketing and far less likely to ask, "How much should we do?" than "How much can we afford?" Worse, under every board member's pinstripe suit is a metaphorical T-shirt that reads, "I don't know anything about advertising, but . . .." If they focus on marketing at all, it's usually on its upstream manifestations such as the TV commercials that caught their spouse's attention.

CHIEF MAYBE OFFICER?

According to one CMO who has been living with all these challenges, "It makes for a deadly cocktail of high expectations, resistance, and complexity."[11] Indeed, CMOs at companies large and small have been succumbing to that lethal potion. Spencer Stuart's Greg Welch says forty of the country's one hundred biggest consumer companies changed their top marketing officer in 2006, only three by promotion. And in the past three years, seven out of ten companies have reorganized their marketing departments.[12] Things have gotten so bad that marketing weekly *Advertising Age* editorialized: "Perhaps we should just call for the end of the CMO position. . . . At the very least, let's change the title to chief maybe officer—as in, maybe he'll stick around; maybe he won't. Maybe her new initiatives will be well-received and move the needle; maybe they won't."[13]

Even if mostly tongue in cheek, such a Kervorkian approach is probably premature, but it does give one pause. Especially considering that, according to the Institute of International Research, senior executives in the United States consider marketing the most important expertise required of the next generation of business leaders.[14]

In an era of consumer uncertainty and corporate insecurity, we are all marketers. Every businessperson plays a role in creating and keeping customers. And whether or not you have the CMO title, you have to deal with the same ambiguity, complexity, and accountability. The good news is that you can learn from the examples—and even the mistakes—of others. The secrets of the marketing masters are within your grasp.

PART ONE

Think Inside Out

Figure Out How You Fit in Your Company's Business Model

*"Marketing is far too important to leave
to the Marketing Department."*

—DAVID PACKARD

RUN MARKETING LIKE A PROFESSIONAL SERVICE

"Gettin' good players is easy.
Gettin' 'em to play together is the hard part."

—CASEY STENGEL

Lauren Flaherty lived among scores of other IBM executives in Darien, Connecticut, and, like them, she had driven herself to Westchester airport hundreds of times. But for the first time in twenty-five years, she was traveling neither on IBM business nor on a family vacation. In fact, she had left her husband and two children at home. After more than two decades at Big Blue, Flaherty had succumbed to a headhunter's call and was seriously considering moving to another company.

LAUREN FLAHERTY

As IBM vice president of global marketing, Flaherty's name was on several headhunters' lists. She knew both technology and marketing, which in itself is a valuable credential. More intriguingly to CEOs suffering through the burst of the dot-com bubble, she had helped the computer giant through a major transformation in the early 1990s. When CEO Lou Gerstner taught the elephant of a company to dance, she had a major role in the orchestra. Like Gerstner himself, Flaherty is direct, forceful, and stubborn—all of which helped when the chief

3

marketing officer Gerstner installed, Abby Kohnstamm, decided to narrow IBM's roster of ad agencies from more than eighty to one. Under Kohnstamm, Flaherty managed the global brand advertising that resulted, including its iconic "e-business" campaign, and eventually moved through a series of other senior marketing jobs.

Flaherty loved IBM and enjoyed her job. But, "When you do what I do for a living," she says, "you're really attracted by the prospect of taking a company with potential to the next level." That prospect put her on a plane to Chicago to meet with another company's chief executive. He had only had the job himself for about a year and still hadn't moved his family to the company's headquarters city. If that gave Flaherty pause, she didn't show it.

TURNAROUND CANDIDATE

The company itself had recently sold its million-square-foot corporate campus, complete with 2.5 kilometers of walking trails, basketball court, Zen garden, and indoor climbing wall in Toronto's suburbs and moved down Canada's Highway 427 to an industrial park on the outskirts of the city. About seven miles from the airport, the company's new headquarters was a boxy eleven-story building that might have been an IBM warehouse. In fact, the matching building next door was a food warehouse. The company was Nortel and it's a toss-up whether the "potential" Flaherty saw was the product of her optimism or of her supreme confidence.

Once a high-tech darling, Nortel had suffered more than most through the bursting of the dot-com bubble and the industry meltdown that followed. Nortel's previous CEO and CFO had been charged with accounting fraud and fired. It had laid off two-thirds of its workforce, paid $2.5 billion to settle a shareowner lawsuit, and seen its market capitalization plummet to one-fiftieth of its peak just six years earlier. The new CEO, a veteran of GE and Motorola, was changing out most of the company's top leadership, and he was looking for a world-class chief marketing officer.

Flaherty was intrigued. On the surface, she thought, Nortel and IBM seemed to share many characteristics—both were high-tech companies dominated by (largely male) engineers. Both were iconic companies that "had gone off the tracks and had to be rebuilt." Like IBM in the 1990s, Nortel had brought in an outsider to rebuild it. And, as at IBM, marketing would play a big role. Flaherty was excited at the prospect of applying all the lessons she had learned at IBM, this time in the top marketing job. But first she had a few questions.

"What's your marketing budget?" she asked Nortel's CEO. "I don't know," he replied. "I hope you'll tell me."

"Well then," she went on, "how many people are in Nortel's marketing organization?" "Wish I knew," he said. "Could be 500. Could be 3,500." Pause. "Still want the job?"

Flaherty ultimately took the job and even managed to outlast the average CMO in an industry suffering the equivalent of a nuclear winter. But the financial crisis of 2008 pushed Nortel's board to hunker down in its three most viable business units, eliminating most corporate staff positions, including the chiefs of technology, sales, service, and marketing. Some analysts suspected the move was intended to make it a more attractive acquisition target. In any case, within two months, in early 2009, the company filed for bankruptcy protection. But even though Nortel's transformation was less successful than IBM's, marketing executives can still draw a number of lessons from Flaherty's experience, whether they are joining a new company or have been in the same place for decades.

GET IN SYNC WITH THE CEO

Chief marketing officers used to promise TV commercials that people would talk about at the country club. In a hypercompetitive world, that's hardly meaningful anymore. Executive recruiter Jane Stevenson has helped some of the nation's leading CEOs find marketing talent. She says, "The biggest complaint CEOs have these days is that marketing isn't practical, isn't focused on relevant business issues—who are our customers, what do they want, how can we get out there first, and how can we differentiate ourselves from the competition."

The Association of National Advertisers' Bob Liodice is continually amazed by how many top marketing people "don't know how to link what they do to what their CEOs care about." Unless it's going to cause some kind of consumer backlash, CEOs most definitely *don't* care about ads and commercials. They care about the sales those ads are supposed to produce. The dullest CEO knows that a brand is more than the company logo, but he or she doesn't really care about the brand as an end in itself. CEOs care about the benefits that are supposed to flow from a strong brand—greater customer loyalty, willingness to pay a premium, getting the benefit of the doubt in tough times, and so forth.

As her interview with Nortel's CEO suggested, the company was essentially a blank slate when Flaherty joined. But she made it her business to understand her boss's expectations and to get aligned with them.

Nortel's CEO understood that the company couldn't possibly grow again until it won permission to put the past behind it. That's how he and Flaherty defined her job. "The work of the CMO has to align to the CEO's objectives," she says. At first, that attitude created some consternation within the company. After she had been in the job for about four months, people inside the company started asking where Nortel's new ad campaign was. "You can't advertise your way out of this situation," she told them. "You have to show sustained positive results."

Flaherty also skipped two other changes new CMOs typically make. Most radically, some change the company's name or at least its logo. Most often, they at least change the ad agency. Flaherty ultimately consolidated the company's advertising at a single agency and she briefly considered the benefits of a name change. But both moves were far down on her list of priorities. Before considering those moves, Flaherty decided to change Nortel's marketing *system*. That meant answering the very first questions she had asked of her new boss— what's the marketing budget and how many people are in the department?

GET THE RIGHT TEAM

The answer to the first question—what does Nortel spend on marketing?—should have been fairly straightforward. Every company codes its expenditures by function. Go to the general ledger, look under "marketing expenses," and there's the answer. It turned out that Nortel's marketing expenditures were consistently 50 percent higher than budgeted. It seems that any of Nortel's 30,000 employees could authorize spending on marketing. Working with the purchasing department, Flaherty quickly reduced the approval authority to fifteen people.

The answer to the second question proved more slippery. Human Resources said there were 2,200 marketing people on the company's organization charts. Finance said that marketing was paying 2,700 people. And the marketing leaders themselves counted 500 people in their organizations. Flaherty brought in some outside consultants to survey the troops. They came to the conclusion that Nortel had 3,500 marketing people, more than 10 percent of the company's total workforce.

Flaherty decided both the consultants and the marketing leaders were right. There *should* have been only 500 people in marketing, but an additional 3,000 people thought they were marketers. Flaherty took those 3,000 people off her books, sending them back to their original organizations, and turned her attention to the 500 with legitimate business cards. She put the entire marketing department through a skills assessment, which led her to replace virtually all her direct reports. "When you're going through a recovery, time is not your friend," she says. "You have to make decisions quickly." Once she had the right people in place, she moved to the development of standardized job descriptions, work processes, and metrics. She partnered with the company's information technology (IT) department to develop an online system for setting goals and tracking results across the entire organization.

MEASURE EVERYTHING

Flaherty is a big believer in measurement. "You have to measure whatever you can and benchmark against best-in-class operations," she says. But the goal is not to document the past. "It's about the headlights, not the taillights," she says. "You've got to measure real time, looking at the future, not historical data." Nortel now uses market tests and real-time analytics to measure everything from customer satisfaction to global communications capabilities.

Unlike in finance, where both the R and the I of return-on-investment calculations are measured in dollars, the "return" on marketing investments is a mix of qualitative and quantitative measures that vary by industry and company. Highly differentiated consumer goods tend to use awareness and image-related forms of measurement, in addition to market share. Capital goods with long purchase cycles rely more on measures of lead generation and customer lifetime value. The key is to identify the few key measures that truly drive the business and to get the whole senior executive team to buy into them. Then make sure that all the *I* is pointed in the right direction and has sufficient critical mass to make a difference where it matters—in the marketplace.

MAKE A DIFFERENCE

In fact, Flaherty launched her first marketing campaign for Nortel in just four cities within each of the company's sales regions—Chicago, London, Mexico City, and Singapore. Flaherty explained the unorthodox approach to a marketing trade magazine:

> When you're at Nortel, and a lot of your competition is bigger and mightier in terms of scale and size and investment, you've got to execute better. When I go into a market I want to go in with full force. I want to go in with my sales team fully enabled, my channel partners fully enabled and engaged, and every cylinder of the marketing engine firing: PR, communications, direct marketing, events, basically a consolidated hit into a focused market. That's just not something that was happening here, and as a result we had a lot of tactics spread very thinly. So up front we did the media relations, the analyst relations, then we started to come in with the sellers and the channel partners to pump the leads and opportunities, then the air cover with the advertising and the events. And what you got was mobilization and momentum, and that's what marketing should be.[1]

Greg Welch, who leads the marketing practice at executive recruiter Spencer Stuart, says that having a shared vision with the CEO is necessary but not sufficient for CMOs. "We often find a disconnect within the chief marketing officer's peer relationships," he says. "It's not unusual to find situations where, despite what appears to be an ironclad relationship between the CEO and the CMO, the CMO's peer group is not always as enthusiastic about the CMO's chances of survival." Part of the reason is the job's growing importance and difficulty. "It's no longer simply about driving marketing programs. It's about creating a truly customer-centric mind-set across the enterprise," Welch says. "And the data suggest that fewer and fewer CMOs have been able to drive such a massive shift in thinking. Today's top performers must have an extremely strong grasp of adjacent functions like IT, finance, and customer service, not to mention sales and supply-side management." The masters of marketing understand business goals from the perspective of a general manager. They can interpret those goals into marketing programs that deliver results. And they can win the support of their colleagues on the executive team.

PARTNER INTERNALLY

One of the reasons so many marketers feel like their company's Rodney Dangerfield is because they sometimes act as if they have a higher calling than the drones in sales, finance, or operations. They think of themselves as "creative" people and wear their innumeracy like a badge of honor. The most significant contact they have with other organizations is to argue about the marketing budget.

The problem is not limited to companies or industries where marketing doesn't have much of a track record. Marketers face a different, but equally difficult, challenge even where they appear to rule the roost. Booz Allen Hamilton's Ed Landry quotes the vice president of marketing at a consumer packaged-goods company: "Everybody thinks they are a marketer, and therefore they value the function less."

Whether companies market to consumers or to businesses, practically anybody feels perfectly free to criticize or meddle with a marketing program in a way they would never attempt with the latest IT or human resources initiative. The engineers won't hesitate to tell you that your ads seem to be written for twelve-year-olds. The sales department thinks the ads would be even better if they focused on the particular deal they're trying to close. The "bean counters" see the marketing budget as a large pool of discretionary expenses with an uncertain tie to revenue.

At many companies, marketing is not only disconnected from functions like finance and sales, it's in an adversarial position. When growth is anemic, the marketing and sales departments point fingers at each other. When earnings are sinking, marketing and finance battle over budgets.

Ironically, in today's hypercompetitive world, nearly everyone agrees marketing has never been more important. Booz Allen Hamilton's Landry has surveyed senior executives on both sides of the divide. "Across the nine industries we studied," he says, "a surprisingly high percentage of respondents said marketing's most important contributions are in areas such as driving innovation and encouraging cross-functional collaboration." It seems that marketers are pushing through an open door. They just need to reach out and form strong partnerships with these departments—listening to them, educating them, and finding ways to accommodate their needs and goals.

MARKETING AND OPERATIONS

At IBM, Flaherty had learned how much other departments tend to dislike the marketing organization. Operating units especially resent the "tax" they pay to fund corporate marketing. They covet its advertising budgets, and wish they could redirect it to their own goals. The problem was even worse at Nortel. "When I got here most of the executive team told me they weren't really sure what the role of corporate marketing was in Nortel," she says. "Corporate marketing was pretty disconnected from what mattered to Nortel's business and regional sales leaders."

In fact, when she arrived at Nortel, the marketing people in the business units didn't report to her and the marketing leaders in the regions, who *did* report to her, didn't have marketing backgrounds— they were PR people focused on generic, "big picture" issues. "That wasn't too surprising," she says, "given that the CMO role was considered a 'corporate staff' position."

To make it clear that she considered her role operational, and to make it more relevant to her internal clients, Flaherty changed out all four of the regional marketing leaders in less than a year, replacing them with a mix of outside hires and career marketing people from the business and regional sales organizations. She also eliminated the corporate marketing "tax" in favor of working with the businesses to develop a single, annual marketing budget for the whole company. All the company's marketing people now dually report to her and to their internal clients. She controls their career paths and oversees the professionalism of their work, but they all share concrete, measurable objectives that matter to the business leaders.

MARKETING AND SALES

Flaherty also worked hard to make her organization indispensable to Nortel's sales organization. She conducted focus groups with sales teams to find out what they needed to better do their jobs. As a result, she collapsed nine different Web sales portals into one. She helped the sales organization develop better tools for engaging customers in meaningful dialogue about their business challenges. "Going back say ten years, it was OK for CMOs to talk about brand awareness," Flaherty says. "Not anymore. Now it's about creating lead volume, lead velocity, making the sales job easier. A big part of what I'm doing is related to sales effectiveness."

Finally, Flaherty's credibility with the rest of the top team is based just as much on her general management skills as on her marketing genius. She thinks about the business holistically and describes herself as the business's "chief architect," creating an agenda for the CEO internally and externally, becoming a knowledgeable voice of the customer. She considers "helping the organization stay centered on the customer and on the future" one of her key responsibilities.

BRAND FLAHERTY

Business guru Tom Peters likes to point out that the most important job in business today "is to be head marketer for the brand called You." And properly understood, that's true.

"Brand You" doesn't mean turning yourself into a rock star CMO, but defining your "promise" in terms that are relevant to your number-one client—the CEO. Flaherty was anything but a rock star at IBM. She didn't travel with an entourage and a spotlight. In fact, until she took the Nortel job, her name seldom appeared in the media and she was virtually unknown outside IBM and its agencies. The essence of branding is not "being known," but being trusted to keep a meaningful promise.

Flaherty did not build her brand within Nortel by touting herself in the trade media or by giving self-laudatory speeches at industry forums. Like any strong brand—consumer or business-to-business—Brand Flaherty tells a compelling story. But her narrative is not about ads or marketing stunts; it's about being part of the senior team and helping her colleagues reach their goals. She won the trust of her C-suite colleagues by identifying with the challenges they faced. She demonstrated her marketing expertise, but not a marketing mind-set. She was just as focused on the business as they were and never came across as self-serving or empire building.

The marketing masters build internal alignment by following six key principles:

1. *They get C-suite agreement on their roles, responsibilities, and authorities, including the areas where they can say "no" and where they have to say "yes" before someone else can proceed.* They draw other organizations into constructing a unified marketing budget that balances short- and long-term needs. They share customer insights broadly and frequently.

2. *They ensure they have the organizational capabilities to fulfill their role.* Following Jim Collins's advice in *Good to Great*, they start with who is on the team, then worry about what they do.[2] They look for functional excellence and business acumen in equal measure. They provide training in both.

3. *They make whatever changes they're going to make as quickly as possible.* The president of Wal-Mart's North American operations, Eduardo Castro-Wright, draws an analogy from his engineering training. "An organization is something very solid and when you apply a lot of heat to change it, it becomes fluid. You want to make sure that you don't keep it fluid too long, because liquids move in many directions that you might not have intended."[3]

4. *They treat C-suite colleagues as internal customers, ensuring their organizations have what they need from them to succeed.* They ensure all their team members treat colleagues in other departments, especially sales and product management, the same way. And they

follow up personally with key internal clients to gauge their satisfaction.

5. *They focus their team on concrete goals that will grow revenue and profit.* They make sure their team members understand the business's overall goals and how their individual objectives contribute to them. They give team members a voice in setting direction by soliciting their ideas, but demonstrate through their own actions that execution is key for leaders who are intimately involved in business development and client service.

6. *They measure everything as if their credibility depended on it, recognizing that it does.* They demonstrate their value and efficiency, but share failures as well as successes and focus on giving their partners predictive information they can use.

Flaherty's experience at Nortel demonstrates that, through no fault of their own, even the best marketers sometimes have short runways. But it also shows that, if they run their organizations like a client-focused professional service, they'll have plenty of frequent fliers—and the prospect of exciting flights ahead.

BUILD A MARKETING CULTURE

"If the associates treat the customers well, the customers will return again and again, and that is where the real profit in this business lies, not in trying to drag strangers into your stores for one-time splashy sales or expensive advertising."[1]

—SAM WALTON

Someone at Wal-Mart skipped the passage above when they read Sam Walton's autobiography, *Made in America*. In 2005, the company not only decided it needed to drag "strangers" into the store with flashy advertising, it hired a bunch of outsiders to do it. One was the chief marketing officer of Frito-Lay; another was a top marketing executive at Chrysler. Both were hired by another relative newcomer, John Fleming, who had joined the company in 2000 following nineteen years as a top merchandiser at Target. Fleming had recently been named CMO with a mandate to build a world-class marketing organization. The Frito-Lay executive, Steve Quinn, was given responsibility for marketing strategy, figuring out who Wal-Mart's customers are and what they want. The Chrysler executive, Julie Roehm, was named senior vice president of marketing communications and was charged with finding a new ad agency.

But first Roehm decided to paint her office walls chartreuse with chocolate-brown trim. She went to the local Wal-Mart store after work, bought a ladder and painting supplies, and redecorated the gray, windowless, 120-square-foot office she had been issued at the company's Bentonville, Arkansas, headquarters. There wasn't much she could do about the metal desk that looked like it had seen action on a navy ship during WWII. And unlike her previous office at Chrysler headquarters, this one didn't have a couch or a conference table, unless you counted the folding card table tucked into the corner. But she certainly made a statement.

JULIE ROEHM

To be fair, Roehm had every reason to think her assignment was to help the retailing giant itself undergo a makeover worthy of reality television. Restless investors—who had watched earnings growth stagnate for three years—believed the company's base of rural and blue-collar customers was tapped out; growth had to come from moving upscale. And there were plenty of signs that the company had bought into the strategy. It had opened a ten-person "trend office" in New York City to track developments in home furnishings and apparel. It hired a fashion director to upgrade its clothing lines with new private labels like the *Sex and the City*–inspired "Metro7" line of camisoles and tunics. It ran an eight-page insert in *Vogue*. And it began stocking expensive jewelry, plasma TVs, and fancy wines in some of its stores.

What's more, Wal-Mart had lured Roehm away from Chrysler with an annual compensation package worth more than $1 million, not counting a $250,000 signing bonus and a promise to pay the mortgage on her home in Rochester Hills, Michigan, until it was sold. Surely they knew what they were getting for that price—a self-confessed "envelope pusher" who told the *New York Times* she is like a vacuum that can suck all the oxygen out of the room. "I come in, and I am extremely high energy, and it can be overwhelming."[2]

Surely one of the Wal-Mart executives who interviewed Roehm—if not the headhunters who recommended her—had read her trade media clippings. They must not only have known what they were getting, but *wanted* it. She had made her mark with edgy advertising like Chrysler's proposed sponsorship of a racy "Lingerie Bowl" that was withdrawn under pressure from customers and dealers. She advertised

Dodge trucks with a commercial showing two guys at urinals talking about how "size matters." In another spot, she promoted the roominess of Chrysler sedans by having a mother tell her daughter that she was conceived in the backseat. She signed the rock band Aerosmith to an endorsement deal and liked to tell people that lead singer Steven Tyler was the second person after her husband to learn the sex of her unborn baby because she took a call from him at her gynecologist's office.

With all that, Roehm was not cut from the party-girl school of marketing. She's very analytical, and usually puts as much steak as sizzle in her frying pan. In fact, she was an engineering student at Purdue University when she caught the marketing bug. As a co-op student, she alternated semesters between classroom and corporate internships. Her first assignment was in package engineering at Bristol-Myers Squibb, but she was less interested in the mechanics of printing, positioning, and gluing labels than in the marketing analytics behind them. "I was fascinated by the marketing studies and the insights about why the labels were or weren't appealing," she remembers. She went straight from Purdue to the Chicago Graduate School of Business, and by the time she earned her MBA in 1996, she had job offers from five companies. She accepted the Ford Motor Company's and joined its marketing leadership program. In 1999, she became brand manager for the Ford Focus, and her marketing programs were so finely tuned to the compact car's youthful prospects, it became one of the company's few success stories that year. That attracted the attention of Chrysler, where she was offered an even bigger job and quickly had an even bigger impact—with headlines to match. The headlines at Wal-Mart would prove very different.

A CAUTIONARY TALE

There are a few other blond, leggy, blue-eyed women in Wal-Mart's executive ranks. But Roehm represented sex, fast cars, and rock and roll in a company of pickup trucks, family values, and easy listening. She lasted about ten months. And her story is a cautionary tale for anyone who aspires to be a "rock-and-roll CMO."

In a story that might have been lifted from the *National Enquirer*, Wal-Mart accused Roehm of accepting improper gifts from an ad agency and carrying on an inappropriate personal relationship with a subordinate. They stripped her of her discount card and escorted her out of the building. She sued for improper termination. They counter-sued for abrogation of fiduciary responsibility. She accused the company's CEO himself of taking gifts from a major supplier. The supplier sued for defamation. The business media and bloggers went bonkers, alternately calling Roehm "a bubbly narcissistic princess of self-hype"[3] and asking if the Wal-Mart "old boy's network" did her in.[4] When the ruckus died down more than a year later, all the lawsuits were settled out of court. No one but the lawyers appears to have gotten much, though Wal-Mart did tell Roehm she was welcome to retrieve her ladder and painting supplies. But that's not where the lessons really lay.

There's evidence Roehm herself saw early signs of the problem. Early in her time at Wal-Mart, she gave an interview to the alumni magazine of the Chicago Graduate School of Business where she had taken her MBA. Asked what lessons she wished she had learned earlier in her career, she replied, "That corporate politics were going to play a big role—that having the best intentions and doing really great work sometimes just isn't enough."[5] According to people who knew her during those days, she complained that people were all smiles and said all the right things, but the simplest requests—like getting invited to meetings—seemed to fall between the cracks.

Roehm's friends say that kind of behavior is the antithesis of her own style, and she herself has said, "I'm not good at passive-aggressive behavior. I'm aggressive-aggressive." She talked to the headhunter who recruited her, as well as to her boss. Both counseled patience. She decided to keep her head down and focus on her job. "When you're really excited by the opportunity to make a difference," she says, "you go into it with a sense that everything will be okay."

Just a few weeks after she was fired, Roehm summed up what she had learned in a *BusinessWeek* interview: "The importance of culture. It can't be underestimated."[6] She almost certainly meant that it can't be "*over*estimated." Indeed, culture is fundamental to the trade in which Roehm is reputedly a whiz—marketing. It's the key to getting things done.

GETTING THINGS DONE

In a 2008 survey of recent college graduates embarking on marketing careers, four in ten (42 percent) said their single biggest challenge was adapting to their firm's corporate culture. Culture is not what you hear from the senior team—it's how the entire organization behaves. As Roehm puts it, it's "how we do things around here; what we care about; what we value; how we define success." Heidrick & Struggles's Jane Stevenson points out "in any C-level role, it's all about cultural fit—who the person is will trump the experience every time."

WAL-MART CULTURE

Few companies have as strong a culture as Wal-Mart. The company was founded in 1962 to bring low prices to small-town, rural America, which the large discount chains like Kmart, Woolco, and Target were bypassing. The store's culture perfectly reflected that business objective in its frugality, team spirit, and "traditional" family values. Wal-Mart not only squeezed suppliers, it asked executives to share hotel rooms. At every shift change, store managers would lead "associates" (not "employees" or "staff") in a cornpone cheer of "Give me a W. Give me an A . . ." and so forth—all in the best tradition of a high-school pep rally. The stores themselves were vast warehouses with concrete floors and fluorescent lighting, not unlike the workplaces of many of the customers, except for the "Happy Face" price tags hanging from the ceiling. And while Wal-Mart would happily sell its customers as many shotguns as they could fit in their pickups, it refused to stock rap CDs or "beer and babes" magazines like *Maxim* unless they had been "sanitized" by wrapping them in plastic with opaque banners covering any "naughty" parts. At one point, many stores even put a modesty shield on the covers of women's magazines like *Elle* and *Cosmopolitan*.

Wal-Mart's principal spokesperson, Mona Williams, is not a product of that culture—she spent most of her career in sales and public relations at AT&T—but she considers it very special. "Wal-Mart people have the strongest sense of mission I've ever seen," she says. "It sounds corny, but they literally believe the company exists to help change people's lives by making it possible for them to buy things they couldn't otherwise afford."

If Wal-Mart's culture grew naturally from its humble beginnings, the company goes to great lengths to perpetuate it today. It sends managers to training sessions at places like the Walton Institute where, among other things, they hear senior executives discuss Wal-Mart's "unique company culture and how to sustain that culture."[7] All store employees attend weekly meetings on subjects taken from a "culture topic index" issued to their managers.

Wal-Mart's culture *is* unusual, both in its strength and in its tenets. Some consider it a homely anachronism at best, a self-righteous exploiter of working people at worse. The company's size and influence put it in the crosshairs of activists across a wide spectrum, from unions eager to organize its employees to food elitists suspicious of the organic milk and vegetables it purveys. Its size also invites oversimplification. Like any large company, Wal-Mart houses a series of fiefdoms that have developed their own subcultures. And as Williams once told the *Today* show's Matt Lauer, some "knuckleheads" do dumb things in the name of that culture.

The strongest strands of any corporate culture run through a Gordian knot of sometime-competing mental models and patterns of behavior. The trick is to move everyone in the same direction by pulling on the strands that tie them together without becoming ensnared in the threads of competing interests.

That wasn't a trick that Julie Roehm had learned earlier in her career. It was only after being fired that she realized it might have been a good idea to attend the Friday morning sessions Wal-Mart's CEO held with the company's officers. She also didn't pick up on two other things that loom large in the Wal-Mart culture—a relentless focus on cutting costs and on spending lots of time with customers in the store. Legend has it that some executives have used hollow doors on sawhorses as desks so they wouldn't have to buy office furniture. Williams laughs at the notion now, but Wal-Mart's executives are anything but flashy.

Most of them, including the CEO, try to spend two days a week visiting stores and talking to customers. Every new executive is expected to work in a store for as much as several weeks to get a feel for the business. Instead, for much of her ten months at the company, Roehm jetted around the country visiting the forty-five or so ad agencies that were bidding to win its advertising account. The only time she was in a Wal-Mart store appears to be when she bought the painting supplies to redo her office.

CULTURE CHANGE

Roehm considered herself a "change agent." But as executive recruiter Kurt O'Hare points out, "When (outsiders) enter a new culture, they don't have the political capital to make the global changes they were brought in to make. When you don't know the history and the culture, there are minefields and banana peels everywhere that are hard to avoid."[8]

You've got to know the territory for several reasons. First, you have to understand how far the existing culture can be stretched before it snaps back in your face. Second, you have to start the change from a place that isn't so foreign people can't function effectively. You can only change a culture if you can identify the behavior and values that *shouldn't* change. And third, you need allies in helping people make the trip. You also need to be sure that you have enough high-level internal support to make the change stick. As a general rule of thumb, if your boss has an office window and you don't, you don't have enough political clout to effect the kind of change Roehm was attempting.

Roehm complained that her counterpart, Steve Quinn, who was responsible for setting marketing strategy, wouldn't return her phone calls or invite her to important meetings. Their mutual boss, John Fleming, refused to resolve the issue, she told *BusinessWeek*, telling her to "take the high road." That should have been a hint of what was to come if she persisted in attempts to give the culture "more edge." But that was the least of her problems.

Merchandising is arguably the most important organization within Wal-Mart. Roehm had no friends within its ranks. If anything, she had alienated the company's powerful merchandisers with her open disdain for their corny "happy face" store signage and crowded displays. In the absence of new advertising everyone could get behind, and despite Fleming's efforts to upgrade and unclutter the stores, the merchandisers ordered up more happy face signage touting low prices.

If somehow none of this had happened, and Roehm retained her responsibilities, it's questionable that she would have been able to move Wal-Mart very far. She didn't have the internal muscle to do it. Despite her lofty title of senior vice president, she was too low in the organization, and she had few, if any, internal allies. But more importantly, she didn't have a feel for the Wal-Mart culture; she was trying to change something she didn't understand.

Roehm admits to learning some important lessons in the first decade of her marketing career.

☞ *"Job interviews are a staged process,"* she says. "You meet only with the best people and they tell you what you want to hear. You don't know how much fortitude they'll have when they get pushed." She advises anyone being wooed by another company to undertake mergerlike due diligence, perhaps talking to vendors and former employees, to get a better feel for the real working environment. "What motivates people, how do they deal with failure, what are they proud of? Are they hungry for change or are they nostalgic for the good old days? Do tough questions make people uncomfortable or do they embrace them?" Some prospective employees pose as customers to get a feel for the company through the behavior of its sales and service people. How long it takes to work your way through a company's service department phone tree will tell you volumes about its customer focus.

☞ *"Be clear about what makes you happy and measure new opportunities against that,"* she says. "Typically, it won't be what your office looks like, who your boss is, or even what's on your pay stub. It will be more intangible, like the people you work with every day or the way decisions get made. If you try to squeeze a square peg in a round hole, you shave the edges off and end up with a wobbly cylinder. Know yourself. It's not a question of right or wrong. It's a question of fit."

☞ *"Building a marketing culture takes more than creating a marketing department,"* she says. "It takes top management that understands the real value of marketing—that it's more than advertising—and is willing to let the customer drive the company. That attitude has to penetrate every corner of the organization in a way people can relate to their own job, from the CEO to the guy who sweeps the floors. It's not easy, and it's not for the faint of heart."

But it can be done. Consider another company with a very different culture arguably as strong and as distinctive as Wal-Mart's—Microsoft.

MICROSOFT

Like Wal-Mart, Microsoft is so big and successful it's a fashionable target for critics of every stripe. It also has a distinctive culture, dominated by engineers. Most Microsoft people are very smart, intense, and analytical. They suffer nonengineers with impatience, notwithstanding the fact that the CEO, Steve Ballmer, began his career at P&G marketing cake mixes.

Microsoft's top marketer, Mich Mathews, is a petite Brit who doesn't have an engineering degree. In fact, she went to college one day a week while an apprentice at General Motors in the U.K. following high school. In 1989, she left GM and joined a U.K. PR agency that did work for Microsoft. She did so well that the company tried to hire her. It took until 1993, but she finally agreed to move to Seattle, joining the Microsoft corporate public relations department. She was soon overseeing communications about everything from the company's financial results and new products to Bill Gates's marriage, the birth of his three children, and the U.S. government's unsuccessful efforts to split the company apart in antitrust court.

In July 2002, with the antitrust suit behind it, Microsoft began entering new markets and found itself competing with marketing powerhouses ranging from Sony to Time Warner and Google. Ballmer reorganized the company around market segments rather than product lines and decided that Microsoft's marketing needed to be at least as good as its engineering. He centralized marketing and put Mathews in charge. But he wasn't looking for better ads. He wanted her to help the company's fabled engineers develop deeper insights into customer needs, and to help the organization respond to the implications wherever the company touched a customer.

MICH MATHEWS

In hindsight, Mathews knows why Ballmer picked her for the job. "The reason I'm in this job," she says, "is because of my network. In PR, you get very little done by fiat. It's the same in marketing—you never have all the levers or all the budget authority you need. You get things done by capitalizing on the credibility and trust you've built with all the people involved." After years of handling the company's most important and sensitive issues in public relations, Mathews had built sufficient credibility and trust to tackle a major reorganization of the company's marketing. She also had one other advantage—she was close to the company's CEO and everyone knew it.

It wasn't something she used as a cudgel, but as a source of leverage. As the head of public relations, she had to know what was on Ballmer's mind, what he was worried about, what was important to him. And he, in turn, expected her to serve as his peripheral vision, to be willing to tell him when she saw trouble brewing somewhere within the company. "In PR, I learned to be a truth teller to the CEO," she says. "It also forced me to develop a broader perspective, to try to see the big picture. It was more than media relations, it was using information about customers and other stakeholders to galvanize change."

It was this ability to build bridges within Microsoft and between it and the outside world that made Mathews the right candidate to lead marketing. When she took over, marketing at Microsoft was largely a communications function. "Marketing was always out launching something or doing an event when it should have been back under the hood with the engineers figuring out the next version of a product that's not going to be on the market for another two years," she said. Interestingly, as she met with her colleagues on Ballmer's staff, she discovered that they agreed. "Steve's staff is dominated by engineers," she says, "but they were telling me, 'I need the engineering ranks to have customer insight and it's not going to come from the engineers alone. We need marketing to do something in partnership with engineering.' They got it. They wanted help in better understanding customers."

Having managed Microsoft's U.S. subsidiary for several years, Mathews also experienced firsthand how tempting it was to cut investments in positioning the brand to meet short-term profit goals. "I realized it was an unhealthy trade-off, but I also understood why people made it," she says. She looked at other industries for models, talking to people in consumer packaged goods, banking, and pharmaceuticals. "Some companies think of marketing as communications—ads and brochures. Others use it primarily to support sales," she remembers. "Microsoft needed both of those, but what really resonated was the strategic relationship between marketing and R&D in pharmaceutical companies. It's a relationship focused on creating intellectual property, and that's what Microsoft needs."

REIMAGINING MARKETING

Mathews began reimagining the marketing organization as two complementary centers of competence—a centralized go-to-market group of communications experts in disciplines from digital media to viral marketing that would work as an internal agency for the various lines of business, and a cadre of high-tech marketing experts embedded in the businesses themselves who could help the engineers plan the next generation of products based on customer research. Mathews would oversee professional and brand standards, as well as career planning.

It would be a major shift for a company that was used to throwing projects over the wall to the ad and publicity people only when the engineers decided a project had an acceptable number of bugs and didn't have room for any more bells and whistles. Mathews knew that moving the company in that direction would take time and require everyone in the top ranks to pull in the same direction. "If you're going to change things," Mathews says, "there has to be a lengthy dialogue about what you're planning to do and why. You can't cook this stuff up in isolation and hope no one catches you meddling in their backyard."

Everything came to a head at an October 2003 meeting Ballmer called for all his top lieutenants to discuss the state of the company's marketing. Mathews outlined what she had found in her survey of the company's existing capabilities, the gaps she saw, and her general approach for closing them. The widest gap she needed to close was between marketing's existing competencies and the ones her new model assumed. That required an extensive investment in customer research practices, and in a comprehensive training program for the company's marketers—veterans and new hires alike.

BUILDING A COMMON LANGUAGE

Working with Northwestern University's Kellogg School of Management and Duke University, Mathews's team created an entire curriculum around eight core competencies, ranging from value proposition design to segmentation and customer insights. Marketing recruits from college campuses are required to attend a two-day-a-month "mini-MBA" on Microsoft's marketing practices during their first two years of employment. Marketers hired from other companies attend a two-day "boot camp" to learn the basics of Microsoft marketing. Existing marketing employees are encouraged to take a self-assessment test as part of their annual appraisal to identify skill gaps. Everyone is expected to build new muscles by embracing a broader mandate than functional specialties such as media relations or speechwriting.

Mathews's marketing organization also partnered with the business units to develop a common approach to customer research. The idea was to emphasize the kind of analysis that can drive decisions about product features and capabilities at the front end of development. "The notion of concept testing or defining thresholds that had to be met before something went out the door was culturally different for our engineers," says Mathews. "They'd say, 'What do you mean you're going to test my product?'" It was a seismic change, but it was key to developing a strong customer value proposition.

Beginning in 2004, the depth of that change was most apparent in the meeting rooms of Building 34 on the vast Microsoft campus in Redmond, Washington. That's where a small team of developers and marketers met every week to hash out the features of new server software not scheduled for release until late 2006. The team members compiled a manual—dubbed the "Book of E12"—to define the software's DNA, from market outlook to how potential customers might value possible features. Involving marketing so early in the product-development cycle was a significant change for a company historically dominated by engineers. "By giving marketing a seat at the table with engineering from the very beginning of the product-development process, we've fundamentally changed the way that we create products and bring them to market," Mathews says.

The change did not go unnoticed by the professional Microsoft watchers and pundits. Based on the beta, or test, version he saw, one consultant deemed it "one of the most impressive upgrades to Exchange that Microsoft has ever released." What especially impressed him was the company's decision to abandon a "purely technical path" in favor of "addressing customers' key pain points and upcoming business trends."[9]

While proud of her team's accomplishments, five years in, Mathews says Microsoft's marketing transformation is only halfway complete. "I know ten years sounds like a long time," she says, "but you can't have some corporate mandate and expect everyone to dance to it." And it takes even longer for people outside the company to pick up the beat.

By late 2008, Microsoft had just begun to respond to Apple's successful campaign to cast it as the overweight, plodding fuddy-duddy of the computing world. It put hundreds of specially trained employees, dubbed "Windows gurus," in retailers such as Best Buy and Circuit City. It opened a new Windows website to demonstrate its own mobile and multimedia capabilities. It hired a new ad agency noted for transforming perceived negatives into positives for clients like Burger King and Volkswagen. And it launched a $300-million ad campaign to take the "PC narrative" back from Apple. Initial ads in the campaign featured a Microsoft engineer who is a dead ringer for the awkward "PC" character in Apple's mocking ads, from his penny loafers to the sharp part in his slicked-down hair. "Hello, I'm a PC," he says, "and I've been made into a stereotype." Then the ad introduces viewers to PC users around the world, from an astronaut and an environmentalist to celebrities like "desperate housewife" Eva Longoria Parker, hip-hop producer Pharrell Williams, and holistic health expert Deepak Chopra. The campaign's slogan, "Windows, Not Walls," is intended to communicate Microsoft's commitment to break down the barriers that prevent people and ideas from connecting. But it could just as aptly refer to the major reengineering of Microsoft's entire approach to marketing.

Before Microsoft could reframe what people thought of the company, it needed to reframe thinking within its own walls. And that's precisely what Mathews set out to do. Mathews had the advantage of a fourteen-year career at Microsoft before assuming leadership for marketing. But what she took on—refocusing an engineering-dominated culture on customer needs rather than on technical accomplishments—was no less daunting.

How the masters of marketing instill a marketing culture:

☞ *They take time to understand the company's existing culture, finding potential points of friction with an externally focused marketing culture.* Mathews knew the Microsoft culture inside and out, which gave her a distinct advantage. Nevertheless, she spent about a year talking to people inside and outside the company, trying to define her role. "It's important to be very specific about your job—not only 'What do I do?' but also 'What do I *not* do?' "

☞ *They ensure they're empowered to make the necessary changes.* If they're not, they don't attempt them until they are. Empowerment can't come only from the top (though it's a good first step). They engage the entire leadership team in the change so they have allies in pushing it through the organization. "Steve (Ballmer) doesn't think of himself as a technologist, but as a marketer," Mathews says. "But he doesn't think in terms of ads. He sees marketing as a catalyst for change."

☞ *They anticipate a multiyear journey when making major changes.* As Mathews puts it, "Don't try to boil the ocean all at once." She acknowledges that there's a strong temptation to do "high fives down the corridors" after every success. And it's important to celebrate when things go well, but it's also critical to keep perspective. "One of the things I learned in PR," she says, "is the importance of thinking two or three steps ahead."

☞ *They look at change from the key players' point of view, getting their buy-in at every step of the journey.* If you're not working on the pain they feel, they won't put up with the cure you recommend. "Another thing I learned in PR," Mathews says, "is the importance of understanding the perspective other people have and tailoring your message to it."

☞ *They build systems to institutionalize the approach they want people to take, from marketing best practices to brand standards.* They recognize that a marketing culture can't be built on rhetoric alone—they make sure they're not all mouth and no hands. They hire the best people available and give everyone the best training. They partner with internal clients to develop standardized approaches to key processes such as research to ensure that actionable data can be shared across the company.

As for Wal-Mart, it abandoned plans to "go upscale" and, in 2007, Roehm's former boss, John Fleming, was moved to a new job leading the company's U.S. merchandising organization. Her nemesis, Steve Quinn, was promoted to executive vice president and chief marketing officer. A new ad agency developed a campaign that seemed in perfect sync with the company's culture. In fact, the theme line—"Save more. Live better."—was inspired by one of Walton's early employee speeches. Wal-Mart's financial results were one of the few bright spots in the economic turmoil that gripped the United States in late 2008.

As of this writing, Julie Roehm leads a marketing consultancy, Backslash Meta, based in Bentonville, Arkansas, where she continues to live with her husband and two sons. The family home has been on the market for nearly two years. Meanwhile, she's still flying around the country for clients as diverse as *Sports Illustrated,* Credit Suisse, and a Las Vegas real-estate developer with ties to a Sultan from Dubai. She also signed on as one of the judges on a CBS television game show in which contestants try to write and perform commercial jingles. In between all this, Julie gives talks about managing one's career reputation—a lesson she admits she learned the hard way.

BECOME KNOWN AS THE VOICE OF THE CUSTOMER

"Consumers are statistics. Customers are people."

—STANLEY MARCUS

Early in her ad agency career, Mary Lou Quinlan had the temerity to ask her boss if she could join the team pitching the Maidenform lingerie account. She was the highest-ranking woman at the agency, had previously been advertising director for the Avon cosmetic company, and actually wore Maidenform bras. She was told the team pitching the account would include only the agency's top leadership, which at the time was all male. She still smiles when she thinks of "those six guys sitting around a conference table passing lacy underwear to each other." The agency didn't win the account, but Quinlan learned a valuable lesson. As she puts it, "smart marketing comes down to having smart listening skills."

MARY LOU QUINLAN

Quinlan's bosses had not only failed to listen to her, they weren't really listening to the women who bought Maidenform's products. They had plenty of company data segmenting the market by demographics, psychographics, product type, fabric, and fashion. They had sales figures by segment and distribution channel. They had competitive data, trend data, and industry forecasts. They had even done their own focus group research among small groups of women paid a modest sum to talk about underwear in a windowless, fluorescent-lit room.

To Quinlan, little of that constitutes real listening. Focus groups have all the spontaneity of speed dating except they're done in front of a two-way mirror with a moderator who has the patient earnestness of a third-grade school teacher. "Some Chatty Kathy inevitably dominates the discussion," Quinlan says. "The shy women shrink into their skins, casting furtive glances at the two-way mirror and wishing they had put lipstick on. When the time is almost up, every woman reaches for her purse and gets ready to make a beeline for the door."

Quinlan stayed in the advertising business long enough to become one of the few female CEOs of a major agency. But she never forgot the pitch she wasn't allowed to make. In 1999, she founded Just Ask a Woman, a leading consultancy dedicated to women's marketing. She's the author of two books on the subject and the women's correspondent for CBS's *The Early Show*. She still has the sparkling smile, bright blue eyes, and red hair of a colleen marching in the St. Patrick's Day parade, which ironically she has never done. Not that she lacks the necessary enthusiasm; she's a very "up" person. But she's not crazy about the faceless uniformity of parades. They're too much like the "target demo" in a lot of marketing plans—lots of bodies moving in unison. Count them as they go by. Compute their average weight and height, if you want. No need to know much more.

KNOW YOUR CUSTOMER

Quinlan bridles at the arrogance of such approaches to market research. Many marketers, she believes, are out of touch with their customers, both female and male. "Too many marketers assume the first thing customers say is what they mean," she warns. "Instead of asking questions, they should watch what people do. That's actually a deeper level of listening."

Part of the problem is socioeconomic. "It's really hard for the average marketer to identify with the average customer," Quinlan points out. "The average household income in the United States was about $48,000 in 2006. That's really hard for someone making in the mid six figures to relate to." She remembers talking to one CMO about the demands that pull working women in different directions. "Why don't they just get someone to clean their house?" he asked, entirely sincerely. When she explained that simply wasn't a realistic option for most working mothers, he sheepishly conceded, "I guess there are people like that."

In Quinlan's opinion, that was a man who should hang out more at the laundromat or in the local mall's food court. "Marketers need to spend time in the real world," Quinlan says. "Sit at the playground with moms, wipe a few runny noses with them, see what it's like to keep track of two kids on a jungle gym and a slide. Read what they're reading; watch *Oprah*. Get out of the office and get in touch with the real people who are buying your products, or should be."

Part of the problem is also that many marketers simply don't like the customers they have. "They want their customers to be thinner than they are, sexier," Quinlan says. "A lot of the marketers I've dealt with really want customers who stepped out of *Sex and the City*." In reality, few of their customers could stand in for Sarah Jessica Parker. "The customers most marketers visualize for themselves are hardly ever real," Quinlan observes ruefully. "Their self-esteem is shot, their kids say they hate them, and they're carrying ten pounds they can't lose for their life."

But real people are much more interesting and a richer source of insight. For example, in discussions with literally thousands of women, Quinlan discovered that losing weight was not an end in itself for most of them. "When a woman is trying to lose weight, she's not just trying to get thinner," she says. "She's trying to reconnect with who she was, three or four years ago—and with who she can still be."

She particularly remembers a session in which a weight-loss client asked women to bring in the clothes "they could almost wear." "The revelation was not that the clothes were in a smaller size," Quinlan says. "But that they reflected a personality you wouldn't have guessed the women had based on the clothes they were wearing now. What their old clothes said was 'this is who I really am.'" To really understand your customers, you have to understand their aspirations and connect with them emotionally. The tallest mountain of statistics is only the tip of the iceberg called your customer—a rich vein of data waiting to be prospected.

BUSINESSES SELLING TO BUSINESSES

One might expect business-to-business marketers to have less difficulty identifying with their customers. After all, they're other businesspeople. But Donovan Neale-May, executive director of the CMO Council, maintains that most business-to-business marketers—especially of high-tech products and services—can be just as clueless as their counterparts in consumer marketing. "Many of these guys don't even know who their customers are," he says. "They sell through two tiers of distribution. They don't have real insight into the customer; they haven't interacted with him; they don't know his problems or his opportunities."

In fact, many technology marketers communicate with their customers through sales or engineering. Too many are locked into programs that have been around ever since their first business cards were printed—trade shows and ad schedules that give them even minimal insight into their customers' real-world needs. While many business-to-business marketers are dipping their toes into the world of interactive media with blogs and social networks, Neale-May says that few have the "data-mining and database smarts" to take full advantage of them. "That's one of the challenges many marketing organizations face," he says. "They have to reskill and bring in people with analytical backgrounds." They apparently also need to tap the resources just down the hall. One consultant was amazed, for example, to discover that the CMO of a large recruiting firm had never met the company's chief information officer.

On the other hand, when Arun Sinha joined Pitney Bowes as chief marketing officer back in 2004, the first thing he did was talk to 2,000 customers in eight countries, as well as a broad swath of the company's own employees, salespeople, and executives. "That's how marketing has changed," he says. "It used to be more downstream—warm and fuzzy. Now it's upstream analysis and relationships. Companies that succeed do these things well."[1]

BECOME YOUR CUSTOMER'S VOICE

Heidrick & Struggles's Jane Stevenson points out that one of the most effective ways to develop a personal brand as a results-oriented team player is by becoming "an influential voice regarding customer behaviors, wants, and needs." Marketing masters connect the dots between customer needs and the firm's capabilities, between customer desires and firm profitability. They represent the customer's voice at the board table and move the entire organization's center of gravity in the customer's direction.

Unfortunately, according to Forrester Research, less than a third of CMOs believe interacting with customers is critical to their jobs and only one in ten considers personally interacting with customers to be important.[2] In Stevenson's view, this may be the source of many marketing leaders' credibility problems. "The business needs to be able to count on the head of marketing to know the most about its customers," she says. "It's not something that can be delegated to sales. The head of marketing has to get out and talk to customers. Then use that personal knowledge and experience to bring the customer to life." In other words, the head of marketing has to become the voice of the customer within the company.

Being the voice of the customer doesn't mean becoming a hectoring presence at the CEO's conference table. It means becoming the acknowledged expert on who customers are and what they need. Plus, it means spreading that word inside the company, involving everyone else in the customer's world. "CMOs who can acutely tap into customer needs and evangelize them throughout the organization will be able to drive growth and strategy for the business," says Stevenson.

The "voice of the customer" is the kind of corporate poetry that sounds good in a CEO speech or framed and hung on conference room walls, but it's essentially meaningless at most companies. USAA, the giant insurer specializing in the needs of military members and their families, may be an exception that proves the rule. USAA goes to great lengths to train its employees to empathize with its customers' unique needs. "We want to cover the light moments, the heart-wrenching moments, what it's like to be bored in the field," says Elizabeth D. Conklyn, USAA's executive vice president for people services. "We try to develop empathy, not only for our members, but also for the family side."[3]

Eighty-five percent of USAA employees have no military experience, but the company does whatever it can to help them identify with their clients in uniform, from using military time to handing out MRE (military Meal, Ready-to-Eat) packets for lunch, to asking phone representatives to read actual letters home from soldiers deployed in Iraq, including some who later died in the war. It seems to work— USAA topped the *Business Week*/J.D. Power list of "Customer Service Champs" in both 2007 and 2008.

Sam Walton, the founder of Wal-Mart, intuitively understood the importance of keeping in touch with customers. He didn't ask new headquarters employees to work in one of the company's stores for a week so they would understand how the registers worked, but so they would get an appreciation for their customers, as well as for the associates on the front line who serve them. Similarly, knowing that the economic gap between executives and customers would widen over time, he insisted that they spend at least one day a week in the company's or its competitors' stores.

Wal-Mart so accurately reflects the tastes of Middle America, as well as its strains, that it can gauge swings in the economy by the number of displaced items in store aisles. If hair barrettes start appearing in the dairy section, it's probably because a cash-strapped mom remembered she needed to buy milk and had to take something out of her cart so she could afford it. Twenty percent of Wal-Mart customers have no bank account or credit card. They deal strictly in cash.

Walton, a billionaire who wore baseball caps and drove an old pickup truck, was more sophisticated than he appeared. But he never lost touch with his core customers and he made sure his executive team did the same, no matter how wealthy he made them.

CORE CUSTOMERS

The biggest mistake marketers make is to try to be all things to all people. All customers are important, but some customers actually drive your business. These are your "core customers," the enthusiasts to whom your brand is most meaningful. They are passionate, vocal, and unreasonably loyal. Meet their needs, and much of the mass market will usually follow.

Most successful marketers start out with a pretty clear idea of their core customer. In fact, their success is built on a value proposition that appeals to a core group of people in ways other offerings don't. But, over time, many marketers drift away from the customers who made them successful, either because they fail to keep up with their changing needs or get distracted by other attractive prospects. There's a seven-year itch in the corporate world too.

The Gap

The Gap, for example, began life selling stylish and affordable casual clothes from a converted church near Stanford University. Its core customer was an undergraduate who felt comfortable in jeans and a crisp, colorful pocket T-shirt. When businesses went casual in the 1990s, the Gap was perfectly positioned with khaki pants and polo shirts for its core customers who were then in the workforce. Life was good. By the end of 1999, there were 1,767 Gap stores in the United States, and it had launched other branded stores, including babyGap, GapKids, Old Navy, and Banana Republic, each with its own set of core customers.

But people's taste in clothes change as they get older, and every generation has its own style. The Gap failed to anticipate its core customers' changing preferences and found itself in an uncertain middle ground. College kids and others who had to watch their pennies bought their clothes at Old Navy, but also at H&M or Wal-Mart. Urban office workers looking for affordable luxuries shopped at Banana Republic, but also J.Crew or Nordstrom. The Gap lost its distinctive edge.

The Gap's same-store sales declined at a time when it could least absorb the blow—management was in the midst of an aggressive expansion. For the 2001 holiday shopping season, the Gap de-emphasized jeans, khakis, and tees and started featuring a fast-changing selection of hip fashions, including sequined camisoles, rhinestone encrusted jeans, and tight-fitting tops in a wide palette of offbeat colors. The hip new fashions confused existing customers and failed to attract new ones. Same-store sales continued to decline, a trend the company has yet to reverse despite changing CEOs three times. Once you lose your core customers, it's hard to win them back.

The Gap's biggest problem is that it doesn't have a clear picture of just who its core customer is. Meanwhile, Anthropologie is tightly focused on vintage-loving, thirtysomething urban women, and Abercrombie & Fitch has preppy, trend-obsessed teenagers in its crosshairs.

By the end of 2007, Marka Hansen, the new president of Gap's North American operations, had canceled television advertising to recalibrate its product mix to the needs of a newly defined core customer of twenty-five to thirty-five-year-olds. "When I got here, I think the team was more focused on 18 to 24," Hansen told the *Wall Street Journal*.[4] "Twenty-five to 35 covers you from kind of post-college to getting married to maybe having the first child. That puts you from The Gap itself into the babyGap and GapMaternity, but it's not trying to be everything to everyone." The retailer's traditional aesthetic of stylish casual clothing rooted in the classics fit perfectly with this customer segment, but reversing a four-year sales decline in same-store sales will take time.

Customers for fashion are notoriously fickle, but the principle of identifying, understanding, and anticipating the needs of a core set of customers applies across industries and in both consumer and business marketing. McDonald's core customers are families with young children, whether it's serving a Big Mac in Boston, a veggie McAloo Tikki in Bombay, or a Samurai Pork Burger in Bangkok. Its advertising has never wandered far from the promise of "food, family and fun."

Burger King

Burger King—the second-largest fast-food franchise in the world—defines its core customer differently. Russ Klein, who joined the company in 2003 when its fortunes were less than stellar, hired a cultural anthropologist to figure out where the company stood in the fast-food jungle. What he found is that McDonald's is perceived as a "childhood oasis, ripe with playful innocence." Wendy's is the "realm of the adult, signifying quality, peace, and being cared for." Klein decided the only place left for Burger King was adolescence.[5]

That doesn't mean Burger King targets adolescents exclusively. And it defines the term rather loosely, emphasizing psychological rather than biological characteristics. It wants to appeal to the adolescent in all of us. That state of mind seems to run deepest in eighteen- to twenty-four-year-old males. As it happens, they patronize Burger King restaurants five times a month, but they're promiscuous—they eat fast food elsewhere an additional sixteen times a month. While they represent less than 20 percent of the chain's customers, they account for more than half of its traffic. Klein says that convincing that core group to eat at a Burger King just one more time a month would increase traffic by 9 percent. Plus, it's a lot easier than getting a regular at the local fern bar to drop in for a burger and fries. "What defines (our core customers) is that they are the most prolific eaters-out in the market," he says. "They're time starved."

In a nod to its core customers, Burger King now keeps most of its restaurants open until midnight or later. And its menu seems to be bathed in testosterone: BK Stackers, with up to four patties of meat; the aptly named Enormous Omelet Sandwich; the Double Croissan'-wich, with two meat portions and two slices of cheese; and the Oreo BK Sundae Shake. There are salads there too, but they seem to be an add-on for any girlfriend or wife who may be in tow.

Now look at Burger King's sponsorships: the National Football League and NASCAR, plus tie-ins with the *Indiana Jones* movie and an Xbox game that sold more than 3.2 million copies in 2007. It even resurrected its iconic "Burger King," once a children's character in the mold of Ronald McDonald, but now used in settings, such as running onto a football field mid-game, that make him seem like something off a misguided Mardi Gras float—festive, but slightly creepy.

One BK Web video says it all: a "subservient chicken" in a garter belt responds to commands typed by the viewer. The video harkened back to the company's "have it your way" theme, but it clearly didn't have "food, family, and fun" in mind. The result? Burger King is considered a hip, fun place with the kind of food that can satisfy the outsized appetites of young men. On that foundation, Burger King enjoyed sixteen consecutive quarters of same-store sales growth from the time Klein joined the company through 2008.

Klein's boss, CEO John Chidsey, told the *Wall Street Journal* the key to the company's turnaround was "finding who our target customer was, figuring out who was the superfan and not wasting our time trying to be all things to all people."[6]

CORE CUSTOMER MEANING

When Klein speaks about Burger King's core customer, he's not winging it or projecting the customer he'd like to have. He has a very specific picture of Burger King's core customers in mind. He knows generally how old they are, how much they make, what they do for fun, what movies they like, what video games they play, who they think is "hot," and what cracks them up. He tracks them like a big game hunter not just through the fast-food jungle, but also in the underbrush of popular culture. Most importantly, he tracks a carefully considered set of attributes that tell him how his core customers relate to the Burger King brand. How well do they understand the brand? How much do they like it? How does it fit into their lives? What is its point of difference?

Those are the values Klein tracks most closely because they are the spark plug of the Burger King brand, igniting synapses in the more intuitive, feeling-oriented part of his core customers' brains. Brands are not concerned so much with what you think, but with what you *feel*. That distinction can make all the difference. Brain scientist Donald Calne argues that the "essential difference between emotion and reason" is that "while reason leads to conclusions, emotion leads to action."[7]

The power of the Burger King brand is not only in its information content, but also in the emotions it evokes. Some of those feelings derive from past memories—Friday evenings hanging out in the Burger King parking lot with your friends. Other feelings are based on the company's own efforts to shape the way you think of yourself as a user of its products. The Burger King's plastic head, several sizes too big for its body, reminds you of your innocent youth, but the character's antics on a football field appeal to the freewheeling adolescent in you too. When the company established a MySpace page for the King, he attracted 120,000 "friends" in a matter of months.

Strong brands have an element of aspiration in them, whether it's the prospect of romance (Victoria's Secret), adventure (Patagonia), or luxury (Jaguar). Burger King puts you in touch with your adolescent side if you're an eighteen- to twenty-four-year-old male (or have the sensibilities of one).

BRANDING

Branding is not the same as advertising. The family-owned Chelsea Milling Company hasn't advertised its Jiffy muffin mix in more than fifty years, but it still dominates its category with a 55 percent market share by unit sales. Betty Crocker and Pillsbury have spent decades and untold millions on advertising trying to catch up. Caterpillar built a strong brand with relatively little advertising by painting all its giant earthmoving machines a bright yellow and marking them with bold black graphics.

Caterpillar's earthmoving machines—many as big as highway billboards—are its most effective branding tool. Over time, seeing them at heavy construction sites created an aura of "toughness" that the company could eventually transfer to a $1-billion line of footwear and clothing. When rival John Deere entered the market for construction equipment, its dealers actually advised it to paint its equipment yellow rather than the green of its farm equipment. Such is the power of a brand.

A brand is a promise made to a very specific set of customers. Its strength comes not from the breadth of that promise, but from the depth of a customer's trust that the promise will be kept. A brand is not simply something stuck at the end of an ad or on the side of a building. It's the "golden thread" that runs through every internal process and through every interaction with customers.[8]

Disney and Apple spend millions on advertising, but the strength of their brands stems more from their unique products and services. When either company has struggled, it wasn't because their advertising was weak but because their products or service slipped. Richard Branson has been able to stretch the Virgin brand from airline to music store and mobile phone service because he made sure it always reflects a somewhat cheeky, fun-loving, unconventional style, not only in its advertising, but also in its operations. The brand's meaning has value in and of itself. For example, every well-known brand has a catalogue of tchotchkes emblazoned with its logo, but companies from

Caterpillar to Harley-Davidson and BMW have leveraged their brand meaning into multimillion-dollar clothing and accessory lines.

The masters of marketing bring their core customers to life for everyone who shares responsibility for delivering the brand promise. They are their customers' voice.

☞ *They know more about the company's customers than anyone else.* They use all the expert data they can get, but they also spend time out in the field, listening to and interacting with customers. For example, senior executives at Wal-Mart and U.K. retailer Tesco spend at least one day a week visiting their company's stores, as well as their competitors'. If this sounds more like anthropology than traditional consumer surveys, it is. In fact, companies like P&G, Whirlpool, Volvo, Campbell's, and Microsoft have had anthropologists on staff for years. They've discovered that observing what consumers do, rather than what they say, gives them insights into their latent motivations.

☞ *They bring the voice of the customer to strategic business discussions.* They can draw a straight line between customer behavior and future financial performance. They help the senior management team understand what's really going on with customers—for example, how their needs, desires, and values are evolving, how their decision-making processes are changing, what trends are influencing their lifestyles or business strategies.

☞ *They find ways to amplify their customers' voices within their companies.* They are as obsessed with stats as the most avid baseball fan, but they make customer data user friendly. MTV's researchers once recreated the bedrooms of four typical teenagers at a senior management meeting, complete with dirty laundry and the teens themselves, so the executives in attendance could better understand the kids' lives and aspirations.

☞ *They ensure that their brand promise is reflected at every point of customer interaction.* For Burger King, that meant not only advertising, but also the restaurant menu, hours of operation, and product promotions. Online retailer Zappos does very little advertising, but it ensures that every customer's shopping experience is so positive it almost guarantees word will spread. CEO Tony Hsieh reminds employees that Zappos is "a customer service company that just happens to sell shoes." To back that up, he encourages call center employees to engage in "random acts of wowness," for example, free upgrades to overnight shipping or directing customers to competitive sites if a product is not in inventory.

CHAPTER FOUR

SHARE THE RESULTS THAT MATTER—GOOD AND BAD

"What gets measured gets funded."
—ANONYMOUS

"Bollocks," said the great bear of a man, shaking the shaggy brown hair around his balding pate. "The notion that marketers invent and create stuff, and accountants measure it, is bollocks!"[1]

Rob Malcolm was not having a flashback to his college accounting courses. Nor was he caught in some Dickens-era time warp. He was delivering the third annual "brands" lecture to the British Brands Group, an association of the United Kingdom's top marketers, and he felt the need to translate his full indignation in terms that would be unmistakable to his audience. But it wasn't really the accounting profession he was defending. He was taking issue with the prevailing attitude that marketing is all smoke and mirrors, more art than science, with little rigor and even less accountability.

ROB MALCOLM

As president of global marketing, sales, and innovation for Diageo, the London-based alcoholic drinks marketer, Malcolm is steward of some 200 brands in more than 180 countries. In fact, Diageo dominated the first Millward Brown "BrandZ" report on the top 100 spirit brands in 2008, with Smirnoff in the lead, followed by Bacardi, Jose Cuervo, Johnnie Walker, and Baileys. Other iconic Diageo brands include Bushmills, Captain Morgan, J&B, Tanqueray, Guinness, Crown Royal, and wines from the Beaulieu and Sterling vineyards.

Malcolm could be forgiven if he still felt a bit like a Yankee in King Arthur's court, even after a decade at Diageo. A native of southern California, he joined Procter & Gamble right after receiving his MBA from the University of Southern California. He spent twenty-four years at P&G, in Cincinnati and in seven overseas assignments, before joining Diageo's United Distillers unit in 1999 to manage its scotch businesses. He was elevated to CMO of the whole company less than a year later.

The company itself was only three years old, the product of a merger between Guinness and Grand Metropolitan that was still in the process of divesting noncore assets such as Pillsbury and Burger King. Its name, which comes from the Latin word *dies,* meaning "day," and the Greek word *geo,* meaning "world," suggests that, like the British Empire of old, the sun never sets on Diageo. Somewhere, someone is drinking one of its beverages at any given moment. Malcolm's job is to spread that urge.

RESULTS THAT MATTER

Malcolm has lasted in his job for nearly a decade because he has developed a reputation as someone who gets results that matter in a company known for its financial prowess and discipline. He has avoided the twin dangers that have bedeviled so many of his peers—measuring what's easy to measure (revenue, costs, head count, and so forth) or measuring what they've always measured (share of voice, message awareness, market share, and the like). He measures these things of course, but he built his reputation on measuring what matters, that is, the metrics that impact business goals.

There have always been pockets of marketing that lend themselves to hard financial measures. Direct-response ads, for example, can be versioned, tweaked, and sequentially reiterated based on replies to different offers, creative approaches, target lists, and media. Search-word advertising enables marketers to track responses from click to click rather than trying to extrapolate from intermediary data like frequency and reach. But other methods, such as brand campaigns, are black boxes—a torrent of money in, a thin stream of warm and fuzzy data out. The return on those investments requires a group leap of faith.

But as Bob Liodice, president of the Association of National Advertisers, says, "No longer are soft measures like 'brand awareness,' 'brand preference,' and 'intention to buy' acceptable. Brand building from the CEO's perspective is about business building—generating higher revenues and profits, which in turn will lead to greater shareholder value." The upshot in recent years has been a flow of marketing budgets to "below-the-line" media, such as coupons, sampling, trade allowances, and direct marketing. While strong on the R side of the ROI (return on investment) equation, such media also tend to be focused on the short term.

DEATH BY DATA

This has kicked off a sharp debate in the marketing community. Some claim that marketing ROI is more complex than financial ROI, where both the R and the I are measured in dollars. Effective marketing, they say, involves qualitative factors, such as awareness and affiliation, as well as quantitative factors, such as cost per incremental volume. Others are afraid that the "art" of marketing is being smothered under the weight of so-called "scientific data," and multivariate regression models are sucking the creative genius out of advertising. For example, one observer frets, "With all the talk of measurement and flowing spreadsheets, the creative-service departments have begun to act more like accounting departments."[2] And to be honest, some big-time brand managers, knowing they have less than two years to make their mark, reject what little hard data they do have in favor of their own intuition. Kevin Clancy, CEO of Copernicus Marketing Consultants, accuses them of having "high testosterone to IQ ratios."

But while the debate rages, nearly 70 percent of marketers in a recent Booz Allen Hamilton survey identified "improved ROI analytics" as the advertising capability they covet most.[3] They know they can't keep saying "marketing is an investment" without subjecting it to the same financial discipline their company uses for its other investments, such as being clear about financial returns, finding and exploiting points of economic leverage, managing risk, and tracking results. "CEOs are focused on tangible results, such as sales numbers, while

CMOs tend to use proxies such as brand awareness and purchase intent to measure their success," says Jim Speros, senior vice president and chief marketing officer of Fidelity Investments. "But at the end of the day, marketing people have to learn the language of the CEO."

Malcolm believes growth is a function of making the company's brands more relevant to consumers. Lots of people say that, but he has drawn a tight connection between "soft measures" such as awareness, preference, and purchase intent and "hard measures" such as revenue, profit, and market share. And he's willing to be accountable for both ends of the equation.

The foundation of Malcolm's ability to quantify connections that are still fuzzy for many of his peers is a bedrock belief that marketing is the "engine room of demand creation." If you really believe that, you start looking for the gauges that tell you how the engine is performing, as well as the knobs and dials that allow you to fine-tune it. You ensure that all your people are working from the same owner's manual, and you give them the tools they'll need if they ever have to get under the hood.

START WITH FINANCIAL GOALS

Diageo's marketing budgets flow from the company's overall financial goals, as determined by investor expectations. These days, Diageo is looking for top-line growth of 5 to 7 percent and earnings growth in the double digits. That's what it takes to be in the top third of consumer goods companies against which it benchmarks itself. Interestingly, Diageo has never been out of the top half in its entire existence.

With those goals in mind, Malcolm's team looks at "the gearing" of the business, asking such questions as: What categories seem to have more momentum than others? Which brands are generating the greatest profit? Are advertising and promotional investments becoming more efficient? And, finally, What mix of brands in which geographies should be able to deliver the targeted financial returns? At the end of this "macro" analysis, Malcolm and his team set a series of revenue and profit targets for the brands that, taken together, could add up to the company's financial goals for the next year.

The individual brand managers then build their budgets by asking what changes in behavior they need to influence within each of their regions. For some brands, that may mean capturing more occasions. For others, it may mean convincing new users to try the brand. It all boils down to "How many consumers have to change what behavior by how much?" For help in figuring that out, brand managers can turn to a vast data bank of consumer information that segments consumers within each geography by level and frequency of consumption, as well as by levels of loyalty (what Diageo calls the "Four As"—"availables" are aware of the brand but don't buy it, "acceptors" occasionally buy it, "adopters" buy it most of the time, and "adorers" would never buy another brand). Plus Diageo is always testing incremental investments and reallocations of its marketing mix, searching for new growth drivers. That gives it ten years of history, shedding light on what works and what doesn't in different geographies and situations.

Malcolm and his senior team add up the individual budget requests and make choices based on affordability and an assessment of each brand manager's business case, including the brand manager's track record in similar situations, the competitive environment, market trends, and so forth. Historically, Diageo's overall marketing expenses have averaged 15 to 17 percent of sales, but spending in different regions or by different brands can vary widely depending on their individual potential.[4]

MOMENTUM AND INNOVATION

"We have a philosophy of fueling brands that have momentum," Malcolm says. For example, the growth of China's middle class, combined with a reduction of import fees when the country joined the World Trade Organization in 2001, prompted a sharp increase in the local marketing budget for Johnnie Walker scotch. In short order, according to trade publications, Johnnie Walker Black Label sales in China were growing 85 percent a year. And in 2008 Johnnie Walker's worldwide sales topped £1 billion for the first time, making it the largest international spirits brand in the world.

On the other hand, Diageo doesn't just go with the flow. It also knows how to *build* momentum under brands. "When we first introduced Ciroc vodka," Malcolm recalls, "it was struggling to find its voice in a sea of luxury vodkas." Ciroc shouldn't have had a problem distinguishing itself as a superpremium vodka—it's made from expensive French grapes, cold fermented and distilled five times, once in copper vats. But people weren't asking for Ciroc, even though luxury vodka sales were among the fastest-growing segments of the liquor industry.

Malcolm says he learned how to build momentum under a brand during his P&G days working on Folgers coffee. "If you find the generic benefit in your brand's category and co-opt it, you can lead the category," he says. For Folgers coffee, the benefit was literally help in waking up. That insight led to an enduring slogan—"the best part of wakin' up is Folgers in your cup"—as well as to a doubling in market share.

"Premium vodkas are part of celebratory enjoyment with friends," Malcolm says. "But we didn't really connect the brand to the idea of luxury and celebration until we joined up with Sean Combs." Also known as Puff Daddy or P. Diddy, Combs is arguably the "icon of luxury" for club-hopping urban professionals who are the category's best customers. Diageo negotiated an unusual marketing and development agreement with Combs that gave him a fifty-fifty share in Ciroc's profits. It turned out to be a good deal for both parties. "In the first eight months," Malcolm says, "sales grew 100 percent."

Customer insights also lead to new product innovations. For example, when the company discovered that many people find it challenging to prepare mixed drinks, it introduced a line of premixed cocktails, such as Jose Cuervo Golden Margarita with Grand Marnier and the Smirnoff Mojito. Not all its innovations succeed. Captain Morgan Gold, a rum-based malt drink, proved too sweet for most U.S. consumers, and it was taken off the market in 2003. But overall, the "premixed" category has been a source of innovation and growth for Diageo.

TRACKING RESULTS

Diageo's key tracking metrics are deceptively simple though they pack a wealth of information. "Simple tools get used," Malcolm says. "Complex ones don't." Malcolm has reduced the key measures of Diageo's return on marketing investment to something that is fondly referred to as the "Dogs and Stars" chart (see Figure 4.1).[5]

It's a simple two-by-two matrix that tracks marketing and financial performance. The vertical axis displays marketing's return on investment by brand—that is, the brand's earnings over the past five years divided by the associated marketing expense. The horizontal axis depicts the effect of those investments on the brand's "health," measured by its impact on consumers.

The "brand health" metrics vary by product category. For example, beer competes in affiliation, that is, where guys get together, so one measure of Guinness's brand health might be its share of those occasions. Scotch whiskey, on the other hand, is a drink of discernment, so loyalty is a key measure of brand health. Other measures of brand health might include awareness, trial, loyalty, or repurchase, as

Figure 4.1. Sample "Dogs and Stars" Chart, used by permission of Diageo.

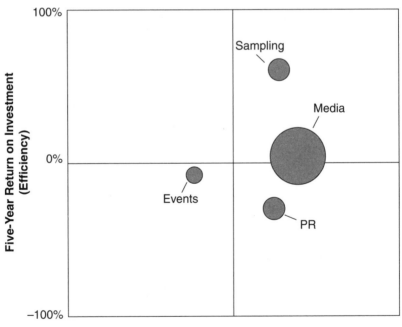

**Measuring Efficiency and Effect
Diageo's "Dogs and Stars" Chart**

well as image perceptions such as "it's the brand for me," or "it stands for success and achievement."

Every marketing program finds a home somewhere on the chart, as a circle whose size reflects the amount spent on each activity. The "stars" occupy the upper right-hand corner and the "dogs," the lower left.

If a marketing program has improved brand health but isn't yet realizing a good financial return, the brand managers are told to find ways to be more efficient. On the other hand, if a brand is producing high financial returns but its health isn't improving, the brand manager is asked to figure out why and to go to work on that. Marketing programs that end up in the bottom left-hand corner aren't repeated.

It's as simple as that—a visual tool that makes sense to both marketers and accountants. "The simpler you make the measurement tools," Malcolm says, "the more likely they are to be used, the more focused people become, and the easier it is to instill best practices." Over three decades in marketing and general management, Malcolm has come to the conclusion that marketing people are naturally curious. "Unfortunately, that also means they have a natural tendency to complicate things," he warns. "In today's world of media and audience fragmentation, that can be dangerous. It's hard to choose what to do out of the thousands of things you *could* do. We try to give our people a framework to help them simplify and focus."

Diageo's marketers nearly always learn something by studying the charts. For example, they discovered that whether or not a brand is "getting more popular" is a leading indicator of momentum and growth for alcoholic beverages, which is a social category. That insight prompted them to expand sampling in selected markets. "In our business, good marketing can affect the business in three to six months," Malcolm says. "I expect our marketers to constantly track their results and to reallocate their spending accordingly."

MARKETING CREDIBILITY

Tying marketing to financial results is critical to building credibility with other C-suite executives. When Malcolm became the company's chief marketing officer, he was virtually a stranger to most of his colleagues on the executive team. So every quarter, for three or four years, he reviewed his results with his colleagues on Diageo's Executive Committee. He showed them how effective advertising had been for the company's top brands, in each of its markets worldwide, warts and all. Malcolm is frank in admitting that when he put the first chart up in the company boardroom, he was a little nervous. He was about to "open his kimono" on a question that most marketing people dance around—does our advertising really work? Does it really grow the business?

He used another simple chart—columns of color-coded rectangles with a few easily identifiable icons. Green rectangles were good. Yellow meant "we don't know," and red meant, "we have a problem and we're working hard to solve it." Arrows pointing up or down indicated the direction of change from the last quarter. The first charts Malcolm put up on the screen for the Executive Committee showed an uncomfortable number of yellow and red rectangles. But his CEO's reaction could not have been better. "This is the most honest and transparent presentation I have ever seen for marketing," Malcolm still remembers him saying. "And I really do trust that you are on track to making the progress we need."

Malcolm was never able to show a solid green chart. But his willingness to share the bad with the good helped him earn the trust of the entire senior management team. Eventually, his quarterly charts gave way to periodic deep dives into areas requiring senior attention, and Diageo brand managers are no longer required to use the Dogs and Stars charts (though many still do). But tracking marketing effectiveness in the context of CFO-friendly operating results is deeply inculcated in the company's culture because it works:

☞ It clarifies and defines marketing's role in the company, as well as everyone's role within marketing.

☞ It enables marketers to make decisions based on hard facts supplemented by experience and intuition, rather than the other way around.

☞ It gives marketing people greater credibility within the company by expressing their accountability in terms that matter to the business.

The genius of Malcolm's approach is that it constitutes a metaphorical "dashboard" that displays all the key measures of the company's marketing growth engine. But just as you can't rip the dashboard off a Honda and expect it to be helpful in driving a Porsche, Diageo's charts are not plug-and-play portable. A marketing dashboard is not a "thing," it's a process. It begins with a clear understanding of the company's financial goals, the drivers of financial success, the business strategies necessary to achieve them, and marketing's role within those strategies.

MARKETING'S ROLE

At a generic level, marketing's role is to move people to think, feel, and behave in a certain way. It might be attracting new users to a category, getting people to use more of your product, or convincing them to remain loyal to you in the face of competitors. The marketing dashboard turns those generic goals into specific objectives, brand by brand, program by program. It ties them to specific financial goals the CFO will recognize, mapping marketing initiatives to business outcomes. And it isn't something that is only read once or twice a year.[6]

"One of the worst things a marketer—or, for that matter, any business leader—can do is say, 'Just trust me; I'll show you when I make my numbers,'" warns General Electric's CMO, Beth Comstock. "You need to have progress reports—benchmarks that force you to ask, 'Are we giving it enough juice? Are we really being successful? Should we pull back?'" At the same time, marketers need to be careful not to get myopic about marketing investments, looking only for a short-term payoff. Diageo's approach balances its financial returns with the health of its brands. A company that looks only at the financial side of the equation might lard its marketing with programs to boost short-term profits at the cost of differentiation and customer loyalty.

Two marketing professors at Northwestern University's Kellogg School point to Starbucks as the most recent company to fall into this trap. "Over the past several years, the ubiquitous coffee chain has rolled out a series of initiatives (with positive ROI)," they note. "But as CEO Howard Schultz admitted, the initiatives have hurt the brand and weakened the company overall. The new breakfast sandwiches, for example, might generate incremental revenue, but leave the stores smelling like cheese factories and make the baristas feel like they are working at McDonald's."[7]

On the other hand, Diageo has run magazine ads for its superpremium Johnnie Walker Blue scotch whiskey, even though the stuff's so expensive every bottle bears a serial number and comes in a silk-lined box. The idea wasn't so much to sell a scotch that has a maximum volume of 20,000 cases worldwide as to cast a bright halo of status and prestige over the entire Johnnie Walker line, including the high-volume and affordable "red" label. It worked. Scotch is all about sending signals of success, power, and achievement. Sales of Johnnie Walker whiskies have consistently grown at a faster pace than the overall category.

MEASURING MARKETING ROI

There is no single "best" way to measure marketing's return on investment. Four Wharton School professors have developed a set of more than fifty key marketing metrics.[8] Which ones are appropriate depends on the category, the brand, and the business goals. What an auto company measures is going to be very different from a packaged-goods company whose products, such as laundry detergent or toothpaste, have a more predictive purchase cycle. The key is to validate the linkage between nonfinancial and financial measures. Use metrics that matter, not just the ones that are convenient.

For example, the famous Net Promoter[9] score is easy to use. Ask a sample of customers how likely they would be to recommend your product. Based on their responses on a 0 to 10-point scale, group them into "promoters" (9 or 10), "passives" (7 or 8), or "detractors" (0 to 6). Subtract the percentage of detractors from promoters, and, voilà, you've got a Net Promoter Score suitable for a one-page memo.

Unfortunately, one is reminded of Einstein's admonition to "make everything as simple as possible, but not simpler." Though Net Promoter scores are reputed to have three times greater correlation to loyalty than customer satisfaction, their practical value probably lies somewhere between predictive and irrelevant, depending on the brand and its category. The key is to calculate how an individual brand's Net Promoter score correlates with sales growth. And to understand *why* customers are promoters, passives, or detractors.

One should also be careful with metrics that sound right, but may be misleading. Acquisition and retention rates might seem like useful marketing performance metrics, but if they result from expensive promotional discounts or steep contract penalties, they aren't telling you much about the effectiveness of your marketing. And when pricing becomes your only source of difference, you are no longer marketing; you're liquidating your business. Amazon is known not only for its low prices, but also for its broad selection, convenience, and fast delivery. Even Wal-Mart has discovered that "everyday low prices" will only get it so far.

People with experience constructing marketing dashboards caution that what really works is seldom what they initially thought would work. Only about half the metrics that seem to make sense initially prove useful in the end. The others need to be fine-tuned, segmented differently, or even discarded. Some metrics don't have sufficient variability to be predictive. Others turn out to cast a bright spotlight on the obvious or trivial. And still others become lightning rods for criticism. If you inadvertently gore the favorite ox of someone politically important, you may find it more productive to remove the lance and aim it elsewhere, rather than press forward and risk the aggrieved party trying to undermine the whole project's credibility. Be prepared to make quick changes in response to feedback during the first three to six months. Then take a tip from the best software companies—develop a fixed and predictable schedule for updates.

Your best partner in building a marketing dashboard is your CFO.[10] The most elegant dashboard will amount to nothing but an interesting accessory unless your company's chief financial officer agrees on which marketing programs are most significant to the bottom line, how to measure their effectiveness, and how to interpret results. At Diageo, finance people play an important role in gathering the data for Malcolm's performance charts, but, more importantly, the company's CFO buys into their logic. He can draw a straight line from Malcolm's charts to the company's financial results.

The masters of marketing follow three simple rules in measuring the return on marketing investment by brand:

1. They keep the process simple, focusing on three or four metrics that can cascade throughout the organization.

2. They choose metrics that are particular to their brand and that reflect marketing's impact on consumer behavior.

3. They compare their performance to their best competitor's and review the metrics they track at regular intervals to ensure they're still
relevant.

MAKE EVERYONE A MARKETER

Diageo's CFO is not the only C-suite colleague who understands what
marketing is up to. Malcolm set in place a system to ensure that everyone at the company knows what they need to do to produce strong
brands and healthy financial results. This really means everyone—not
just the people in marketing.

Diageo was still a corporate toddler when Malcolm became chief
marketing officer—not quite a blank slate, but not totally fixed in its
ways either. On the other hand, because it was the product of a series
of mergers—Seagram's spirits and wines were added in 2001—the
company's marketers had all been trained in different ways and used
different languages. Diageo needed a coherent approach to marketing
and to building brands.

The company drew from the best practices and learning at its con-
stituent companies, including the ones being spun off, as well as from
academia. "We spent a fair amount of time developing a language and
a set of tools and a philosophy of building brands," Malcolm says.
The resulting product is called the "Diageo Way of Brand Building,"
(DWBB, pronounced "dweeb," as in "have you been dweebed?").
Basic "dweebing" happens in a five-day, interactive training program
that teaches a common framework so Diageo brand managers approach their work in the same way, while also having the freedom to
develop very distinct personalities, positioning, and value propositions
for their individual brands. A series of thirteen books codifies the approach and provides useful references and examples.

So far, Diageo has invested more than $70 million to "DWBB" its
employees. Of course, all the company's marketers have attended, but
in addition more than 500 have been trained as course facilitators.
Diageo's CEO and its executive board attended an early session, followed by the leaders of every function in every market, as well as
agencies and joint-venture partners. All told, more than 10,000 people
have attended the training course, which has been given in twelve languages across eighty countries. Malcolm himself teaches one week of

the DWBB program every year, as do other senior Diageo marketers. In fact, the program is entirely staffed from within the company's ranks; no outside trainers are involved.

There has been surprisingly little pushback, even from the "creative types" who are notoriously resistant to structure. "I've discovered that you don't have to push people to use something that makes their lives easier and that works," Malcolm says. "Maybe 20 percent of the new people we hire want to do their own thing. Eventually, they either come around or we agree to part ways."

The Diageo Way of Brand Building has permeated every function and level of the company. "I knew we were beginning to get on the right track, that we had started to arrive," Malcolm says, "when one of our senior sales directors said, 'Hey, we need a DWBB for sales. Please develop it fast as the marketing folks are moving ahead of us.'" In fact, about a third of the people who attended the course were from outside marketing.

When everyone thinks of themselves as marketers, there's a good chance it's because the marketers think of themselves, first and foremost, as businesspeople:

☞ *They speak the language of business, a language of returns on investment, hurdle rates, and operating margins.* They know how to read a balance sheet and an income statement as easily as a media plan or a creative brief. "If a marketing person can't speak the language of the business in a credible way," warns Heidrick & Struggles's Stevenson, "it's impossible to get recognition or respect."

☞ *They define their success in terms that matter to the business.* When asked to identify the most important attributes of a successful chief marketing officer, 65 percent of respondents to a Spencer Stuart study cited an ability to influence the bottom line, followed by strategic orientation (44 percent) and customer orientation (33 percent).[11]

☞ *They work on their personal development as businesspeople.* The masters of marketing "don't spend a lot of time on self-promotion," Stevenson says, "they focus on self-improvement." They take on responsibilities outside of their comfort zone, participate in strategic cross-functional initiatives, and leverage the expertise of younger members of their team for "reverse mentoring" in areas like new media. Marketing leaders don't have to know how to optimize page rendering. But in a Web 2.0 world, they should know what it is and how to get it done.

☞ *They see their primary responsibility as leading a strong team, not serving as the company's principal "ad maker."* "Functional skills are nice," notes Spencer Stuart's Greg Welch, "but for the top marketing job, leadership is more important. No one can do everything. The marketing head's job is to build a team that can." Such a team has a good balance of creative and analytical skills. It's diverse, from a variety of industries and backgrounds. And it shares a common approach to marketing, based on business acumen and tight alignment with the company's financial goals.

☞ *They "infiltrate" the company's other organizations.* They don't spend a lot of time in their offices, meeting with their own direct reports. They spend it with their business colleagues, educating them about marketing but also learning about their functions, their concerns, and their goals. They look for opportunities to add value to their colleagues' functions. For example, Forrester's Cindy Commander likes to tell the story of a CMO who worked with his company's chief information officer on an internal campaign to improve perceptions of information technology's value.

☞ *Finally, they tie everything they do to the company's financial results, not metaphorically, but in reality.* They make the business's financial results the gauges and knobs by which marketing is run. At Diageo, finance people within each brand group support the measurement systems. At companies like Yahoo! and Home Depot, the finance department "owns" the marketing ROI dashboards. But in all cases, finance and marketing work in close partnership.

PART TWO

Think Outside In

Connect to Your CEO's Highest-Order Goal—Profitable Growth

"The aim of marketing is to know and understand the customer so well the product or service fits him and sells itself."

—PETER DRUCKER

CHAPTER FIVE

DEVELOP INSIGHT INTO PEOPLE'S NEEDS

"It takes little talent to see what lies under one's nose,
a good deal to know in what direction to point that organ."
—W.H. AUDEN

According to *Advertising Age*, the best marketer of the twentieth century was Procter & Gamble. The recognition seems appropriate enough for the company that invented brand management, pioneered in consumer market research, and became the most pervasive advertising voice of the century. P&G even created an entire category of entertainment—soap operas—to promote its detergents and other household products. But A.G. Lafley, who took over as the company's CEO at the dawn of the new millennium, suspected that the skills of the past would not sustain P&G in the twenty-first century.

P&G FOLLOWS CONSUMERS

When Lafley became CEO, half of P&G's top fifteen brands were losing market share, the company's stock price was in free fall, and employee morale was in an even steeper nosedive. Consumers were changing—the proverbial "little homemaker" had shed her apron and left the house. The world was fragmenting into countless market segments defined by changing demography and what *BusinessWeek* called "increasingly nuanced product preferences."[1] David Martin, president of brand consultancy Interbrand, put it succinctly: "All the research we're doing tells us that the driver of demand going forward is all about products that are 'right for me.'"[2] Those changes put a premium on understanding who the consumer is, perhaps more deeply than the consumer does.

Consumer understanding was a lesson that the company had already learned the hard way in foreign markets. In 1956, P&G introduced Crest, a new mint-flavored toothpaste with cavity-protecting fluoride. While other toothpastes, including P&G's Gleem, promised whiter teeth, Crest advertised therapeutic benefits under the slogan "Look Ma, no cavities." Crest quickly captured 10 percent of the U.S. market and the company decided to sell it in England as well. But, while the toothpaste flew off shelves in the United States, it gathered dust in the United Kingdom. When P&G's researchers looked into it, they discovered why. In England, people associated mint with "spearmint," the aromatic oil used in liniment. They could imagine rubbing it on aching muscles, but not on their teeth.

When P&G entered China in the late 1980s, one of its first steps was to dispatch hundreds of researchers to live with Chinese families and observe how they approach everyday tasks, from changing the baby to brushing their teeth. The knowledge they gathered informed everything they did, from what products the company would offer to how it formulated them. Wherever possible P&G used local flavors, colors, and textures. A jasmine-flavored Crest toothpaste, for example, capitalized on the Chinese belief that tea is good for controlling bad breath.

Two decades later, the company was still following the same play book. P&G researchers noticed that the Chinese who lived in small rural villages did their laundry by hand, putting just enough detergent in the basin to create light foam in the water. That made it easier to rinse the clothes and used less water, which had to be carried in buckets from a neighborhood pump. That observation led to the development of single-use packages of low-sudsing Tide Clean White.[3] The suds rinsed out completely in just one bowl of clean water so it was more convenient and saved trips to the village pump. As a result of paying close attention to what its customers in China do, as well as what they say, P&G today is the most successful foreign marketer in the country. It actually sells more Crest toothpaste in China than in the United States.

JIM STENGEL

In 2000, Lafley could see that P&G's U.S. home market was becoming as "foreign" to the company as any country overseas. To grow sales, he decided to send the whole company back to school on U.S. consumers. He took the company off "transmit" and put it on "receive," vowing to "put the consumer at the center of everything the company does." It might have remained just another corporate cliché except for the executive Lafley chose as P&G's global marketing officer, an eighteen-year veteran of the company named Jim Stengel.

Trim, bespectacled, and a youthful-looking forty-five years old at the time, Stengel could easily have been confused with the cool high-school English teacher all the kids like. In fact, he considers teaching central to his role. Just before being named the company's global marketing officer, Stengel had been working with two Cincinnati University professors to upgrade the marketing organization's skills. When the profs trailed P&G marketers to get a better fix on their development needs, they discovered that the company's vaunted marketing people felt disconnected from the marketplace. They were so busy attending meetings, sitting through conference calls, filing reports, and responding to e-mail that they could only squeeze out six hours a month to spend with consumers, whether in formal focus groups or by informally approaching them in stores to ask what they were buying and why.

Stengel had learned the importance of staying close to customers in four different foreign assignments. In 1995, he was general manager of the company's business unit in the Czech and Slovak republics. To give Secret deodorant a boost in the market, he decided to give away free samples. Unfortunately, he didn't realize that in those days Czech women used deodorant as a perfume, not as part of their daily routine. They were more likely to dab it on their necks before a date than roll it across their armpits after a shower. His sampling program had given potential customers enough deodorant for a year. Sales didn't budge. "It was a classic case of not being close enough to the consumer," he now admits. "It wouldn't have taken much to understand that Czech women don't use deodorant every day." Stengel never made the mistake again. And when he became the company's global marketing officer, he made sure P&G wouldn't either.

CONSUMER RESEARCH

P&G literally invented the field of consumer research back in 1925 when it sent teams of recent female college graduates door-to-door to interview housewives about laundry, cooking, dishwashing, and any other chore for which it might have a product. By the 1960s, its research moved to the telephone and focus groups, but the company continued to collect reams of data and it expected the brand managers to make good use of it.

P&G runs a "Marketing University" where teachers from in and outside the company educate its 3,000-odd marketers on best practices and marketing innovations. It holds an annual brand-building symposium that brings everyone together to recognize, and learn from, outstanding work. Stengel convenes quarterly meetings of the people working on the company's fifteen biggest brands so they can learn from each other. The company periodically holds internal trade shows where brand managers display storyboards explaining recent successes and new ideas.

Abe Jones, a principal in the AdMedia Partners merger and acquisition advisory firm, notes that "P&G pushed responsibility down, forcing brand managers to be more entrepreneurial, long before Tom Peters made it a consultant's bullet point." In fact, Procter & Gamble has so refined its approach to marketing that it is a source of intellectual leadership for the entire economy. "GE and McKinsey people might take issue with this," says Jones, "but in my opinion, the P&G way of doing things is so disciplined and runs so deep, it has made its alumni more successful than those of any other company in the world."

But by 2000 Stengel's internal research suggested that the company's marketing people were barely able to stay afloat in the quantitative analysis flooding their offices and PCs. Worse, reading about consumers, rather than meeting with them in person, is like trying to type with boxing gloves on. "Without that direct contact," he wrote in a later report, "it was difficult to build an emotional connection, which is what ultimately leads to brand loyalty."[4]

Stengel also questioned whether moderated focus groups were really all that useful when P&G and its competitors were already addressing consumers' most obvious needs, and growth would only come from meeting needs that customers had difficulty articulating. Customers can tell you how to improve the products they use, but few know enough about the art of the possible to describe the next generation. If you had asked a farmer in the nineteenth century what he needed, he would have described a larger horse that ate less, not a tractor. Akio Morita, the cofounder of Sony, is reputed to have said, "We don't ask consumers what they want. They don't know. Instead, we apply our brain power to what they need, and will want, then make sure we're there, ready."

UNARTICULATED NEEDS

The holy grail of consumer research is understanding unarticulated needs. Spreadsheets don't come with a column headed "insight." Real insights are seldom that obvious, or they're *so* obvious few people ever see them. And many times, it's not what the data say, but what they don't say that matters. Consumer research has moved far beyond the homely definition Henry "Buck" Weaver gave it in his early days at General Motors—"finding out what people like, doing more of it, finding out what people don't like, doing less of it."[5]

Convinced that all the slicing and dicing of data was stifling customer insight, Stengel flipped the company's approach. He instructed his people to start with direct observation of customers in their natural settings, followed by quantitative analysis based on those observations. And he ensured that they spent time outside the middle-class suburbs where they themselves lived to observe a wide range of customers with diverse backgrounds, values, and cultural reference points.

Furthermore, instead of asking consumers what products they use, he focused his researchers on figuring out *how* consumers use them to uncover latent needs they might not even know they have. "What the customer buys and considers value is never a product," Peter Drucker pointed out. "It is always utility, that is, what a product or service does for him. And what is value for the customer is anything but obvious."[6]

People sometimes find uses for a product that the manufacturer never anticipated. Who knew that parents would use Cheerios as an easy-to-carry snack for restless toddlers? Or that gardeners would spray cooking oil on lawnmower blades to keep cut grass from sticking? People also unwittingly mask their real needs behind compensating behavior. For example, when P&G researchers hung out with people cleaning their homes, they discovered that dustpans are really a way of compensating for the fact that while brooms can sweep dust and dirt into a pile, the pile still needs to be disposed of. The result was the Swiffer floor-cleaning system, which combined broom and dustpan in one product.[7]

Sometimes what people really want may not be functional, but aspirational and emotional, such as the need to feel with-it, pretty, or athletic. There was no general outcry for an upscale coffeehouse before Starbucks began opening stores that served a high-quality brew in a socially and aesthetically pleasing environment. Similarly, at the height of its success, Victoria's Secret wasn't selling lingerie; it was putting romance, glamour, and fantasy in a box. And today, more than two decades after they first landed in shoe stores and ten years after their namesake left the basketball court for the last time, Air Jordans are more than polyurethane encapsulated air; they're the essential part of a uniform that identifies the wearer as fit and active—even if he or she is lying in a hammock.

Few people realize they're buying something so intangible. If you ask them, they'll say they're attracted to good-tasting coffee, luxurious fabrics, and comfortable feel. And those qualities are important, but they don't tell the whole story. To identify people's *real* needs you need to immerse yourself in their lives, from where they play and work to where they learn and worship.

CONSUMER UNDERSTANDING

Stengel's goal was to make P&G the world's foremost "consumer understanding" company, so he urged the company's marketers to spend lots of time with consumers, experiencing their morning routine, helping them with chores, and asking them about their habits and frustrations. "What we're trying to do is let people, without a filter, really be with our consumer in her life," he says.

Such "consumer immersion experiences," as Stengel calls them, have become commonplace at P&G. It was a technique the company was already using in foreign markets that it knew it didn't understand. Applying it in the United States and other so-called developed countries was a powerful new idea. The technique owes more to anthropology than polling, but P&G's goal is not so much to understand where consumers have been, but where they're going—to find new uses for existing products and breakthrough ideas for new products.

For example, P&G originally marketed Febreze as a product to remove unwanted odors such as smoke from fabrics and textiles. But when the company's marketers began observing how consumers were using Febreze, they discovered that some men used it on their gym bag, teenage girls used it on everything in their closet, and teenage boys sprayed it on the seats of their cars. Based on their research, they repositioned Febreze from an "odor remover" to a "fabric refresher," increasing the size of the business by 50 percent every year for three years.

Observations like these also contributed to an entirely new spin on laundry—don't do it! Just spray the clothes you've been wearing with Swash, a line of products designed to get stains, wrinkles, and odors out of clothing without putting them in a washer. The products themselves aren't really new. P&G already sold a Downy Wrinkle Releaser spray and a Tide-to-Go stain-remover pen. But the company found that college students hated doing laundry so much they were willing to rewear slightly soiled clothes if they could get away with it socially. Swash products are so singularly focused on college kids' unarticulated needs, they're only available online.

MARKETING ON PURPOSE

The real benefit of customer immersion research is that it forces marketers to adopt a radically different perspective. Instead of looking at the world through the lens of their product line, they begin to look at their capabilities through the lens of customers' lives. Instead of focusing on product features and benefits, they try to understand their customers' values. "We really try to get at what we can do through our brands to make a difference in people's lives," Stengel says. "Once that's your goal, everything changes—from the competitors you worry about to the way you interact with R&D, sales, and retailers." Stengel calls that "purpose-based marketing."

For example, a decade ago, P&G's diaper scientists were obsessed with one thing—dry bottoms. Most of their energy went into making diapers stay drier longer. But the company's biggest competitor in the diaper business stumbled onto a more holistic approach. Some consultants convinced Kimberly-Clark that pull-on diapers had a lot of emotional appeal for parents and toddlers, who saw them as a step toward "grown-up" dress. Diapers are clothing with symbolic as well as functional meaning, they told the company. Kimberly-Clark rolled out Huggies Pull-Ups nationally in 1991 and, by the time P&G caught on, annual sales had reached $400 million a year.

As it happens, none of the Pampers marketers had babies. But when they spent time in homes with triplets or shopping with families trailing a toddler, they quickly realized that wet bottoms were only a small part of parents' daily concerns. Moms and dads were far more focused on their babies' overall development and health. And trying to determine how diapers fit into the two- to three-year arc of a baby's initial development kindled an even stronger linkage between the R&D lab and marketing. Instead of obsessing about the technology of fluid absorption as a goal in itself, they began thinking of diapers as clothing, which led to improvements in the diaper's fit, feel, and appearance. They hired fashion designers to work on the brand and made Pampers more stretchy and fabric-like, eliminating the feel of plastic against baby's skin. They asked themselves how they could help babies sleep better, directly contributing to their brain development. And once P&G's marketing and research people understood how frustrated parents can get with toilet training, they developed a line of Pampers Feel 'n Learn trainers that stay wet for two minutes, prompting toddlers to give the potty a try.

What happened, Stengel says, is that Pampers's brand managers began thinking "more holistically" about their role in making people's lives better. The Pampers.com website they created is more about educating parents than selling diapers and attracts 1.5 million unique visitors per month. "Pampers used to be all about drier bottoms," he says.

"Now they're about giving and caring. And that service mentality is reflected in everything from the product design and packaging to the door-to-door health advice we give in developing markets."

Stengel also discovered that when marketers go into the field their whole attitude changes. People get inspired. "Because whatever they're working on—whether it's a life-changing drug like Actonel or Asacol, or it's Tide or Downy—when they understand the product has a role in someone's life, they come back more pumped up," he says.

TARGETED INNOVATION

Once you have spent time with consumers on a shop-along or a live-along, it's hard to think of them as a homogeneous mass. You begin to see how different they are, and how their cultural background influences their behavior. Immersion research begins with "Who is your consumer?" and leads quickly to "What's different about her?" The result is target-based innovation.

In fact, Stengel likes to say that P&G no longer has any "mass-market brands." Take Tide, for example. It's one of the company's oldest brands, dating back to 1946, but it comes in multiple variations, responding to consumer preferences for different fragrances, fabric softeners, or sudsing levels. It even comes in a cold-water version to save energy costs, a concentrated form that saves on plastic packaging, and as a solid stain-remover stick that people can carry around.

All told, in the past eight years, P&G has increased its investment in immersive research more than fivefold and has invested well over $1 billion in consumer and shopper research, twice as much as its competitors. Every year, P&G marketers observe or work with more than four million consumers in sixty countries.

Has the investment paid off? P&G has traditionally spent about 10 percent of sales on advertising. That was the case in 1999, just before Lafley took over, and sales increased about 3 percent over the prior year. In 2007, P&G again spent about 10 percent of sales on advertising, but its revenue increased closer to 12 percent. In other words, P&G spent proportionately about the same amount of money and got four times the lift. In 2000, P&G had ten billion-dollar brands, which accounted for about 50 percent of net sales and slightly more of profits. Today, it has twenty-three billion-dollar brands, accounting for two-thirds of net sales and more than 70 percent of profit.

IMMERSIVE RESEARCH

Perhaps the most objective measure of immersive research's success is the degree to which other companies, large and small, are adopting the technique. Anthropology, or ethnographic research, is no longer restricted to the jungle or outback. Arm & Hammer goes into people's homes to inspect the insides of their refrigerators and the conditions of their cats' litter boxes. Nissan photographs the cluttered trunks and front seats of people's vehicles. And General Mills watches consumers shopping at a faux grocery store it operates in its Minneapolis headquarters.

The result? When Arm & Hammer noticed that consumers missed large clumps of wet litter in cleaning the cat's litter box, they came up with a version that turns blue when it's wet. When Nissan saw how much junk ends up in the average car, they divided the Sentra's trunk into storage areas and added spaces in the passenger compartment for things like CDs. And based on shopper reaction in its pretend grocery store, General Mills redesigned its Bisquick Shake 'n' Pour container from a square tub to a bottle that looks more shakable.

Twenty years ago, Microsoft had two researchers watching consumers on their home or work computers. Today, it has 300. And about half of General Mills's consumer research now involves observing people individually, compared with ten years ago when about 80 percent of its research was done in focus groups. Tesco, the U.K.-based retail giant, requires every executive, including the CEO, to spend one week a year in a junior-level job in one of its stores. And it has been known to have executives trail customers home, watching them cook and eat meals.

It's not easy to discover needs that customers themselves can't articulate. The available tools—primarily focus groups, surveys, and data mining—are relatively crude. Mary Lou Quinlan, who specializes in advising companies on women's needs, likes to quote data from a survey she took on what actually happens on the other side of the two-way mirror during focus groups—67 percent of the observers made phone calls, 24 percent took a nap, and 19 percent were so bored they cleaned out their wallet or purse. Not surprisingly, three out of four left before the session was over. Focus groups can also be misleading. When Herman Miller showed its Aeron chair to a focus group of likely buyers, they asked if they could see the upholstered version.

As chief analyst for Millard Brown, one of the world's leading market research companies, Nigel Hollis is an unlikely champion of customer immersion programs. While he doesn't think they can substitute for quantitative surveys, he does believe most businesspeople would benefit from combining the "shallow view" of most traditional research with the "in-depth view" provided by participating in peoples' lives. "Few businesspeople can extrapolate from a report or set of numbers to thinking and feeling like the person who buys their products," he says. "Seeing someone wrestle with packaging, deliberate between spending the remains of the week's budget on snacks or cereals, or select clothing based on comfort rather than appearance can bring home the results from research in a much more meaningful way."

LISTENING WITH YOUR EYES

The trick is to listen with your eyes as your customer shops, cleans house, or makes dinner. You'll learn more about his or her life, hopes, needs, and goals in one afternoon of what P&G calls a "shop-along" than in fifty one-hour focus groups. But Hollis warns, "Such learning should also be tested further to ensure it isn't based on atypical behavior or a misinterpretation of what people are really trying to do."

Of course, watching customers use your product can also be done under more controlled conditions. Target, for example, pays customers to assemble products in a "user experience lab" at its Minneapolis headquarters. Merchandisers and buyers watch from behind two-way glass as people struggle to assemble a gas grill or a bicycle, and a hidden camera memorializes the process for later analysis. Instructions and even parts are changed based on what they find. For example, when screws kept falling off a screwdriver, Target had the vendor magnetize them.

Sometimes listening with your eyes will lead to apparently naïve questions. For example, the shape of watermelons made it difficult for Japanese storeowners to stock them in their small shops. Someone asked why watermelons couldn't be square, and it turned out that if you place them in a square box as they grow, they assume its shape. Square watermelons are cheaper to ship, they're easier to stock in the store, and they take less space in customers' refrigerators, which means they're willing to pay a little more for them. Similarly, who thought yogurt could come in a tube? But that's what Yoplait did with Go-Gurts. It made yogurt easier and more fun for kids to eat and it helped Yoplait pull ahead of Dannon.

Anthropologists specialize in finding patterns in people's beliefs and behavior that lead to such "What if?" questions. "My clients . . . used to ask me to find the solution (to a known problem)," writes anthropologist Grant McCracken. "More and more, they ask me to find the problem. How, they ask, should we be thinking about this?"[8] The answer, for both anthropologists and marketers, is to immerse themselves in people's lives and to listen with their eyes.

THE BASICS

While it sounds simple, customer immersion requires significant preparation. It's a lot more complicated than hanging out at the mall or shadowing someone around the grocery store. From the top, it's important to specify whom should be observed, who should do the observing, and what the observer should be watching for.

> ☞ *Figure out who your customer is, not in demographic generalities, but in terms of the particular tasks he or she wants to accomplish functionally, socially, or emotionally.* How is he or she different from all the other people who have similar tasks? Virgin Entertainment's primary customers are not simply the CD-buying teenagers you'd expect, but "social fun spenders" who tend to be ethnically diverse females in their twenties. That insight affects everything from Virgin's inventory to store layout and window displays.

> ☞ *Watch for unexpected local tastes and customs.* Predictions of a homogeneous global market were somewhat premature. For example, what could be simpler than selling tortillas in the Southwest of the U.S.? But Gruma, a $2.5-billion Mexican bread company, claims that Texans like their tortillas

fluffy, while Californians like them elastic. It seems each state was settled by Mexicans from different regions.

☞ *Listen for expressions of feelings such as anger, joy, envy, or fear as the customer describes what he or she is trying to do.* Customer emotions will give you a clue as to their unexpressed values. To help senior managers understand how tedious and frustrating simple banking functions can be, Credit Suisse's David McQuillen made senior managers open a new checking account at a local branch, then he had them take the teller's place to get the full experience.[9]

☞ *Schedule face-to-face visits in your customers' natural habitats, whether they accomplish the task in their homes, workplaces, or a laundromat.* Then you can concentrate on figuring out how the task fits into their lives. What are they trying to do? What problems are they encountering? When Scott Cook, one of Intuit's founders, first got the idea for an automated bill-paying system, he called people at random from the Palo Alto, California, and Winnetka, Illinois, phonebooks to gauge their interest. And when he had the first working model of Quicken, he sent programmers into customer's homes to watch how they used the program. This not only led to product enhancements like the electronic paper tape in the Quicken calculator, but also to whole new products like QuickBooks for small businesses. Where did Cook begin his career? P&G.

☞ *Reach out especially to customers you wouldn't normally encounter in your own social circles.* At one P&G Worldwide management meeting, Stengel had each attendee spend an afternoon with a low-income family in the Cincinnati area to see firsthand what role P&G brands played in their lives. Stengel also takes his own medicine—for example, on a recent trip to China, he spent time with both low- and high-income families.

☞ *Send the right people into the field. Cross-functional teams work best because people always interpret what they ob-*

serve through their personal frame of reference. Since the goal is to identify unarticulated needs for which you might have a profitable technological solution, at minimum the team should include people from marketing, R&D, and finance or business strategy. But all team members should be open-minded, naturally curious, and imaginative.

☞ *Provide a native guide to the techniques of ethnographic research.* It takes great skill to put personal views aside, and not only listen to what others are saying and doing, but also to ask the right open-ended, neutral questions—such as "Why are you doing that?"—to get the right input. Give team members the benefit of a disciplined process so they surface from their immersion in customers' lives with useful information.

☞ *Schedule enough visits with enough different customers to ensure that you are not misled by atypical situations.* It's easier to spot meaningful patterns if you have sufficient data points. When P&G marketers videotaped men (wearing swimsuits) in the shower, they were surprised by how many used body wash on their hair. That led to the development of Old Spice High Endurance Hair & Body Wash, a combination shampoo and body wash.

☞ *Be open to input you weren't expecting.* Levi Strauss invited a group of mothers to bring their fourth-grade daughters in to discuss ideas for new girls' jeans. While the girls talked denim with a moderator, the mothers were cooling their heels in a nearby conference room. Someone brought up how hard it is for women to find jeans that fit. That wasn't exactly news to the Levi's people, but they were impressed by the level of emotion in the discussion and by the fact that every woman there seemed to have the same set of concerns, no matter what her body type. Thirty designs and a year later, that discussion led to the introduction of Levi's "Totally Slimming" line of jeans.

☞ *Ensure that the information gathered from these interactions doesn't get filed away in the bottom drawer of a mid-level planner.* It should be disseminated throughout the company to give context to intelligence accumulating elsewhere, including on the Internet, in mainstream media, and in your own customer service channels. The biggest hole in most companies' research programs is a lack of history and case studies that provide perspective and help avoid reinventing the wheel.

☞ *Be prepared to capture visual, auditory, and sensory cues.* Audio recorders and video cameras are extremely helpful to capture actions and comments that might be missed the first time around. When Tesco entered the U.S. market with a new chain of Fresh & Easy convenience stores, it videotaped people's refrigerators and pantries in its initial markets. Analyzing the tapes helped it with everything from store layouts to inventory. It even suggested private-label goods like its Fresh & Easy Smart Box packaged snacks—clear plastic boxes with crackers, cheese, raisins, carrot sticks, and organic milk. With the consumer's permission, some research services can even outfit a home with lipstick cameras that are unobtrusive and capture candid behavior.

☞ *Schedule debriefing sessions for all the participants.* Include a few knowledgeable people who didn't accompany the field teams. Their questions and reactions can help uncover insights that might otherwise have been missed. Design firm IDEO trains its people to follow five rules: defer judgment, build on the ideas of others, hold one conversation at a time, stay focused on the topic, and encourage wild ideas.[10]

Of course, none of these techniques will have a lasting effect unless companies keep marketers and researchers in their positions long enough for them to develop a significantly deeper understanding of the consumer. That understanding required major changes at P&G, where, before he became global marketing officer, Jim Stengel had ten different assignments in eighteen years.

Finally, companies need to act on the insights their people develop. Ed Landry, a Booz Allen Hamilton consultant, has studied hundreds of marketing organizations. "There is a world of difference between knowing and doing," he says. "P&G walks the talk."

CHAPTER SIX

DEVELOP INSIGHT INTO BUSINESSES' NEEDS

"A rational person is someone you don't know very well."
—ANONYMOUS

Prematurely bald with a brush mustache, bushy eyebrows, and piercing eyes, the late Ted Levitt looked like the demanding overseer of a busy loading dock through much of his unusually productive life. But for more than forty years, he trafficked not in goods but in ideas, great pallets of ideas that are still taught at business schools around the world. Officially, he chaired the marketing area at the Harvard Business School, but through a prodigious output of books and articles, including a four-year stint as editor of the *Harvard Business Review*, Levitt influenced generations of the world's business leaders.

As a lecturer, Levitt had an easy wit and a knack for memorable aphorisms packed with meaning. Lecturing his marketing students, he famously thundered, "People don't want to buy a quarter-inch drill. They want a quarter-inch hole!" Few business-to-business marketers would argue with Levitt's insight. Yet they continue to push drills, not holes. And they segment their market by the equivalent of drill types, not by the kinds of holes different customers might need. But, from a customer's perspective, the structure of a market is very simple. As Clayton Christensen—one of Levitt's students and now a Harvard

Business School professor himself—put it, "Customers just need to get things done and they hire products to help them do it."[1]

THE BUSINESS-TO-BUSINESS CUSTOMER

Successful marketers figure out what jobs customers need to get done and then develop products to do them. But it is precisely at this point that consumer marketers and many of their business-to-business counterparts part company. Many business-to-business marketers assume that their customers understand precisely what products and services they need, have reduced it all to a set of carefully crafted specifications, and make entirely rational decisions about their purchase.

But even sophisticated business customers can't always articulate their real needs and they don't necessarily get more eloquent when they gather in committee. The purchasing department may send out exquisitely detailed requests for quote, but the specs they're working against probably originated elsewhere. Everybody who touched the requests probably added their favorite options or the latest bells and whistles they read about in the trade media. The in-house lawyers undoubtedly added legalese designed to prove their worth as much as to protect the customer if anything goes wrong. The people who actually use the material being ordered probably never got near the bid documents, so many significant features were never mentioned. And, if the end users somehow did get to put their two cents in, their input could be misleading unless you understand the full context of the circumstances in which they work.

For example, Becton, Dickinson (BD) is a leading supplier of medical devices, supplies, and technology. It introduced the first disposable syringe, the first defibrillator, the first pacemaker, and the first patient-monitoring system. Among the innovative products it introduced in the 1970s was a portable electrocardiogram monitor that communicated with a central nursing station wirelessly. Nurses told BD they wanted a waterproof case for the transmitter the patients carried. Every competitor, except BD, had a waterproof case.

At first, this request seemed to make little sense. Heart attack patients don't typically swim while in the hospital. And when patients shower, they remove the transmitter and electrodes. Moreover, a nurse is always standing outside the shower stall, so he or she wouldn't really need help finding the patient. After a little probing, BD discovered that patients would sometimes drop the wireless transmitter in the toilet and their nurse would have to clean the unit. The nurses didn't so much want a waterproof transmitter as one that was easy to clean.

BD's answer was anything but easy. They showed the nurses how to snap open the wireless transmitter and clean it by pouring saline solution over the electronics inside, and then how to dry it with a hair dryer. One wonders if BD really understood what a cardiac intensive care unit is like. Nurses don't have time to dry electronic components by hand. In any case, the company soon sold its medical systems unit to another company that ultimately went bankrupt and was acquired in turn by Litton Industries.[2]

SUN MICROSYSTEMS

Sometimes, end users know exactly what they need. It just doesn't show up in the bid documents. For example, Sun Microsystems sells sophisticated technology to highly knowledgeable customers. When Sun engineers met with a large customer's data-center managers to discuss their plans for the next generation of computer systems, they expected to discuss processor architectures, memory capacity, and input/output options. So they were surprised that the discussion turned quickly to connectors and command lines—that is, the little plugs that go into the back of the computer and the instructions a user types to get the thing to do something.

It seems that in Sun's then-current high-end products, the connector between the user console and the data-center racks became easily unplugged. Not a big deal normally, but the data-center racks are off-limits to most people and in a locked cage. Putting the plug back in was a hassle. "Why couldn't you use a captive connector, like an RJ11 or DB9?" they asked. The Sun engineers had no answer. It could have been a requirement in the purchase specs, but no one placing the order thought to ask the people who actually run the data center.

Then the customer asked why every Sun product family used different commands to run the system. Even when two product families happened to have the same top-level command, the options and subcommands were often different. "We have to train our employees on three different command sets," the customer explained, showing a "cheat sheet" issued to systems administrators with the commands for the most common tasks on each product line. "Why can't you have one set of commands for all your products?" Again, the Sun engineers had no answer.

"We had created a great command line interface for our product line, with exactly the features and options our product needed," development engineer Bob Hueston later explained in his blog. "The engineers working on the other product lines did the same thing for their products."[3] Like most high-tech companies, Sun's salespeople spent lots of time with their customers' purchasing people and probably even took some of the information technology executives to lunch. But until Hueston showed up, no one bothered to meet with the people who were actually using their products.

Furthermore, not everyone who handles a Sun computer along the way is an electrical engineer or software programmer. To its credit, Sun wanted to understand what a customer's "first encounter" with the company was like—that is, from the time when the crated computers were dropped off on the customer's loading dock until they were up and running. It sent cross-functional teams to shadow some new computers as they arrived at fifty customer sites worldwide.

What they discovered ranged from the mundane to the serious. Just getting the computers out of the box was a chore and figuring out what to do with the packaging was a trick. In some offices, the packing material literally covered every lateral surface and couldn't be thrown out until the computer was safely booted on. They discovered that desk and office layouts vary significantly in different parts of the world, making it difficult to hide all the computer's connections. And not all the components shipped with the computers were as easy to install as they thought.

Because Sun had sent cross-functional teams into the field to observe these problems firsthand, most of the issues they identified were resolved relatively quickly. But if Sun hadn't gone looking for those problems, not many of them would have made their way through the corporate hierarchy in all the companies involved to get resolved.

Sun engineer Bob Hueston calls this whole process "breaking down the fourth wall," using a theater term that describes the invisible wall separating the audience from what's happening on the stage. Too many product development engineers, he argues, toil alone in their cubicles, hunched over their workstations, relatively oblivious to the customers who will eventually use what they're designing. The same could be said of marketing people, who should be the customer's voice within their companies.

SATISFYING UNMET NEEDS

The key, long before anyone starts throwing contract boilerplate around, is to understand what your customers are trying to do and how you can help them do it. Understanding and satisfying unmet needs is the real source of competitive advantage because, in the end, your customer is not buying a product, but the ability to make a profit, either by generating more revenue or by lowering costs.

Consider Seagate Technologies. As the first company in the world to manufacture computer hard drives, it clearly knows its business. But as the company's CEO, Bill Watkins, explained to the *Wall Street Journal*, as Seagate grew it lost touch with what its customers were trying to get done. He said:

> I got involved with trying to sell DVR drives to Scientific Atlanta. And we had shifted our whole focus from 5,400-rpm drives to 7,200-rpm drives. Well, they didn't want 7,200 [revolutions per minute]. And we kept telling them, "You are all screwed up. You don't understand this. This is so much better performance." In their mind they didn't need performance. They wanted the quietest storage device they could get their hands on because this box was going to be in the bedroom. They wanted absolutely no noise. And because of that they couldn't put a fan in the box to cool it down. And we didn't get the business.[4]

Seagate engineers and marketers had improved the price performance of their hard drives by 30 percent, but they lost the sale because they didn't really understand the job their customer needed to accomplish. If they had, they would have focused their energy on size and noise reduction rather than speed.

That's why Hewlett-Packard often sends engineers out to watch customers use their products. Their only instruction is to watch with open eyes and ears, but closed mouth. They can ask an occasional question, but they are never to guide or direct the customer. What they invariably see helps them design better products—whether they observe problems that arise, work-arounds customers devise, or capabilities that go unused.

Sometimes they ask the customer to describe what they're doing while they're doing it to get insight into their thought processes, which can often be very different from what the people who designed the equipment assumed. Often the customers will even express needs that only occur to them in the context of what they're doing and would never come up in a structured interview. For example, when a product developer from Hewlett-Packard watched a surgeon performing an operation, she noticed that the doctor guided his scalpel by watching a television screen that displayed a close-up image of the operating field. But the surgeon had to pause as people moving around the operating room periodically obscured his view of the screen for a few seconds.

That prompted the developer to think of ways to suspend the images a few inches in front of the surgeon's eyes. It would never have occurred to the surgeon to ask for such a product. He might not even have been aware of the problem. But when HP later introduced a lightweight helmet with a small TV screen attached at eye-level, it improved surgical productivity, increased medical accuracy, and made the surgeon's task easier.[5]

John Schiech, president of Black & Decker's DeWalt division, also understands the importance of observing customers on their own turf.

When his marketing people visited construction sites in the 1990s, they noticed that the McMansions many contractors were building had huge moldings. The most popular miter saws in those days, which retailed for about $200, had ten-inch blades and could cut only halfway through those big pieces of trim. "They had to pass a 16-foot piece of molding out the window, flip it around, pass it back in, and make the rest of the cut," he remembers. Schiech's people realized that if DeWalt offered a twelve-inch blade, which would require a completely different, much bigger saw, contractors could make these cuts in one pass. "So we developed and launched the twelve-inch miter saw, and charged $399. It became the number-one-selling miter saw by a huge margin, and remains so to this day."

DeWalt's engineers and marketers spend lots of time at job sites, talking to people who make their living with power tools and watching how they use them. Back in the office, they put all the information they've gathered into a database of tool features and customer contacts that engineers can draw on to help design new products. Once they have prototypes of new products, they take them back to the same job sites, leave them for a week or two, and collect feedback on how they performed.

Sometimes, the customer's needs are not so functional. Hill-Rom, which originated as a casket and hospital bed manufacturer, put its market researchers to work as hospital orderlies to better understand how it could improve its customers' profitability. It didn't take long for Hill-Rom's people to notice how much time they and the floor nurses spent on duties that were only tangentially related to patient care, such as lowering and raising beds and chasing TV remotes. Their observations led to the development of a new line of hospital beds with built-in controls that free nurses from nonnursing duties. Hill-Rom also extended its design excellence to the critical care environment, leading to the innovation of the power column and critical care beds. Eventually, Hill-Rom spun off its casket business and concentrated on an even broader line of medical equipment, but it describes its business as "partnering with health professionals to meet their care goals."[7]

In contrast, in the 1970s before Becton, Dickinson discovered market research, the company invested $1 million in today's money developing a Lojack-like wireless "patient locator" for coronary care units. The idea was that it would give medical staff instant information on the whereabouts of any patients who wandered off. The only problem—which didn't occur to BD until after the product was introduced—is that there was no market for it. Coronary care patients don't typically "wander off."

UNDERSTANDING YOUR CUSTOMER'S *GEMBA*

You can't really understand a company unless you understand the larger landscape in which it operates. The Japanese call this *gemba*, which is the term for the manufacturing floor. In Japan, if a problem occurs on the line, engineers swarm all over it to understand the full impact of the problem. Quality consultant Glenn Mazur first used the term to refer to any customer's place of business or lifestyle. The idea is that, to really understand a customer, you have to visit their *gemba*. Otherwise, you'll only have secondhand data and won't really relate to the customer's daily life, with all its challenges and opportunities.[8]

DuPont, for example, is one of the world's leading chemical companies. It sells very little directly to consumers, but it puts a lot of emphasis on understanding how its products fit into its customers' operations and how it can develop new products that address their long-term opportunities and challenges. For example, DuPont surveys automobile designers and engineers every year to identify their top concerns. At the top of the list in 2007 were environmental issues, followed closely by fuel economy. It was the first time in fourteen years that cost reduction didn't win. DuPont got lots of good publicity for the survey and associated itself with issues of importance to its customers. But more importantly, the company added to its understanding of customer needs. It wasn't just coincidence that the company figured out how to replace the steel in exhaust systems with a reinforced nylon resin. When used in the Volkswagen Golf, it reduced the component's weight by nearly half—and helped reduce the car's fuel consumption.

DuPont issues an annual report on the most popular car colors. (Silver led in the United States for six years straight until it was edged out by white in 2007.) Sure the company sells paint to nearly every car manufacturer, but the survey drives home the point that DuPont understands what consumers are looking for. Similarly, DuPont's plastics division sponsors an annual Oscars-like awards event to recognize the best packaging innovations. Not all the entries use DuPont plastics—and it isn't a requirement to win—but it highlights the company's leadership and innovation.

This isn't simply a matter of generating publicity. Understanding its customers' customers has been built into DuPont's DNA ever since it introduced nylon to the world during the Great Depression. In fact, DuPont didn't unveil the world's first synthetic fiber to scientists at an academic conference but to 3,000 women's club members at the 1939

World's Fair. Nylon is suitable for fishing line, medical sutures, and toothbrush bristles, but DuPont decided to focus on nylon as a replacement for the silk in women's hose. The company didn't plan on entering the hosiery business—it would sell nylon thread to garment companies—but it understood the importance of knowing end-user needs and helping to create demand for its immediate customers. When the first nylon stockings were introduced nationally in May 1940, women literally lined up to buy them. The company sold four million pairs in four days.

After World War II, a succession of synthetic fabrics, such as Orlon, Dacron, and Lycra, flowed out of DuPont's laboratories, and the company redoubled its efforts to better understand consumers' tastes in fashion and style. It also opened an office in the Empire State Building near New York's garment district so staff could feed information on trends and innovations back to the labs. All of this on-the-ground intelligence helped the company improve the performance of its fibers while also increasing their appeal.

Although DuPont sold most of its textile business in 2004, the company still puts a premium on understanding the needs of its customers' customers. For example, before introducing a new line of medical fabrics, DuPont tested them in operating rooms to better understand how surgeons and nurses define comfort and what they look for in medical gowns and drapes.[9]

WHAT BUSINESSES WANT

On the surface, it would seem that business customers all want the same thing—a fatter bottom line. But in reality they all have different ways to get it. Companies in the same industry can have wildly divergent views of value and how to create it. Consider Target and Wal-Mart. The former is looking for style and innovation at a good price; the latter wants reliable delivery at the lowest possible price.

Furthermore, the purchasing specs that are supposed to put all suppliers on an equal footing can be just as overwhelming for the buyer as for the seller. With more data than anyone could evaluate, let alone absorb, the typical business buyer falls back on rules of thumb and past experience to simplify decision making. Whether conscious or unconscious, much of the buying process then becomes an exercise in justifying the initial decision. No one who has ever been on either end of a major contract bid believes the dance is totally free of emotion. The saying "no one ever got fired for buying IBM" sustained the company for years until technology changed the competitive field under its big blue feet.

Emotion is not the opposite of reason. They are separate mental processes that often intersect and influence each other. Business customers are not a different species; they are people just like us. And like us, they want the same feelings of satisfaction, pride, and self-esteem from their jobs. Smart marketers understand the human context within which their customers operate. Then they focus on helping them achieve their business goals. Marty Homlish has been the chief marketing officer for the giant German software company SAP for more than seven years. It would be hard to find a more technical market, but Homlish believes the line between business and consumer marketing is disappearing. "Behind every B-to-B company is a consumer," he says. "The way you communicate to that person . . . [is] as an informed consumer."[10]

CUSTOMER SAFARIS

Ed Petrie is an expert on adhesives and sealants. In his thirty-year engineering career, he has written over 100 technical articles on the subject, as well as two popular reference books; holds a number of patents; and consults for a wide range of businesses and government agencies. If anyone can talk glue, it's Petrie. But that subject is far down on his list of topics when he's talking to a customer. He'd much rather talk about the customer's business. The reason is not exaggerated humility, but survival.

"Adhesives and sealants are complex products whose performance depends on how they are used," he explains. "Many material and processing variables can be tweaked to improve the finished product. You can't do that unless you know what your customer needs and how much he's willing to pay for it." Petrie believes marketing to businesses is more complex than to consumers because buyer and seller are more interdependent, the purchase process is more complicated, and everything is highly dependent on a third party—the end user.

That's why Petrie is a big proponent of what he calls "customer safaris,"[11] carefully orchestrated visits to gain insight into what customers really want, how they perceive value, and how you can help meet their unarticulated needs. In the business-to-business version of P&G's customer immersion process, managers and technical staff leave their offices and laboratories to travel to their customers' operations. They interview buyers and users. They tour the facilities where their products are used, asking open-ended questions about their business challenges and opportunities. They listen to the tone of people's voices, as well as to the content of what they're saying. They follow the flow of their customer's operation all the way from R&D to end user.

The main goal of a customer safari is to uncover what your customer—and, perhaps even more importantly, your customer's customer—needs. "Walking in our customer's shoes forces us to look at their problems, not our own," Petrie says, "and what inevitably follows are ingenious ways that we can make their business better." As Petrie has advised his clients in the adhesive industry, "It's important to bring business solutions to the customer and not just a bottle of glue."

But walking in a customer's shoes without stumbling requires careful choreography and orchestration. "You can't just throw people together and hope that magic happens," Petrie warns. The process has to be creatively managed with expert facilitation and results-oriented follow-up. Unfortunately, customer visits are not featured in marketing textbooks, and the subject is not taught in school. But the masters of marketing seem to share the same secrets:

☞ *They visit customers who use (or could use) their products in similar ways even if they are in different industries.* Their goal is to find the intersection between their customers' needs and their own capabilities. They make sure to include power users who stretch the limits of their capabilities, as well as small users who never ask for anything special. Whenever possible, they even include customers they've lost as well as customers they'd like.

☞ *They don't limit participation on their side to executives.* They bring people from a variety of functions and at different levels. As Jim Guerard of Macromedia put it, "product marketing, product management and engineering need to be present at all customer visits—like a jury in a court trial, they must all share the same information and weigh the same evidence in making product decisions."[12]

☞ *They meet with all team participants prior to the first customer visit to make sure everyone understands the goals.* They establish a few standard questions to ask all customers, for example, What keeps you awake at night? Where do you want to see your business in five years? What are your company's biggest opportunities? They encourage follow-up on the initial answers, asking for examples. They caution team members not to ask for solutions, but to probe for business problems. And they ask them not to talk about their product or company, but to make the customer's task the center of conversation.

☞ *They don't turn the visit into a sales call.* For that matter, they ask any salespeople on the visit to limit their participation to making introductions and taking notes. Good salespeople are trained to respond to customer objections and complaints. Should any complaints surface they don't want to push them aside, but to dive into them, prodding for more information.

☞ *They don't stay in their customers' conference rooms.* The whole idea is to observe how customers use the product, to see firsthand how it fits into their business process, and to ask open-ended questions about their operations and business goals. They try to meet customers at every level in a variety of functions so they can find out what's on their minds. They know they can't do that on mahogany row.

☞ *They don't expect lightning to strike in the first visit.* It takes a number of visits to accounts of all sizes to develop real insight into their business. But masters of marketing end each visit by debriefing all the participants while the visit is still fresh in their minds. They document the team members' observations and begin compiling an archive of customer visit data that they can share with others within the company.

☞ *When all the visits have been accomplished and people have had an opportunity to reflect on the data accumulated, they schedule a final brainstorming session to identify customer needs they can profitably address.* They're careful to include people who didn't participate in the visits in this final session. People who are fresh to the project will focus on the data and not on the personalities involved. They'll ask questions that probably won't occur to people who participated in the visits.

CHAPTER SEVEN

TURN INSIGHT INTO FORESIGHT

*"The most exciting phrase to hear in science,
the one that heralds new discoveries,
is not 'Eureka!' but 'That's funny . . . .'"*

—ISAAC ASIMOV

Nokia was a paper, rubber, and cable company for the first century of its life; it didn't manufacture its first mobile phone for another two decades after that. If it had stuck to its knitting, today it might have had a good business in rubber boots and toilet paper. But it wouldn't be the world leader in wireless handsets.

The path from paper to wireless was not as nonlinear as it may seem—rubber and paper are used in making cable; electronics was a logical offshoot of the cable business; and wireless was just an application of a certain type of electronics. But Nokia's transformation had less to do with clever R&D (though Nokia has plenty of people in white lab coats). Nokia owes its success to an uncanny ability to read where customers and technology are going, often before the customers themselves realize it. Most importantly, Nokia excels at what Peter Drucker considered one of management's most difficult tasks: "to abandon rather than defend yesterday."[1] The growing realization of that task's importance may explain one of the biggest shifts underway in marketing—the integration of marketing into companies' innovation processes.

According to research by the Association of National Advertisers (ANA), 70 percent of companies have reorganized in the last three years to give marketing a bigger role in strategy and innovation. While retaining responsibility for communications, fully 35 percent of consumer marketers and 47 percent of business marketers report that they are now also responsible for strategy and innovation. Additionally, nearly a quarter of business marketers said they also have primary responsibility for new business development. Three out of four marketers said they participate in the development of corporate strategy and half contribute to new product development. Nine out of ten are part of their company's senior leadership team.[2]

The ANA's research described an environment that reflects Drucker's belief that innovation is an economic, not a technical, term. It depends on exploiting changes in demography and values, as well as technology. And the masters of marketing are experts in two of those three areas.

At some companies, marketing is the engine of innovation; at others, it provides critical input. But in every case, there has long been a broad consensus, at least among academics, that "the R&D-marketing interface is one of the most critical" in the product-development process.[3] By translating customer insights into business insights such as revenue and profit potential, the masters of marketing help drive innovation and keep their companies ahead of the curve.

BUYING CUSTOMERS, NOT SELLING PRODUCTS

Harvard Business School professor Ted Levitt suggested that companies think of themselves not as selling products, but as buying customers. "An organization," he said, "must learn to think of itself not as producing goods or services, but as doing things that will make people want to do business with it."[4]

Consider Kiwi. For the first hundred years of its life, Kiwi was largely a purveyor of a shoe polish named in honor of the inventor's wife, who was a New Zealander, or "kiwi." The British and American armies adopted Kiwi polish during the First World War and spread its name around the world, just as new production methods made leather boots and shoes widely affordable. Eventually, Kiwi was sold in more than 200 countries and accumulated a 53 percent market share worldwide.

The Sara Lee Corporation bought Kiwi in 1984, but sales stalled as people began switching from leather shoes to sneakers or to footwear made from canvas and synthetic materials. In 2005, a new CEO began divesting nonstrategic units and lit a fire under management to accelerate growth. Kiwi interviewed 3,500 people in eight countries about shoe care in its search for new avenues of growth. It discovered that people would rather throw out an old pair of shoes than polish them. People no longer cared so much about the shine on their shoes; they were far more concerned about how fresh and comfortable they felt. On a list of more than twenty attributes in shoes, shine ranked seventeenth. Smell trumped shine. To grow, Kiwi had to "abandon yesterday" and learn about foot anatomy and bacterial growth. It had to become a foot-care brand, not simply a polish.

The name the company chose for the growth initiative that followed—"Project Galileo"—indicated what a break with the past it would be. Within months, Kiwi introduced fragrant shoe inserts for women, fresheners for men's footwear, gel inserts for greater comfort, and a raft of products to protect shoes from nasty weather. They also remade the shoe-care aisle, developing displays that grouped products by function. The new lines were first rolled out in Spain and, based on that success, around the world. Kiwi's sales rose more than 4 percent in 2007 to $310 million. By focusing on its customers' needs, rather than the products it happened to make and the technology it happened to know, Kiwi—in the words of Sara Lee's CEO—"drove growth on something that hadn't been growing for some time."[5] Marketing thinking provided the foresight on which its innovations were based.

STARTING WITH THE CUSTOMER

Larry Huston thinks he knows why many innovations fail. It's not the technical part—most engineering problems are relatively trivial. Yet, seven out of ten new consumer packaged goods fail in the first year. As a member of P&G's technical staff for more than two decades, Huston has seen his share of market flops. "I've looked at hundreds of products," he says. "Probably 60 to 70 percent of the time, the source of the failure is that they didn't understand the consumer."[6] The trick to successful innovation, it seems, is getting really clear on the consumer need. If you can do that, the technology to get it done is someplace—finding it is the easy part.

Consider the iPod, one of the most successful product innovations in recent memory. It doesn't represent new technology. In fact, Apple sourced the components from other companies and contracted out the manufacturing. What was new was its concept, which sprang from the insight that consumers want an easy and safe way to buy individual songs on the Internet and save them on an easy-to-use player without worrying about all the technology involved. Apple's innovation was the user interface and the business model. "Getting the customer insight at a profound level is enormously important," Huston says. "What you really want to understand is one consumer in terms of mind, body, soul and task."[7]

NEW INNOVATION MODEL

P&G had long prided itself on understanding consumers. Yet in 2000, Huston concluded that his company's innovation model was broken. P&G's research and development operation was one of the best in the world—7,500 engineers, more than the combined science faculties of Harvard, Stanford, and MIT, spending upwards of $2 billion a year. But as the company grew to a $70-billion enterprise in the twenty-first century, the innovation model it devised for the twentieth century was not up to the task. Only 35 percent of the new products the company introduced were meeting financial targets. Research budgets were growing faster than sales, which had obvious limits. And to grow at 4 to 6 percent annually, P&G would have to add sales of $4 billion a year—an unlikely prospect under the circumstances.

A.G. Lafley, who had been appointed P&G's CEO in 2000, had come to the same conclusion and asked Huston to develop a new innovation model that could sustain high levels of top-line growth. To do that, both men believed the new model should tap technical capabilities outside the company. The strategy wasn't to replace the company's 7,500 researchers, but to better leverage them. Lafley set a very public goal that half of P&G's new products would come from its own labs, and half would come *through* them. Huston was galvanized.

"As we studied outside sources of innovation," he remembers, "we estimated that for every P&G researcher there were 200 scientists or engineers elsewhere in the world who were just as good—a total of perhaps 1.5 million people whose talents we could potentially use."[8]

Huston built a set of systems that gave P&G access to scientists from around the world. Five years later, the benefits of the new approach were dramatic. P&G's innovation success rate more than doubled, while the cost of R&D declined as a percentage of sales. And external collaboration plays a role in nearly half of the company's new products, up from about 20 percent in 2000. For example, the highly successful Mr. Clean Magic Eraser was based on a product found in a market in Osaka, Japan, and the technology that makes it possible to print messages on Pringles potato chips comes from a bakery in Bologna, Italy.

P&G has enjoyed another benefit—collaboration between marketing and R&D has grown closer, as has cooperation between the company's different technical practices. Aroma experts working on Millstone coffee and Herbal Essences shampoos contributed ideas for new toothpaste flavors and helped develop a scratch-and-sniff feature on Crest packages. Each marketing group is encouraged to develop a list of the top ten customer needs that can drive the business. And they're encouraged to look at the customers' needs holistically— "mind, body, soul, and task" in Huston's words—not simply as isolated product attributes. If the customer needs are defined well enough, P&G is confident it can marshal the resources internally and externally to fulfill them. For example, the technology behind Clairol's Nice 'n Easy Perfect 10 hair coloring actually originated in the company's laundry labs. The development of Crest Whitestrips teamed people from the company's oral-care area, who obviously knew about whitening teeth, with people in corporate R&D who had developed novel film technology, and people from fabrics who were experts in bleach.

Other companies have taken the same approach to "open innovation," creating a new industry of contract product developers in the process—from industrial designers like IDEO and Nottingham·Spirk to electronic clearinghouses like InnoCentive and NineSigma. The result: products such as P&G's Swiffer floor-cleaning system, Palm's

Treo wireless phone, and Sherwin-Williams's Twist-n-Pour paint containers.

DEVELOPING CUSTOMER-MADE PRODUCTS

Marketing is also at the center of an important trend in new product innovation—customer participation. Some companies go further than consulting their best customers on the design of new products; they actually involve them in the process of innovation. This is more than brainstorming, which is designed to produce a stream of ideas that can later be winnowed down. It's more than beta testing, which is largely about finding and fixing software bugs or testing human factors like the position and size of knobs. And it's more than personalization, which happens after a company has decided what options it will offer and is still essentially a one-way conversation. This is a two-way approach to innovation that starts from a clean slate or a rudimentary prototype and asks users to collaborate with the pros to take it from there to production.

Nokia, for example, launched "Nokia Beta Labs" in mid-2007 to give users an opportunity to contribute to the design of new wireless phone applications. In little more than a year, it had posted about two dozen cell phone applications to the site, most in very early, pre-beta stages of development. One application counts your steps as you move around town and another turns your cell phone into an audiobook.

One of the first applications posted on the site, Sports Tracker, lets runners record their workout data, such as their average speed and total distance. Tapping into the global positioning system (GPS) on some phones, it even let users plot their routes. More than a million people downloaded the program, and thousands suggested improvements that would never have occurred to the developers. For example, users wanted to be able to share favorite routes with others and post photos they took along the way. Nokia's developers also discovered that people were using the application for sports other than running, including motorcycling, paragliding, and hot-air ballooning. Sports Tracker was still in development in mid-2008, but another application that uses the phone's global positioning capabilities, Nokia Maps, "graduated" to full application status. The Nokia Maps application serves up basic navigation instructions, satellite maps, and multimedia city guides to people on the go.

Nokia has also taken codevelopment to the very real world of refugee camps and urban slums. For example, the company's ethnographers have set up "open design studios" in places like Buduburam, Ghana, home to 40,000 people, most of whom had fled from the civil wars in neighboring Liberia, Sierra Leone, and Ivory Coast. They strung a banner in front of a concrete hut and invited people to come in and describe or draw a picture of their "dream phone" in exchange for possible prizes. In the first two weeks, more than 140 people did just that, even though few of them actually owned a phone yet. Over the course of a year, Nokia's researchers gathered several three-ring binders of drawings. Muslims wanted a phone that could orient them toward Mecca for prayers. In the Mumbai slums, people wanted a phone that could forecast the weather since they had no radios. In a Rio shantytown, someone suggested a phone that could monitor air quality.

But this is not just an elaborate promotional stunt. Research just like this led Nokia to introduce a mobile phone with a dust-resistant keypad, antislip grip, and built-in flashlight to appeal to the hundreds of thousands of truck drivers who travel India's poorly lit highways. It all stems from a business philosophy that the company's chief marketing officer, Keith Pardy, says is "very Finnish"—observe then design. "You see it in the furniture, the glassware, and the architecture," Pardy says. "It's a balance between function and form. It is the thread that connects everything we do."[9] Plus Nokia has invited its users to help pull that thread.

Other companies have taken similar approaches. Xerox asks its product developers to spend one or two weeks shadowing customers to see how they use the company's products. When the engineers noticed that 44 percent of the paper that comes out of its printers and copiers is thrown out in less than a day, they started working on paper that can be erased and printed on again. That kind of on-the-spot recycling saves money and trees, both of which make for happy customers.[10]

PLAYING WHERE THE PUCK WILL BE

Famed hockey player Wayne Gretzky used to say, "A good hockey player plays where the puck is. A great hockey player plays where the puck is going to be." That's also the difference between good and great marketers. Target, which grew from the Midwest's Dayton-Hudson department stores, built its greatness on an uncanny ability to anticipate customer wants, needs, and values. That very nearly defines the essence of "trend spotting." And, in fact, Target has had a "trend department" since its earliest days in the 1960s.

Originally staffed with fashion scouts from the Dayton-Hudson department stores that Target would ultimately subsume, the new trend department's first initiative was to expand the color palette for T-shirts. Within a few years, staffers were traveling from corporate headquarters in Minneapolis to Europe, New York, and Tokyo several times a year to scope out fashion shows, trade shows, street trends, rock concerts—anything that could help them identify and anticipate new trends. Today, the department not only provides guidance for buyers and merchandisers, it also feeds the company's own product development group.

The trend-spotters report to Target's chief marketing officer, Michael Francis, a stylish Midwesterner who has been described as brimming with so much enthusiasm, "he looks as though he might eject out of his seat at any moment."[12] In fact, when he was a young buyer, he recreated the famous Paris flea market at a Marshall Field's store in Minneapolis, filling its eighth-floor auditorium with millions of dollars of merchandise shipped over from the French original. After a three-day stay there, he had everything left over shipped to the Marshall Field's in Chicago, attracting such excited crowds that the event was repeated for years.[13] The department store became known as "the Paris of the prairie." In fact, when Macy's—which bought and renamed the Marshall Field's store—wanted to reinforce its local heritage, it recreated the flea market.

That sense of style is what gives Target its cachet and turns it into "Tarzhay," the destination of choice for trendy shoppers on a budget. But Target's approach to design isn't only about fashion; it's primarily about meeting customers' needs. Target's ClearRx prescription bottle is an innovation that responds to the trend of an aging population as well as to people's enduring desire for safety and convenience. It has a wide, flat surface for the label, which is easy to read without rotating the bottle, and the information is presented in a logical hierarchy that can be understood at a glance. The cap is on the bottom and it's easy to grip and open. A colored ring on the neck indicates which house-hold member was issued the prescription so no one takes the wrong medicine. There's even a sleeve on the back for all the printed information that is usually stapled to the bag and thrown out. It looks good—but that's not the point.

Target's goal is to democratize good design, to make it accessible and affordable, while constantly surprising its customers. So, for example, in the fall of 2008, Target celebrated New York Fashion Week by opening four "Bullseye Bodegas" in Manhattan. The rented storefronts, which were only scheduled to be open for a week, featured new fashion, beauty, and home products from the company's partnerships with twenty-two designers. The bodega theme resonated with New Yorkers, who are used to shopping in the neighborhood grocery stores that dot the city. And the prices—which averaged only $25—undoubtedly built anticipation for the company's first full-sized store in the city, scheduled to open in 2009.

TARGETING TRENDS

A trend is a significant, lasting change in people's behavior. Black is not a trend. The trend is that more people are wearing black—in fact, so many people are wearing black that the dullest of us begin to notice. The marketing masters are among the *first* to notice and they capitalize on trends as they grow in popularity. There's nothing superficial about trends; they convey something about people's needs, desires, and values. One of Target's first trend-spotters, Robyn Waters, has gone on to found her own firm and to write extensively on the subject. "Trends are signposts pointing to what's going on in the hearts and minds of consumers," she says. "If you want to be 'on trend,' figure out what's important, not just what's next."[14]

The top new brands of 2007 all benefited from being on the leading edge of what is now a widely recognized trend toward greater interest in products' health and wellness benefits. According to Information Resources, which tracks retail sales of consumer packaged goods around the world, Campbell's Reduced-Sodium Soup was the top new product of 2007. In fact, the top ten new products were all low-sugar, low-carb, low-salt, or otherwise formulated to deliver health benefits beyond basic nutrition, including General Mills Fiber One Chewy

Bars, Dannon DanActive Probiotic Dairy Drinks and Activia Light Yogurt, and Sara Lee Heart Healthy and Hearty & Delicious breads. In the nonfood category, the most successful products were those that made everyday chores and personal care easier and more pleasant, including Huggies Supreme and Natural Fit Diapers, Tide Simple Pleasures Detergent, Gain Joyful Expressions Detergent, and Febreze NOTICEables air fresheners.

Marketing masters specialize in anticipating and responding to people's changing needs. No one asked Target to redesign its prescription bottles, but because the company knows its customers, it anticipated their need and was first to address it. No one at Target takes that ability for granted. The key is to anticipate trends, and Francis has five "secrets" for doing that.

THE SECRETS OF TREND SPOTTING

1. *First, Francis ensures that everyone in the company understands the Target brand and what sets it apart from its competitors.* The wide aisles, bright lights, and iconic signage are part of it. So is the absence of clutter, blaring public-address announcements, and piped-in elevator music. But what really says, "Expect more. Pay less," is what's on the shelves—stylish, affordable goods, handsomely presented and often surprising.

2. *Second, he taps the creativity and observational skills of everyone in the company to find products that deliver on the brand promise.* Every quarter, Francis asks employees to compete in finding the next "big idea" for the company within a predetermined area. "We've done everything from what's the next consumable product that we would like to repackage to what product in your pantry frustrates you the most," says Francis. The winner gets cash, recognition, and the chance to see his or her idea on the store's shelves. But even outside the contest, Francis says every Target employee is always looking for trends, from the top down. That's how Target found master sommelier Andrea Immer, who selects most of the wine the company sells and helped create its "wine cube," a colorful box that holds four bottles. A Target employee discovered her while flipping through a wine book she had written. Within

months, she was on the payroll. In fact, all Target managers are expected to constantly grow their own web of contacts. And to keep the new ideas coming, managers have to compete for a portion of their budgets every year. That was the source of 2007's vertical fashion show, featuring acrobats "walking" down the side of a building.

3. *Third, Francis ensures that ideas are shared broadly across the company so good ones that arise in one area can take root elsewhere.* For example, the Simply Shabby Chic line of home goods designed by Rachel Ashwell moved from furniture to bedding to dinnerware to pet bowls over the course of its first three years. Of course, not all the company's ideas work. It admits that its high-thread-count bedsheets were a loser at Target even though they took off in high-end bedding stores. Hermit crabs were a big trend in Japan and the company decided to paint some with the company's bull's-eye logo to publicize a film festival in California. It was good branding until the little critters began biting bystanders who couldn't resist picking them up. Francis still remembers seeing photos of "our well-branded hermit crab hanging off someone's finger." But Target is careful not to penalize people for thinking creatively and trying new things. Even the hermit crab infestation had a happy ending. Rounding them all up proved impossible and they washed up on beaches from Mexico to Los Angeles for eighteen months. The company turned it into a find-the-hermit-crab sweepstakes with Target gift cards as the prize.[15]

4. *Fourth, Target taps the creativity of top-notch design talent outside the company.* It was the first discount retailer to commission work from designers like Michael Graves, Isaac Mizrahi, Zac Posen, and Joy Gryson. It intersperses "limited-edition" collections by famous designers like Rogan Gregory within its own GO International private label line. By mid-2008, eleven internationally famous designers had collaborated on the line with Target's 300-person-strong design staff. It signed a deal with then-fledgling soap company Method based on a drawing for its unique, upside-down dispenser.[16] And it stays in touch with young, up-and-coming design-

ers by sponsoring education programs of the Council of Fashion Designers of America.

5. *Finally, Francis's fifth technique for staying on the leading edge of trends really is a secret.* He has an elite "creative cabinet" of people from all over the country whom he considers "brilliant." It's a rotating panel of people in a variety of disciplines that puts him in touch with developing trends. "They feed in ideas on a regular basis," he says. "I probably have about a dozen of them—trend people, movie people, advertising people. We pay them. They've become invaluable for me, because it's people who we trust, who we know have the right taste level, who understand our brand." The cabinet members file their reports through e-mail, photos, or long memos, from wherever in the world they happen to be. They're also on call to weigh in on new initiatives such as the design for a new cereal box or the growing importance of sustainability programs, but to date they have never met as a group. Francis says it's not necessary. "The power is in their working independently," he says. "We're the cross-pollinator. We're the integrator."[17]

DEMOGRAPHIC CHANGE

A demographic tsunami is roaring down on marketers, and its currents will be felt for generations. It's not news that America's population is growing older. But the combination of lower birthrates among whites and greater immigration from abroad portends a cultural shift even greater than the Baby Boom following World War II. Within the span of a newly minted brand manager's career, ethnic and racial minorities will become a majority of the U.S. population. The Census Bureau calculates that by 2042, Americans who identify themselves as Hispanic, Black, Asian, Native American, Native Hawaiian, and Pacific Islander will together outnumber non-Hispanic Whites. Four years ago, officials had projected the shift would come eight years later.

The Rand Corporation warns that figuring out the implications of the nation's changing racial profile is "not rocket science . . . it's harder."[18] To start, most scientists agree that the concept of "race" itself carries little biological or genetic meaning. They define it primarily in sociocultural and psychological terms. That doesn't mean race and ethnicity aren't meaningful in themselves, but that they're deeply rooted in the consciousness of individuals and groups. And for that reason they are of overarching significance to marketers.

America has never been a "melting pot," but more of a stew whose ingredients are distributed somewhat unevenly through the broth. The U.S. population is getting even more "lumpy" in that sense—with an aging, largely white Northeast and a South and West growing younger and more diverse. Most heads of household in California and Texas are already Hispanic, Asian, African American, or multiracial. Nearly one in ten U.S. counties already have more people who identify themselves as non-White, than those who label themselves White. In less than a generation, no single race will be in the majority in the United States. The mainstream male of 2042 will likely be a Spanish-speaking person of color.

Members of this new "minority-majority" are less likely to assimilate than to acculturate. As Esther Novak, founder and CEO of multicultural marketing agency VanguardComm, points out, "people select which elements of (American) culture they absorb and which (elements of their native culture) they intuitively retain." They may adopt the dominant culture's language and etiquette, while maintaining their own music, food, and social attitudes. In many cases, they may even switch back and forth to suit their own needs. For example, in the 2000 U.S. Census, about three-quarters of Asian Americans claimed to speak English "very well," yet more than half said they spoke an Asian language at home. Research conducted at Florida State University found that Hispanics prefer to speak Spanish when dealing with emotional issues, so they may speak English at work and Spanish at home, especially if they are a multigenerational household.[19]

As many sociologists have observed, at some point even the most fully acculturated individuals try to reconnect with their heritage in a process called "retro-acculturation." Hispanics who have lived their lives speaking English for decades will start speaking Spanish at home in an effort to pass on their heritage to their children. None of this should be surprising. The great Irish immigration was 150 years ago, but many American cities still hold St. Patrick's Day parades.

MULTICULTURAL MARKETING

Over the next decade, multicultural marketing will leave its quiet niche and become much more mainstream as savvy marketers react to both the size of the market and its distinctive characteristics. The collective buying power of Hispanic, Asian, and African American households in the United States already exceeds $2 trillion. Home Depot didn't need surveys to understand the growth in Hispanic contractors; the evidence passed through its parking lots every day. Now this reality is reflected in Home Depot's bilingual signage, in-store workshops *en español,* and a Spanish-language website that replicates the English-language site's 40,000 product listings.

But effective multicultural marketing requires more than a good bilingual dictionary. Multicultural audiences consume media differently. African Americans are heavier radio listeners than average, and Hispanic consumers spend more time online. At the same time, ethnic media is exploding across the country. In some major markets, including Los Angeles, Miami, and New York, Spanish-language TV stations have higher ratings among the young adults advertisers covet than the mainstream networks.[20]

Multicultural audiences have different social values and consumption patterns. For example, P&G research shows that African American women spend at least three times as much on beauty products as the general female population. P&G also found that 71 percent of black women feel they are portrayed worse in the media than any other racial group. The result was a nationwide "My Black Is Beautiful" campaign, underwritten by Pantene, CoverGirl, Crest, and Always, to share beauty and lifestyle tips within the context of a discussion about issues of concern to African American women. Meanwhile, Kimberly-Clark launched two websites—HuggiesEnEspanol.com and PullUpsEnEspanol.com—so Hispanic mothers can share parenting tips, traditions, and advice *de mama a mama* ("mom to mom"). The best tips are to be compiled in a free book to be distributed in select retail stores nationwide just ahead of Mother's Day 2009.

Finally, the "multi" in multicultural applies within groups that speak the same language as well as between them and others. There are social and cultural differences between Hispanics of Puerto Rican,

Mexican, and Cuban descent, not to mention between people in the nearly two dozen other Spanish-speaking countries. Similarly, besides speaking different languages, the U.S. Asian population includes people who trace their ancestry to countries as diverse as India and Vietnam or Nepal and Japan.

Novak cautions that "multicultural marketing is not only about language, it's about identifying with people's values and traditions. It's about culture." Relevant cultural cues specific to different groups matter. Bill Cosby played the most acculturated of African American pediatricians on television, but he wore sweatshirts from historically black colleges and hung art by black artists on the walls of his TV-set living room. Flavors, textures, and traditional ingredients matter too. General Mills introduced a line of cereals catering to the tastes of Hispanic families under the *Para su familia* brand; Frito-Lay did the same with Doritos in zesty flavors such as Salsa Verde and Flamin' Hot Sabrositos. Revlon and P&G's CoverGirl introduced a wider array of product colors tailored to the complexions of African Americans, Hispanics, and Asians. Even Barbie now has friends of ambiguous ethnicity. According to Mattel, Kayla could be Native American or Puerto Rican; Madison could be Hispanic or African American; Chelsea could be anything.

Marketers have long understood the power of endorsements within multicultural communities. Run-DMC landed a $1.5-million endorsement deal on the back of their 1986 Top Five R&B hit, "My Adidas." More recently, rapper Jay-Z has increased the street cred of a wide variety of products, including Courvoisier, Nike, Motorola, Belvedere, Versace, Chloé, Range Rover, Rolex, and Mercedes-Benz. Consumer brands have long integrated elements of urban culture into their general marketing as well. For example, Target advertises its home furnishings for young people to the rhythm of break dancing. But now, even more diverse multicultural cues are finding their way into mainstream marketing. Sometimes, the cues are as subtle as a commercial's casting. Sometimes, they can be more overt. For example, Toyota featured a bilingual driver in commercials for its Camry Hybrid during the 2006 Super Bowl. But they all add up to marketing that more accurately reflects America's social and cultural stew.

The masters of marketing turn insight into foresight, amplifying their customers' voices in their company's boardroom and labs. They understand that developing culturally and socially relevant new products is as crucial in the rapidly changing U.S. market as it is in developing countries around the world.

☞ *They don't have a static view of their customers' needs, desires, and values, but assume that they are in constant flux.* They constantly measure customer satisfaction for cues on evolving behavior. MTV sends teams of ethnographers to rifle through the closets and music collections of its youthful viewers. They even hang out with them in clubs and on street corners, searching for clues to their shifting likes, dislikes, interests, and values.

☞ *They schedule time to stay in touch with lifestyle and cultural trends.* PepsiCo's CEO, Indra Nooyi, jumps in her car on weekends to visit supermarkets, where she chats up shoppers and salesclerks. In addition to the business press, she reads everything from *People* and *Vanity Fair* to the AARP magazine.

☞ *They are the in-house experts on market changes, deploying a wide-ranging set of forward-sensing mechanisms to stay in touch with popular culture and societal trends.* They look at each new development through the stereo lens of their brand values and their customers' needs. P&G is reevaluating everything from detergents to diapers in an effort to create greener products that will appeal to consumers. In detergents, it is turning to low-temperature washing to save energy and concentrated formulas to reduce packaging. In diapers, it is reducing the amount of material in Pampers as well as in their packaging.

☞ *They consider multicultural marketing a mainstream activity, not a sideline funded in the interests of political correctness.* Their multicultural marketing extends from product development to promotion and across all customer touch points. Pepsi used multicultural marketing before the term itself was invented. It hired a team of black salesmen in 1947 to bring Pepsi to the attention of African American churches and community organizations, and has been a corporate leader in diversity ever since.[21]

☞ *They engage employees in spotting trends and opportunities.* When IBM asked 750 global CEOs where their innovative ideas came from, just 14 percent cited traditional R&D, another 36 percent mentioned customers, and 41 percent said employees. It makes sense—who else knows the company and its customers better? Urban Outfitters, the retailer of insurgent chic fashion, changes the "look" of its inventory with every new generation of teenagers and counts on every employee to help it stay ahead of the curve. It distributes a "style book" companywide and profiles typical customers in a quarterly employee-produced newsletter to define the current look. And it rewards employees with concert tickets for sending reports to the merchandising and design teams on what they're seeing and hearing.

☞ *They find ways to involve customers in their company's innovation process, either by serving as their proxy or by facilitating their hands-on involvement.* Office-products retailer Staples held an "Invention Quest" competition, asking customers for new product ideas. It received 8,300 submissions to the first contest and put the winner—a combination lock that uses words instead of numbers—into production. That was 2004 and the product is still in the Staples catalogue. Lego invited five people acknowledged by the hobbyist community as "master builders" to help design a new generation of little plastic bricks embedded with tiny motors, sensors, and processors. Called "Mindstorm," the new kits enabled hobbyists to construct working robots to roam through the medieval castles they had built with the "dumb" plastic bricks they'd had since they were kids. The approach worked so well that Lego quickly expanded the user panel to fourteen members and most recently to 100. Nearly 10,000 hobbyists applied for the position.[22]

☞ *They consider product innovation a team sport, emphasizing collaboration within the company and with outside development resources.* They have built systems to identify the best technical talent in the world in areas of importance to them and developed processes for managing outside developers while protecting proprietary information.

P&G's CEO, A.G. Lafley, points out that there are different kinds of change and each has its own cost. The easiest changes to make are in response to a crisis, but they're the most expensive. It's a little cheaper to make changes in reaction to problems that don't quite rise to the level of a crisis, but it's also a little harder to mobilize people. The hardest change to make is also the cheapest—changes in anticipation of events. Those are the changes in which the masters of marketing excel.

BUILD CUSTOMER LISTENING POSTS

"The consumer is not a moron, she is your wife."

—DAVID OGILVY

This admonition by David Ogilvy would set off political incorrectness alarms today—and he probably wouldn't phrase it exactly the same way anyhow—but his larger point is timeless. Your customer is not an idiot; he or she is someone like your spouse. Your customer is someone not that different from you. But many marketers commit the sin that has doomed many marriages—they don't listen.

Of course every marketer tests a new initiative before launching it, most field periodic "Do you love us?" surveys, and a few track their brand's image as carefully as their cholesterol levels. But only the masters of marketing have developed listening skills sharp enough to deepen customer relationships and drive innovation.

The first rule of listening is to be there when customers want to talk. That includes key points in your relationship, from the first time they see an ad for your product, notice it on the shelf, buy it, get it home, and first use it, to when something goes wrong, it needs to be serviced, and it's time to replace it. Successful marketers talk to a sample of customers across all these touch points; the best marketers establish consistent entry points across them so every customer can initiate a conversation at his or her convenience. You don't need a sophisticated IT department to gather and manage customer feedback. For example, Tom Heinen, who runs a seventeen-store grocery chain in Cleveland, puts his phone number on every cash register receipt and asks customers to call with comments. He listens to the answering machine as he drives between stores.

CONTINUOUS LISTENING

Networking giant Cisco Systems views listening to customers as a continuous process rather than a singular event. It even has a "chief listening officer," Kirby Drysen, who sees his job as "ensuring the relevance of customer information . . . (and) getting the business to act on the voice of the customer." One way to ensure customer intelligence is relevant is to constantly collect customer feedback and data, rather than waiting for quarterly or annual survey "windows." To ensure that the information is actionable, Kirby's team engages field teams and business units in the survey process and then makes the results available, in real time, all the time, to every Cisco employee. "This creates a sense of urgency every day about how well we're serving our customers," he says. "The most powerful motivator is relevant, compelling information that solves real issues."[1]

But customer communication at Cisco is not limited to surveys. In addition to the standard online newsletter and executive blogs, the company hosts more than two dozen discussion groups on its website, plus a wiki where customers can collaborate in real time on Cisco product applications and issues. Cisco even has seven separate Twitter accounts—CiscoSystems, CiscoIT, CiscoPress, CiscoLive, CiscoDC, CaWebLearning, and CiscoSP360. There's also the CiscoSP360 channel on YouTube, plus the Cisco Facebook group.

On its main website, Cisco runs a regular "ask the expert" feature where different Cisco engineers answer questions in their area of expertise for two-week periods. Other Cisco experts make technical presentations in webcasts and podcasts that are maintained in an online library. Cisco users can add comments to some of the company's product video and data sheets. And the company even publishes user reviews of its products. While the reviews are not exactly hard hitting, they offer a user's perspective on a product's most appropriate applications, installation issues, and so on. Plus, readers are invited to offer suggestions (for example, "Can you publish the documentation in French?") or ask questions. For example:

> Please help me on this we have 2811 router version 12.4(13r)T. There was four emptt HWIC slots on this and we need to add WIC-1ENET on existing HWIC slot. After connecting into WIC-1ENET into HWIC slot router not detecting the card.

In case you're wondering, the answer appeared to be:

> No IOS supports wic-1enet. You need an hwic-1fe, to have a third lan port, or use subinterfac on the existing ones and a switch with vlan support. [*Sic*]

It isn't as titillating as TMZ.com—but it's effective customer communication. And great marketing.

To ensure that its website is as useful as possible, Cisco invites user ideas to improve its functionality and gives users an opportunity to vote on them. The company also closes the loop on customer questions by carefully monitoring use of its website. If a registered user downloads a white paper off Cisco.com or views one of its webcasts, the salesperson who follows that particular account is notified so he or she can follow up as appropriate. No wonder Cisco is the world's leading provider of networking products.

MAKING IT EASY FOR CUSTOMERS TO COMMUNICATE

Cisco's customers, by definition, are Web savvy. In fact, the company prides itself on the amount of business it does strictly online. But not all consumers have easy access to the Web and many who do prefer to conduct business in person or over the phone. Successful marketers make it easy for their customers to ask questions or give them feedback.

AT&T invented toll-free calling in 1967 as a substitute for collect calls and, perhaps more aptly, for the operators who handled them. Sheraton was the first company to use and advertise the service as a free, central reservations number. Other marketers quickly followed suit and, for a while, AT&T had a nice business advising its customers on how to set up call centers. In time, marketers began using toll-free numbers for a wide range of applications from sales to service and general inquiries. About 200,000 rattled cooks call the Butterball Turkey Talk-Line every Thanksgiving. Toll-free numbers began appearing on soup cans, cereal boxes, and assembly instructions, as well as in ads. A few clever entrepreneurs captured alphanumeric combinations like 1-800-FLOWERS or 1-800-MATTRES (leave off the last "s" for "savings").

Those were the days when businesses actually welcomed phone calls from customers. But in time, even though competition brought the price of the actual phone call down, all the other costs—staff, real estate, and so on—went up. Call centers were graded on how many calls they could handle in an hour. Operators were told to get off the phone as quickly as possible. Today, many companies do everything they can to push orders and support issues online where human interaction can be minimized and controlled.

Many company websites make it easier to find the CEO's salary than a toll-free number to reach them. Ironically, even the "Contact Us" icon on AT&T's home page takes you to another page where you're asked to describe the subject of your inquiry (in seventy-five words or less). Type "repair" and you are taken to still another page where you are invited to send an e-mail, peruse a series of frequently asked questions on the topic of "repair," or click yet another icon to see a list of toll-free numbers, one of which actually deals with repairs. Call that number and a recorded voice welcomes you, tells you how important your call is to the company, delivers a pitch for more services, tries once more to get you to send an e-mail, or failing that invites you to use their "automated system." If you persist, you are invited to "press 3" to speak to a "repair specialist." As tedious as that is, at least you can eventually speak to a human being. At the Amazon site, that's not even an option.

Not that online communications are inherently less effective. Many people prefer e-mail because it gives them a record of their communication. But many e-mail systems are black holes. British online service provider Transversal evaluated the ability of 100 leading U.K. companies to answer routine questions via e-mail and by phone. Less than half (46 percent) of the e-mailed questions were answered adequately. Additionally, the average time to respond was nearly four days and a quarter of the questions were never replied to at all. Phone calls, on the other hand, were answered within two minutes.[2]

ZAPPOS

Marketers who are truly customer centered offer multiple contact options and make them easy to find and use. Online retailer Zappos, for example, puts its 800 number on every single page of its website. Phones are answered twenty-four hours a day, 365 days a year. If someone wants to communicate through e-mail, there's an easy-to-use form on the "Help" page, a link to which appears at the top of every screen.

Of course, none of this will make a difference if the people answering the phone or responding to e-mail are measured by the amount of time they spend with customers rather than how well they answer their questions. For example, many companies give their phone representatives two minutes to resolve a customer's issue—every second over counts against them. As a result, they have an incentive to end the call as quickly as possible, whether or not the issue is resolved.

Zappos, on the other hand, doesn't even track how long each call takes, only how many rings it takes for the phone to be answered. There are no scripts, no time limits on calls, and employees are encouraged to do whatever it will take to make callers happy. Call center employees go through four weeks of paid training. By the time they finish, they understand the company's strategy, its product line, and its culture. Then after one week on the job, Zappos offers employees $1,000 to leave. Zappos's CEO Tony Hsieh figures that if someone will take the money and run, they obviously don't have the level of commitment the company is looking for. But only about one out of ten call center employees takes the offer.

Zappos puts all this effort into training its frontline people because it considers word of mouth about its customer service its best marketing. "The way we have grown the company is by focusing on customer service instead of spending a ton of money on paid advertising," says Hsieh. "We take most of the money we would have spent on advertising campaigns and instead put that back into the customer experience so that we can grow through repeat customers and word of mouth." On an average day, three out of four orders are from repeat customers, who also tend to spend more than on their initial visits. Eight out of ten customers learn about Zappos from friends or through online ads. The company does relatively little advertising in other media.

Zappos views each of the 5,000 calls it receives every day as a branding opportunity. "When a customer calls, you have the full attention of that customer," Hsieh says. "That's the time where you have a huge opportunity to shine." And it's one of the reasons Zappos's gross merchandise sales grew from less than $2 million in 2000 to a projected $1 billion in 2008.[3]

As of the end of 2008, Zappos's website included more than 300 pages of customer reviews, and not all of them were unalloyed praise. A few customers complained about "big, clunky clodhoppers" that were two sizes bigger than advertised. Others griped about straps that wouldn't stay put. But even those complaints were softened by Zappos's policy of accepting returns for any reason within a year of purchase. It repeats the policy on every page and even pays for the return shipping.

VALUE COMPLAINTS

Not every customer call is a lovefest, even at Zappos, but you dismiss complaints at your own risk. Some people complain for the entertainment value or to draw attention to themselves. And if others have a chip on their shoulder, corporate America may have helped put it there. Scott Broetzmann, president of Customer Care Measurement & Consulting, believes recent accounting scandals and job outsourcing have created "a swell of corporate distrust . . . that has a visceral effect on how customers approach day-to-day transactions" with companies.[4] But most have a legitimate gripe from which you can learn.

Satisfy dissatisfied customers and they may tell their friends you don't suck after all. Look deeply into their problems and you might discover how to improve your product or customer service. For example, Cabela's, which is famous for its extensive retail and online shrines to hunting, fishing, and camping, tracks customer feedback as carefully as any backcountry guide on the scent of a twelve-point buck. Vice chairman Jim Cabela spends a few hours every morning reading through customer comments. Then he hand delivers them to each department, circling the issues he'd like to have addressed. That's one reason Cabela's grew from a fly-tying business run off a kitchen table to the world's largest outdoor outfitter, with more than $2 billion in sales and a listing on the New York Stock Exchange.[5]

SPECIAL-PURPOSE COMMUNITIES

Some companies use the Internet to tap the creativity and intelligence of ordinary customers. For example, P&G used the Internet as a test market for Crest Whitestrips, one of the most successful products it has ever introduced. The company began selling the teeth whiteners exclusively on the Internet. Sales were only a few million dollars, but the company followed up with people who bought the product to find out why they purchased it, how they used it, what they liked and didn't like. When the brand went into national distribution, the company tailored its marketing to the four groups that responded best in the Internet trial—teenage girls, brides-to-be, young Hispanics, and gay men.

Del Monte, which derives 40 percent of its revenue from pet food, created a private online community called "I Love My Dog," and handpicked its 400 members. The company uses the group to help create products and test marketing campaigns. When Del Monte was considering a new breakfast treat for dogs, it asked the group's members what they most wanted to feed their pets in the morning. The consensus answer was something with a bacon-and-egg taste, so Del Monte began development of something called Snausages Breakfast Bites, which are not only flavored like bacon and eggs, but also contain an extra dose of vitamins and minerals. Del Monte contacted members of the "I Love My Dog" group dozens of times over the six months the product was in development, both as a group and individually. Because it had real-time input from motivated customers, it was able to cut in half the normal time between coming up with the idea for a product and getting it on the shelves. Working with the "I Love My Dog" group also gives Del Monte early insight into the development of new trends. For example, when the company realized that many people now treat their pet as a family member, it introduced Kibbles 'n Bits Brushing Bites, the first mass-marketed oral-care dry dog food, which became one of the most successful new dry dog foods in years.[11]

Virgin Mobile USA uses 2,000 carefully selected online customers to keep abreast of trends. Virgin calls members of the group "Insiders" and it rewards them for responding to occasional surveys with free calling minutes and phone upgrades. When Kraft Foods' Nabisco division used an online community to gather customer opinions on food and health, it came up with its popular 100 Calorie Packs line of snack bags.

Computer maker Dell not only lets customers rate and review its products on its website, it also solicits their ideas and suggestions. In its first year, Dell's "IdeaStorm" collected 8,600 suggestions with 600,000 votes and 64,000 comments (in mid-2008, the leading proposal was to wrap components in less plastic wrap). Starbucks picked up on the idea as its first foray into social media with "My Starbucks Idea." Within the first week, the highest-ranked idea was that customers should get a free cup of coffee after buying a set number. Other suggestions were for more comfortable seating, free wireless, reusable rubber sleeves for paper coffee cups, and an express line for drip coffee. The success of such programs, however, depends on evidence that the company is actually listening to all the input. Dell, for example, claims to have implemented thirty-five of the ideas in the first year of the program, including a computer running the open-source Linux operating system. Several months in, Starbucks had several ideas "under review" and had moved to implement two—more free wireless service and a plastic stirrer that doubles as a splash guard to avoid annoying spills.

CHRYSLER

Chrysler launched an online Customer Advisory Board (CAB) in mid-2008 in an attempt to better understand the driving public. Members were recruited online at a new "Chrysler Listens" website that hung off the company's corporate home page behind a "tell us what you want" hyperlink. The company thought it could do a few online polls, test some new ads and commercials, answer a few questions, and maybe get a few ideas.

So many people expressed interest in joining the Customer Advisory Board that Chrysler decided to expand its size to a potential 5,000 members, from the 2,000 originally planned. The concept originated in Chrysler's marketing department, but from the beginning, CMO Deborah Meyer challenged her colleagues across the company to contribute personnel, topic ideas, and questions for online discussions—and to respond quickly to feedback the company receives through it. The greater customer contact should "give us so much more urgency" across Chrysler, Meyer said. "Our level of motivation will be ramped up."[6]

No one at Chrysler thinks an online discussion can replace talking to customers face-to-face. And, in fact, the Customer Advisory Board is just one of several listening initiatives across the company. Chrysler named the industry's first chief customer officer, who began his tenure by writing to every person who bought a Chrysler in the quarter he arrived. He thanked them for their purchase and asked if there was anything he needed to know. Then the company instructed senior managers to call a customer a day, on average, to get their feedback; they will also take turns in the company's call center and compete in generating sales referrals.

TAPPING ENTHUSIASTS

Enthusiasts are people who have a special affinity for your product category. For Burger King, they're the eighteen to twenty-four-year-old males who eat fast food twenty-one times a month. For Cisco, they're the companies that are highly dependent on data-intensive applications deployed across a wide geography.

Enthusiasts may not spend more with you than other customers. They may not even be particularly loyal to your brand. But they will have the highest standards, be the most demanding, and develop new needs long before the average customer. And they may use your products in ways you had never considered. For those reasons, you should pay special attention to them.

That has proven a winning formula for Burton Snowboards, the best-known brand in one of the world's fastest-growing sports. Jake Burton started selling homemade snowboards out of his barn in Londonderry, Vermont, in 1977. The company now has retail stores from Japan to Austria and makes everything for snowboarders on and off the hill, from snowboards, boots, and bindings to travel bags, belts, and apparel.

The majority of the two million people who ride the slopes on boards every year are teenagers or in their twenties. But when Burton wants to find out where the sport is going, it tunes in to a small segment whose influence far exceeds its size—the pros. Burton listens to 300 professional riders worldwide, thirty-nine on the team it sponsors. "Riders are involved in each step of the product development process at Burton," the company touts on its website. "Pro riders give product managers feedback on everything from the ride and flex of a board to the color of bootlaces and the texture of jacket linings."

Burton staffers talk to those riders virtually every day, whether on the slopes or on the phone. After the 1998 Winter Olympic Games, Shannon Dunn, who won a bronze medal in the half-pipe competition, mentioned that her bindings were bruising her ankles. Within a week, designers came up with an insert that they included in the company's product line. Burton's attitude is that "if they can please the pros, they can please anyone." But just to make sure, Burton also puts about half of its sales reps on the slopes every weekend, loaning gear to amateur snowboarders, riding with them, and noting what works and what doesn't. In addition, Burton has an online community of 25,000 snowboarders who provide real-time feedback in exchange for trying products for free.

LURKING ON THE INTERNET

As the Internet's center of gravity moves from digital catalogues to interactivity and dialogue, savvy marketers are listening closely to what people say. And the best of them are joining the conversation. It not only gives them insight into what their customers think of their product, it tells them what's on the minds of people who prefer their competitors'. Dell has forty-two employees engaging with customers on Facebook, MySpace, and anywhere else they gather. Companies ranging from Comcast and General Motors to H&R Block and Whole Foods Market are following the short messages on Twitter and piping in whenever they can add something useful.

The Internet represents one of the richest veins of opinion about a company and its products. Only 6 percent of consumers believe "companies generally tell the truth in advertising," so they increasingly turn to online sources for information, the only form of media in which trust is increasing.[7] Mary Lou Quinlan, who has spent hours talking to thousands of women, notes that new moms, for example, are "fiends about Internet searches." If they need a stroller, they read all the reviews, blogs, and message boards. Then, when they actually buy one, they post their own reviews. "The chain of influence in those cases is not only faster than ever, it's more crowded," Quinlan points out. "And the social media are more influential than advertising because a mom knows she can trust another mom."

Some sites, such as Epinions and TripAdvisor, were built expressly to provide a forum for comments on companies and their products. Shopping search engines like BizRate and ShopWiki encourage users to rate products, as do almost all online retailers like Amazon, eBay, and Zappos. Gadget blogs like Gizmodo and Engadget invite comments on their professionally written reviews. Others, like Pissed Consumer and The Complaint Station are expressly designed to register—and publicize—customer gripes. The Consumerist has gone so far as to publish the e-mail addresses of an offending company's top executives. And, of course, vigilante websites like "Microsoft Sucks" and "(Fill In The Blank) Sucks" attract people eager to air their grievances and spread conspiracy theories.

According to Internet research firm FairWinds Partners, there are 20,000 websites with the suffix "sucks."[8] (For some reason, only 2,000 end in the phrase "stinks.com.") BankAmericaSucks.com shows up in the top fifteen results of a Google search for the bank. In a preemptive strike, some companies—including Coca-Cola, Toys"R"Us, Target, and Whole Foods—have bought any domain names that might become gripe sites. Companies like Southwest Airlines don't let those sites gather dust, realizing that angry customers will simply go elsewhere. Instead, they link them to their own customer service sites, giving customers an outlet for their fury and gathering valuable data in the process. The idea is to get customers to complain directly to the company, not on the World Wide Web.

MINING CUSTOMER COMMENTS

Between their own customer service channels and the online chatter about them, most large marketers are drowning in data. The best of them become digital anthropologists, using sophisticated techniques to mine the mountains of comments, praise, and criticism that pile up about them. Companies like Biz360 monitor and compile online reviews and customer ratings across websites, providing competitive reports by category. Data-mining services like Anderson Analytics find patterns in comments taken from text-based media like call center logs and user blogs. New software algorithms can even gauge the emotional content, or sentiment, of text messages.

In one project for Starwood Hotels, Anderson Analytics culled through more than one million customer-feedback surveys in twenty-nine different languages. Even assuming Starwood had the staff to read and code all those comments, it's unlikely their approach would have been consistent over time, not to mention across coders. "You can have someone read through 100 comments, and they will likely overstate the importance of some concepts, understate the importance of some concepts and totally miss other things," said Tom Anderson, managing partner, Anderson Analytics.[9]

For example, when Anderson analyzed third-party websites to find words associated with Starwood, the term that popped up most often was "rate," suggesting that prices were an overwhelming concern. But just as many guests commented favorably as unfavorably, indicating that it was *not* a dominant concern. Meanwhile, Anderson discovered that Starwood's guests were more likely to comment favorably about the hotel's beds than were guests of other hotels, and Hilton's guests were more likely to make positive mention of that hotel's food and health clubs. That validated Starwood's multimillion dollar investment in its "Heavenly Beds" and inspired a new initiative to offer more healthful foods.

TAPPING YOUR OWN EMPLOYEES

Your own employees, especially those on the front lines with customers, are often one of the best sources of intelligence. The masters of marketing tap that source, not only to uncover problems, but especially to "center" the company on their customers.

Every Cabela's employee is encouraged to borrow any of the company's more than 200,000 sporting goods products for up to two months. All they have to do in return is to write a review that's shared via a companywide software system when the goods are returned. That's not only a nice perk, it also helps employees better empathize with product issues customers might have. Four Seasons Hotels and Resorts takes a similar approach at most of its properties. After their orientation, every worker—from front-desk to housekeeping—is given a free night's stay for him- or herself and a guest, including meals. In return, employees are asked to grade the hotels on such measures as the number of times the phone rings when calling room service to how long it takes to get items to a room. After six months of service, employees can stay up to three nights a year for free. After ten years, they get twenty free stays.

Mickey Drexler, the CEO of J.Crew, is famous for wandering the retailer's sales floors, asking customers what they're looking for and quizzing salespeople on what shopping bags people are carrying into the store. It turns out that his wandering extends to other corners of the company. A call center operator once told him that a lot of women were buying multiple copies of a summer dress in different sizes. She thought it was an amusing story. Drexler saw an opportunity and launched a new line of bridesmaids dresses.

When a new CEO took over Sara Lee in 2005, she asked executives to meet with employees around the world to get their ideas on new growth opportunities. Among the product ideas that emerged were Soft and Smooth whole-grain white bread, which kids who don't like brown bread will eat, but meets parents' nutrition goals, and 3volution, an air freshener that rotates through three scents every forty-five minutes. Both products are still among the company's best sellers.

SQUEEZING IDEAS OUT OF DATA

Greg Green isn't the typical ad guy. In fact, he's a systems analyst with a PhD in math. The CEO of the Digitas ad agency—himself a former Bain consultant—hired Green to figure out how to apply the analysis of data to the generation of ideas—in Green's words, "to push rigor and imagination together."

Three years ago, when he was still struggling to explain his assignment to agency colleagues whose eyes were visibly glazing over, he happened to be standing in a used-car lot in Framingham, Massachusetts, outside Boston. He needed a truck to haul his boat from his home to the lake on weekends because he had given the car that used to have that duty to his college-aged son. It wasn't a long trip and, aside from an occasional trip to the town dump, it was probably the only use the truck would get. So he was kicking the tires on used trucks when a salesman sidled up and asked, "Why are you looking at used trucks when you could get a new one for almost the same price with GM's rebate?"

Green's first thought was that the dealership must be behind its monthly quota for new truck sales. The profit on used vehicles is usually better than on new. His second and third thoughts were "Hmmm. It's probably a lot easier to move someone from buying a used car to buying a new one than to get him into a dealership in the first place" and "I wonder how big the used-car market is and where do people do their research?"

By the time Green got home, he had scribbled a whole page of questions, ranging from What is the size of the market opportunity? to Which messages would work best? to Is anybody already doing this? Answering those questions would require the resources of the entire agency. And they would need real-time access to rapidly changing, relevant data, if they wanted to test different approaches. Which is exactly what Digitas did, starting with a small ad on the website of the Kelley Blue Book and moving to multiple combinations of different ads on different websites. Green's system gave the client's marketing people, as well as the agency's creative and media people, real-time data on customer responses to each combination so they could refine their approach.

Eventually, Digitas sold the business to General Motors, but it became the first test of the assignment Green had been given—use data to generate ideas. Green demonstrated that, just as a Bloomberg terminal can help money managers develop investment ideas, an online dashboard that gives clients real-time data on their marketing initiatives can help media and creative people develop marketing ideas. The online platform Green developed, called The Global Navigator, gives clients real-time visibility into their marketing initiatives around the world and across all media. It consolidates dozens of complex information streams, including proprietary client data such as website and direct-response metrics. But, unlike a dashboard that adds everything up, the Global Navigator allows clients and agencies to do "What if?" analyses. Sometimes those analyses lead to media cost optimization, sometimes to new business strategies, sometimes to both. "When that happens," Green says, "it's magic."

✧ ✧ ✧

The marketing masters have listening skills sharp enough to drive by.

☞ *They make it easier for customers to reach the company with questions, feedback, and suggestions.* And they make sure someone responds with a message that sounds like it came from an interested, caring human being. They tap the expertise of people on the front line with customers, rather than treating their work as an expense to be minimized.

☞ *They build dialogue into everything they do, creating a community of users whose creativity they can harness.* In many cases, that makes their customers more loyal, but their real goal is to make themselves better marketers, by better understanding their customers' needs.

☞ *They pay special attention to the customers who are most enthusiastic about the product category and are often on the leading edge of new trends.* But they also listen to people's complaints, looking for patterns that can guide product development and service improvements.

☞ *They monitor third-party channels and bring all customer comments, suggestions, and questions together in an integrated database for analysis.* They track their performance in online ratings against competitors' and take action on what they learn.

☞ *They don't confuse creativity with innumeracy.* They use data to confirm their firsthand experience, to inform their strategies, and especially to generate new ideas. They think of data as an idea's best friends.

In short, marketing masters construct a system of listening posts where customer data from multiple points can be captured, organized, and shared. Maybe that's why, by some calculations, customer-focused companies are 31 percent more profitable, twice as fast in bringing products to market, twice as likely to be market leaders, and enjoy 20 percent higher customer-satisfaction rates.[10]

PART THREE

Connect Emotionally

Bring Meaning to the Noisy Confusion of People's Lives

"People who manage to satisfy their personal needs are changed by it. They become seekers of meaning."

—Scott Adams

FIND YOUR BRAND'S HIGHER PURPOSE

"Man is the only animal who must create meaning."

—Ernest Becker

Not quite tall, seldom tan since she moved to London, but still lovely well into her forties, Silvia Lagnado may no longer stroll the Ipanema beaches of her native Brazil. But as global brand director for Unilever's Dove division from 2001 to 2006, she turned plenty of heads in the marketing world.

Dove, of course, is the bar soap that David Ogilvy positioned as "one-quarter cleansing cream" in 1955. His campaign challenged women to wash half their face with "ordinary soap" and half with Dove to see how soap "dries your skin" while Dove "creams your skin while you wash." The campaign was so successful it continued to hammer away at the same functional promise in one form or another for more than four decades.

But in 2000, growing more slowly than its chief competitor, P&G, Unilever decided to change its decentralized ways and winnow its 1,600 brands to about 400. A smaller number of the remaining brands would be declared "Master Brands," spanning broad product categories. One of those Master Brands was Dove and its bailiwick would now extend beyond soap to include deodorant, hair-care products, facial cleansers, body lotions, and other personal care products.

In 2001, Lagnado became one of the company's first "global brand directors" charged with refashioning Dove's meaning so it would apply across the entire range of products within its category. Claiming functional superiority would no longer be sufficient for Dove, because functionality meant different things in different categories. Lagnado decided, instead, that Dove should stand for a point of view and she assembled a small team to set off in search of it.

BEAUTY THEORY

The first thing the Dove branding team did was review fifty years of Dove advertising around the world. "We quickly realized there had been a commonality to Dove's communications over the years and across countries," one of the original team members, Alessandro Manfredi, remembers. "The old and enduring testimonials were rooted in a notion of 'democratic beauty' that was part of our heritage." Indeed, testimonials by real women—or models carefully made to look like real women—had been a hallmark of Dove advertising since the days when Ogilvy himself was writing the copy. "We asked ourselves why women responded so well to that kind of advertising," Manfredi says. "And we wondered if it wasn't because they responded to beauty with imperfection—beauty that was not cold but real."

Over the course of the next nine months, Lagnado developed that idea into a "Beauty Theory" that she took on the road, discussing it with Dove regional brand managers around the world. Not everyone was wild about it. Some brand managers—mostly male—were adamant that beauty products were sold on aspiration. Women don't want to look "real," they said. They want to look beautiful.

Lagnado and her team regrouped frequently, cycling between despair and determination. They knew they had a big idea, but it clearly wasn't going anywhere internally. Then in 2002, Lagnado's entire team of fifteen brand managers and agency people attended a Unilever executive education program in Ireland. The program, called Leaders Into Action, is designed to build a more entrepreneurial culture within the company. One key component is a business project participants present at the end of the program to senior executives for possible funding and implementation. The Dove team decided to present their Beauty Theory and what started as a pure marketing exercise became a very personal exploration for all the team members. "Silvia talked about her personal beauty hang-ups," Manfredi recalls. "Her personal feelings can't be underestimated, but everyone recognized themselves in the discussion. We all admitted to being concerned about how we looked, even the men."

Lagnado didn't want money for the Beauty Theory campaign. She already controlled a good portion of Dove's budgets around the world. She wanted something more valuable—the institutional support for a campaign that would question the standards of beauty on which much of the personal care industry was built. She wanted to change the meaning of beauty.

Then someone had a brainstorm. The Dove team would bring a secret weapon to their meeting with senior management. In addition to the Beauty Theory and the supporting white papers by leading psychologists, they would show the senior executives a short videotape featuring their own young daughters describing how they felt about their appearance. One little girl hated her freckles, a young Asian girl wished she were blond.

Lagnado got senior management's attention and encouragement, but Unilever's new management system split responsibility for the "development" and "building" of its brands. Lagnado was responsible for brand development, which meant conceptualizing new products and setting strategic direction for Dove. But regional brand managers, who were accountable for sales within their territories, controlled brand building, which included advertising. Although they reported to her on a dotted-line basis, Lagnado couldn't force the regional brand managers to run a particular campaign. She had to persuade them through the power of her arguments, presented in a series of white papers, webcasts, and meetings.

REAL BEAUTY

Lagnado caught a break when Klaus Arntz, the brand development director for Dove in Europe, returned from one of her meetings so frustrated at the inaction that he vented to his wife. To his surprise, he discovered that she shared the very insecurities Lagnado had been describing. "My wife, who is quite beautiful, told me she doesn't like to look in the mirror because she thinks there are so many things wrong with her," he remembers. "Suddenly, I understood how big the audience was for this campaign."[1]

Convinced that Lagnado was on to something, Arntz worked with Ogilvy & Mather, London, to come up with ads to reflect the new positioning, using ordinary women rather than models. They cast a plus-sized salesclerk for the first ad. But old habits die hard. The first photographer the agency hired shot her in Marilyn Monroe's classic pose with a billowing skirt. As soon as the proofs came back, Arntz knew it was a mistake. "Our shop girl looked so glamorous, that the whole campaign seemed like some silly look-alike contest," he remembers.

Arntz decided to eat 100,000 euros in production fees (about $127,000 at the time) and start over. The agency came up with a new photographer who specialized in shooting real people. He proposed to photograph the women individually and in groups in front of a plain white background, stripping away any distractions. Initially, he even wanted to strip away their clothes, posing them naked, but calmer heads prevailed and he settled for plain white underwear. The women's love handles, double chins, and dimpled knees set them apart from conventional models, but they also exuded a confidence and vitality that made their "real curves" look beautiful.

Arntz planned to launch the new campaign across Europe in January 2004, but he could only get brand managers in three countries to run what some were calling "the campaign for ugly women." That quickly changed when sales of the Dove anticellulite firming cream featured in the ads increased by 400 percent. Stores couldn't keep it on the shelves. What's more, the campaign stimulated a discussion on the nature of beauty worthy of Greek philosophers, though it played out on talk radio, on television, in blogs, and in viral media.

Meanwhile, Lagnado commissioned a ten-country study of women's self-esteem and the impact of beauty ideals on women's and girls' lives. The study surveyed 3,300 girls and women between the ages of fifteen and sixty-four in Brazil, Canada, China, Germany, Italy, Japan, Mexico, Saudi Arabia, the United Kingdom, and the United States. What it found was a global insecurity complex, especially among younger women. Only 2 percent of the women surveyed considered themselves "beautiful," and only 9 percent felt comfortable describing themselves as "attractive." Ninety percent wanted to change at least one aspect of their appearance. And 71 percent admitted they avoided activities—including applying for a job—because of concern about their appearance.

The research turned Lagnado's Beauty Theory into a worldwide debate via a website, print ads, YouTube videos, a traveling photo exhibit, and billboards. The Campaign for Real Beauty, as it came to be called, was more like a political campaign than advertising. People from forty different countries, speaking twenty languages, discussed what they think is beautiful. And in the process, Dove became a different kind of beauty brand.

The Campaign for Real Beauty was also a commercial success. Through 2008, Dove still enjoyed healthy growth and, according to Manfredi, "consumer research in key countries like Germany, the U.K., and the United States shows that consumers love the brand even more because of the campaign." And befitting an effort that was never solely about advertising, Dove has funded further research into women's attitudes toward beauty, sponsored self-esteem workshops attended by more than two million young girls, and established the Dove Self-Esteem Fund, with a $10 million grant to make resources available to young girls' "moms and mentors." In the United States, the fund works largely through a Girl Scouts program to help young girls counter idealized beauty images.

Dove aims to change the status quo and to replace it with a broader, healthier, more democratic view of beauty. As its website says, "a view of beauty that all women can own and enjoy everyday."[2] Along with Dove soaps, lotions, cleansers, shampoos, and deodorants, of course.

NO GOOD DEED

Dove's Campaign for Real Beauty was not without controversy. Marketing pundits dubbed it the "fat girl's campaign," criticized what they considered a tenuous link to product sales, and, when growth rates slowed in the fourth year, issued "I told you so's" to the trade media. Activists questioned Dove's sincerity, since parent Unilever seemed to have no problem using big-bosomed, scantily clad women to pitch Axe deodorant to perpetually adolescent men. And in mid-2008 there was even a brief kerfuffle when someone claimed to have retouched the very photos of real women that kicked off the campaign in the United States.

Manfredi, who was appointed global brand vice president of Dove in 2007 when Lagnado assumed responsibility for Unilever's even larger "savories" food category, admits that the Campaign for Real Beauty staked out a challenging territory for itself. "You need to find the fine line between being aspirational and inspirational," he says. "If you use images that are ugly for the sake of being ugly, you will not inspire women to feel better about themselves." On the other hand, he insists none of the photos used in the ads were altered to tighten tummies or trim thighs. The photographer, Annie Leibovitz, backs him up, saying all her retoucher did was "remove dust and color correction."

Manfredi also denies that the campaign has run out of steam. "The campaign has won new users, increased the loyalty of existing customers, and increased sales over the last five years," he says. "But it's not solely about sales; it's about developing a brand strategy that has competitive strength for the long term." As for fallout from the Axe comparisons, Manfredi says that while there was some backlash from bloggers and advertising pundits, it never showed up in sales. Indeed, many within Unilever believe any apparent contradiction between Axe and Dove is superficial—both brands are self-affirming. "Axe addresses men in an insecure moment when their self-esteem depends on attracting the opposite sex," one brand manager told me. "What hurts women is showing perfect people and making them feel guilty that they don't measure up."

Axe's definition of beauty may be more superficial than Dove's, but that doesn't negate the new meaning Dove has created for itself. And at a fundamental level, both products are about building their customers' confidence.

CREATING MEANING

Creating meaning is the epitome of marketing. It isn't some kind of smoke screen behind which a marketer can hawk his wares. It isn't some kind of New Age mumbo jumbo for the creation of false needs. And it's certainly more than sloganeering or packaging. It's a commercial process that starts with a deep understanding of a particular set of customers in the full context of their lives and social settings.

Silvia Lagnado led her team in creating a new meaning for a bar soap that had been around longer than any of them had been alive. When they arrived on the scene, Dove was a mild soap that didn't dry out a person's skin. Pressed for a more specific definition, many consumers could probably parrot lines from Dove's advertising, noting, for example, that it is "one-quarter cleansing cream" and has "a lower PH than ordinary soap." When they were done, Dove was a line of products designed to unlock the "real beauty" in every woman.

The secret to their success lay in anticipating two powerful trends. The first was the unexpected by-product of our increasingly celebrity-obsessed culture—a rejection of six-pack abs and size 0 figures as an achievable beauty standard, combined with real concern about eating disorders and performance-enhancing drugs. The second trend was women's growing ability and willingness to spend money on looking after themselves. For example, sales of "antiaging" skin-care products in the United States surged 63 percent between 2002 and 2007.[3] By tapping into women's deepest feelings about the Western media's portrayal of feminine beauty, while validating their own efforts to care for themselves, Dove created a new meaning for itself.

This is more than "positioning," which tries to create an image or identity for a product relative to its competitors. So Volvo is the "safe" car, while Mercedes is a "luxury" car, and Porsche is a "high-performance" car. But they're all still cars. The masters of marketing go a step further—they create new *meaning* for their product based less on its advertising than on its experience. A BMW is not only the "ultimate driving machine," it's the freedom and exhilaration of the open road. As advertising legend Keith Reinhard puts it, "Advertisers need to worry less about their brand image and more about their brand experience."[4]

The president of Wal-Mart's North American operations, Eduardo Castro-Wright, told the *Wall Street Journal* that the company's improved performance in 2008 stemmed largely from deciding it stood for "more than just low prices, but [rather] saving people money to make their lives better. That gave us a unifying marketing message and gave 1.3 million associates a powerful sense of purpose."[5]

P&G's Jim Stengel believes a brand's meaning should come from asking the power question, "What does my brand do to make people's lives better?" Target's answer to that question is "we bring good design to everybody," and it's reflected in everything from its product selection to its store layout, shopping carts, cash registers, lighting, and signage, as well as its personnel policies, marketing strategies, and philanthropy. When all of those activities serve a common purpose, the result is better teamwork, more efficient operations, and clearer meaning.

THE NEED FOR MEANING

As noted in the opening quote to this chapter, cultural anthropologist Ernest Becker once observed that, "Man is the only animal who must create meaning."[6] Our prehistoric ancestors were compelled to label the world around them as they organized into increasingly intricate social groups. Eventually, those labels began appearing on their cave walls and carefully buried with their dead. Those markings signaled prehistoric people's concern with the larger meaning behind phenomena—who we are and why we're here, to be sure, but also the nature of beauty, accomplishment, creativity, truth, community, freedom, harmony, and a host of other abstract concepts that only existed in the firing of particular synapses within primitive human brains.

We are millennia removed from those crude expressions of meaning, but they still speak to us and of us. Modern man's behavior may be more refined, but in many ways it is just as elemental. We still have the same hierarchy of needs—from physical to social to spiritual. The masters of marketing operate at the higher levels of those needs, not simply selling products, but constructing meaning around products so they can be used in the language of social communication and satisfy spiritual needs.

People choose one brand rather than another because it has the right meaning for them. That meaning is not transferred in ads, but by experiencing a brand's ideals. Harley-Davidson, for example, has created a rich body of meaning and sustains it with symbols and rituals as rich as any religious sect's. The Harley Owners Group (HOG, of course) boasts more than one million members who share the same ideals and values.

Amancio Ortega opened a small lingerie shop in Spain in 1963, specializing in knockoffs of the latest fashions. When he noticed the same customers wandering around the store just to see what was new, he realized they considered clothes a perishable commodity, like fruit that is in and out of season. That insight drove the development of a system that can move fashion from a designer's board to a store rack in a matter of weeks. The Zara brand is supertrendy; it ships new styles to its 3,000 retail stores in sixty-four countries twice a week. The stock changes so often that Zara means "freshly baked clothes" to its customers and satisfies the social value of being *au courant*.

French marketing professor Benoît Heilbrunn says a brand is not a "sign" but a "semiotic engine" that constantly produces meaning and values.[7] What he means is that brands operate at the higher ends of Maslow's famous hierarchy of human needs—providing not just survival and safety, but esteem and self-actualization. For example, in 2007 the number-one reason people gave for buying a Toyota Prius hybrid is "it makes a statement about me."[8] The relatively new science of neuro-marketing is compiling substantial evidence that brands operate at a "preconscious" level in ways we don't yet completely understand.

Researchers have even been able to track the phenomenon on brain scans. Reed Montague, the director of the Baylor School of Medicine's Center for Theoretical Neuroscience, dreamed up an experiment that duplicated the Pepsi Challenge to keep his teenage daughter occupied as she helped out in the lab over summer vacation. Montague had volunteers lie supine in a functional magnetic resonance imaging (fMRI) machine, which shows blood flow within the brain. Then he had them sip both Coke and Pepsi through a tube while he watched their neural activity. Without knowing what they were drinking, about half of them said they preferred Pepsi. But once Montague told them which samples were Coke, three-fourths said that drink tasted better, and their brain activity changed too. Their dorsolateral prefrontal cortex and hippocampus lit up like Christmas trees. Both of these areas are implicated in modifying behavior based on emotion and affect. Montague theorized that the brain was recalling images and ideas from commercials, and the brand was overriding the actual quality of the product.

Montague's research, which was published in the October 2004 issue of the journal *Neuron,*[9] showed how deeply Coke's brand has actually insinuated itself into people's nervous systems. In particular, Montague said his findings demonstrated how Coke's brand imagery "biases preference judgments."[10] Your taste buds may say you prefer Pepsi, but your hippocampus overrules them. Over time, Coke has assumed new meaning, completely separate from its formulation, its packaging, and even its taste. The phenomenon is so real that in 2008 Burger King researchers fanned out to remote parts of the world, like the frozen tundra of Greenland and the hinterlands of rural Transylvania, to conduct a taste test between its Whopper and McDonald's Big Mac.

THE CREATION OF MEANING

We'd wear out the nation's fMRI machines before we could completely understand these phenomena, but it seems certain that some brands have assumed meaning they did not anticipate. Sometimes that meaning accretes to a brand simply because it's been around a long time. Johnson & Johnson, for example, still means "babies" to most people, even though the company derives less than one percent of its revenue from baby products and less than 3 percent from the sale of children's products overall. However, the company carefully cultivates and reinforces that meaning because it casts a warm and friendly halo over all its other businesses. Who doesn't like babies?

Brands can also acquire unanticipated meaning because they perfectly capture the ethos of a particular time. That's how a simple pair of denim blue jeans—Levi's—took on mythic quality. First, in America, as a retelling of Gold Rush stories, then in postwar Europe as a symbol of the youthful, fun-loving country of its liberators. By the 1980s, used Levi's were so packed with meaning they were a form of currency in parts of Eastern Europe for traveling Americans.

The masters of marketing don't leave the creation of meaning to chance. They begin by understanding a particular customer's needs within the context of social trends, especially at points of tension or conflict. Then they make sense of the apparent contradictions within the context of their product. What they do is akin to political scientist Alan Wolfe's definition of meaning as "making larger sense out of smaller bits." Such meaning is a cultural phenomenon, not an issue of linguistics or semantics.[11] Rather than simply associating their product with customers' aspirations, they create a world in which people's collective anxieties are resolved and then invite them in. In Silvia Lagnado's words, they offer "inspiration, rather than simply aspiration."[12]

Because such meaning is a cultural product, it often contributes to the creation of identity. Indeed, recent research suggests that a product's meaning not only demonstrates who its customers are, but who they are *not*.[13] For example, Nike couldn't break into skateboarding shoes because, in the rebel world of skaters, it was considered "corporate." So the company turned to hard-core skaters with street "cred" to design a shoe customized for skateboarding. It assembled a Nike skateboarding team and brought in maverick young artists to depict their exploits on the sides of the shoes. And it sold the shoes only to the right small shops at first. When recognized skaters began wearing the shoes, kids began asking for them and Nike expanded distribution.[14] It created meaning for the shoe, not through advertising, but by making it part of the culture.

Similarly, Black & Decker had been making power tools since 1910 when it purchased General Electric's small-appliance division in 1984. After a few years of peddling irons and coffeemakers with the GE logo, the company decided to bring everything under the same roof so Black & Decker mixers were on the shelf just one department over from the power tools. Naturally, the company supported the rebranding effort with plenty of consumer advertising. Sales increased—for consumer appliances. But power tool sales declined. Black & Decker had changed the meaning of its name—from masculine and tough to feminine and domestic. Contractors were embarrassed to walk onto a job site carrying a Black & Decker drill. "The contractor doesn't want a tool that has the same name as his wife's toaster," says Dan Gregory, vice president of marketing for DeWalt.[15]

So in 1992, Black & Decker launched a line of portable electric power tools under the DeWalt name in distinctive black and yellow housings. At first, it concentrated on sales to professionals, sending an army of tool guys in bright yellow trucks to construction sites around the country asking workers to test and critique DeWalt tools on the spot. Professional contractors account for nearly 70 percent of purchases, but more importantly, the company needed their endorsement to get do-it-yourselfers to buy the tools. In just a few years, DeWalt became one of Black & Decker's most profitable divisions, with a 35 percent share of the professional-tool market. Black & Decker created new meaning for a brand it had bought and discarded, decades before.

People have always derived meaning from considered purchases, like cars. What's new is that now even consumables have meaning. Clorox redefined itself as a health and wellness product, tripling sales between 2005 and 2008. Instead of touting bleach's whitening power in the laundry, TV commercials celebrated its cleaning power on every household surface that might gather germs. Clorox commercials feature little girls pretending to be mermaids in bathrooms so pristine you could do a heart transplant in the bathtub. The company's website is crammed with tips for disinfecting surfaces to ward off colds, flu, and a critter called methicillin-resistant *Staphylococcus aureus* that can do nasty things to your skin.

Of course, some efforts to create meaning never amount to more than word association. ConAgra weaved its consumer brands through a website it created with all kinds of nutrition and exercise tips. Healthy Choice, Egg Beaters, and PAM seemed right at home. Orville Redenbacher looked a little uncomfortable. But the whole effort didn't amount to much more than a media buy with good placement.

Creating meaning requires more than clever advertising. Until recently, Starbucks did very little advertising, yet it defined itself as more than a cup of coffee. Starbucks is a total experience. Customers order in an idiosyncratic language where "tall" means "small," "grande" means "medium," and "venti" means "large." But that's just the beginning. Every beverage comes in a bewildering range of options—like a marble mocha macchiato, one-third decaf, triple shot, with sugar-free vanilla, 2 percent milk, no foam, and an extra drizzle of chocolate. And a "barista" makes the coffee fresh—customer-by-customer, face-to-face, right across the counter. Patrons can take their cup to a comfortable chair or a sofa, and if they pass someone on the street carrying the familiar cup in a safety liner they know they're members of the same club, what many brand experts call a "coffeehouse" community.

THE POWER OF STORIES

Stories are a powerful tool for creating meaning, particularly if the story is dramatic, easy to tell, and easy to remember. In those cases, consumers become the primary authors of a brand's meaning through the retelling of its story. Emotional attachment becomes the consequence of creating meaning, rather than a tool in its construction.

Ever since the Magdalenians drew on cave walls in southern France around 32,000 years ago, we've told stories to make sense of the world.[16] Marketers recognized this from the earliest days. Aunt Jemima and Uncle Ben became the symbols for a new pancake mix and a particular brand of white rice not only because they gave the products personality, but because they subtly told a backstory of "happy slaves" who were dedicated to their "family's" well-being.

For example, Roy Raymond, a Stanford business school grad, founded Victoria's Secret in 1977, because he found it awkward to buy lingerie for his wife in the typical department store. He built the kind of store he'd like to shop in—lots of wood-paneled walls, oriental rugs, Victorian vanities, and a helpful staff. Instead of hanging bras and panties in every size on racks, he framed single matching pairs in each style on the walls. That spared men from pawing through the unmentionables looking for the right size. They could just point to the style they liked and a salesperson would help them estimate the right size before fetching it from the back room. He also stocked it with the kind of lingerie a man would like to see on his wife or girlfriend, not something from a "French postcard" of the nineteenth century, but more romantic than plain white granny panties and bras. Stepping into Victoria's Secret, whether in one of the three original stores or in the pages of its lavishly illustrated catalogue, was to step back in time to a more glamorous, romantic era. Victoria's "secret" was that there was plenty of lace beneath that erect, somewhat suppressed Victorian posture.

In 1982, just five years after opening the first Victoria's Secret in the Stanford Shopping Center across from the university, Raymond sold out to The Limited, which adhered closely to his formula as it expanded into shopping malls across the country. Through much of the 1990s, Victoria's Secret meant glamour, beauty, fashion, and romance. Victoria's Secret lingerie became a covert sign of femininity as the proportion of women in the professional and technical workforce accelerated during the 1980s and 1990s. In that sense, it resolved the tension between appearing "businesslike" and retaining one's sexuality.

However, as Victoria's Secret entered the new millennium, many of the tools it used to reinforce its meaning—from enlisting supermodels as silent "spokespeople" to staging high-profile lingerie "fashion shows"—became too sexually charged. Some towns even tried to ban the store's provocative window displays. The brand's meaning had devolved from "romance and glamour" to "sex and sleaze." When profits declined 12 percent in the fourth quarter of 2007, the company's CEO said the chain had "gotten off" its heritage and become "too sexy." She said it would return to more sophisticated and less overtly seductive styles.[17] By drifting away from its heritage, Victoria's Secret contradicted its own meaning. It became inauthentic and phony. In marketing, that may be the biggest sin of all.

On the other hand, the makers of the American Girl line of dolls have never been confused about their meaning, and the stories they create about each doll only enhance their meanings. Most dolls toymakers produce today are aimed squarely at little girls. But the American Girl line, which is a subsidiary of Barbie's Mattel, targets these girls' parents and grandparents. The dolls' prices reflect this—while Barbie costs about $20, a new American Girl doll will set a doting grandmother back about $95. But what she gets for that price is not only an eighteen-inch-tall plastic replica of a real girl, but a whole experience.

Each doll represents a period in history and comes with a book that tells its backstory and describes its personality. There's also a full line of period-correct costumes and accessories. Grandma can even take granddaughter and doll for tea at one of five American Girl stores. Some hotels near the stores even offer "American Girl Getaway" packages, including use of an American Girl doll travel bed, a free American Girl–themed dessert for a girl (and one for her doll) in the hotel restaurant, and a complimentary limousine ride to the local American Girl outlet. Everything is designed to give little girls and the people who love them an imaginative experience that they can share. It's all made up, but very authentic. And it pays off. While Barbie sales have been declining in the United States, American Girl dolls remain wildly popular. The *American Girl* magazine is one of the top ten children's publications in the country, and the stores have higher sales per square foot than Tiffany's.

"DESIGN THINKING"

When A.G. Lafley became CEO of P&G, he didn't consider the company's reputation for "making goop that does what it's supposed to" particularly high praise. A stint in Japan had taught him that fusing function with meaning and pleasure was a higher order source of competitive advantage and growth. Ironically, the world's largest packaged-goods company had never put much emphasis on package design. But Lafley considered how a consumer reacts to the product on the shelf as a brand's "first moment of truth" and an integral part of the brand experience. He thought P&G should market not just products, but the consumer's experience with them—how they look, smell, and feel.

Lafley set out to inject good design into the company's DNA and, as a start, established the company's first corporate design office, reporting directly to him. He staffed it with a mix of company veterans and outside hires. And adopting an expansive definition of "design," he gave the design office a mandate to teach P&G's managers a new way of thinking. Lafley calls it "design thinking," or imagining what could be possible, rather than being constrained by an analysis of directly observable facts or past evidence. That's a lot more than putting racing stripes on a tube of Crest and, in fact, P&G has applied the discipline to a wide range of thorny problems from business strategy to office design.[18] Designers who once labored on logos and packaging in humble anonymity found themselves deeply involved in all aspects of product development.

But the design office's first order of business was to convince the company's brand managers that aesthetics are more than fluff and design is more than drawing. In their initial meetings, the new vice president of design would typically ask groups of brand managers how they would package Altoids mints if P&G purchased the iconic lozenges from Wrigley. They said they would change the expensive tin to a plastic tube, scrap the paper lining that didn't seem to serve any real purpose, and make all the mints the same shape so they would stack neatly. Then she would ask them if they would pay a 400 percent premium for mints in their new package. They almost always said "no way," and suddenly lightbulbs went off—they now understood the value of aesthetics.

Through workshops that teach the principles of "design thinking" to cross-functional team leaders, as well as an external review board that evaluates the company's new products three times a year, the central design office has stimulated a steady stream of innovations. It helped restage the Herbal Essences line of hair products by chucking the flower-child daisies on the label and putting the shampoos and conditioners into neon-colored, unusually shaped bottles that nested comfortably together. It helped with the formulation and fragrance of Olay Regenerist. In fact, it helped design everything from new ergonomic bathroom-cleaning products to a new tampon applicator. It even helped Oil of Olay design an online beauty service that guided women to a personal skin-care regimen tailored to their particular skin type.

Whether they use anthropologists and ethnographers or their own intuition and experience, the masters of marketing find their brand's higher purpose at the intersection of its competencies and people's needs, desires, and values. They build their brand's meaning around that higher purpose. And they recognize that being true to their meaning requires more than graphic guidelines and advertising standards. It requires widespread understanding and constant vigilance.

☞ *They understand their brand from a customer's perspective, in terms of task, benefit, and emotions.* IKEA has babysitting because it's all about helping young families furnish and decorate their home without worrying about the kids wandering off.

☞ *They find their brand's purpose in their customers' higher-level emotional and social needs.* Silvia Lagnado's initial goal was to move Dove out of the "soap" category into the much broader "beauty products" category. She did that by giving the brand a distinctive point of view on the definition of "beauty" and a higher purpose—helping women achieve greater self-esteem.

☞ *They ensure that their higher purpose is meaningful to their customers and believable coming from their brand.* They are not afraid to stretch their brand's boundaries in the interests of creating a higher purpose. By starting a conversation about the nature of beauty, Dove won consumers' permission to change its meaning from a bar of soap to a full beauty line.

☞ *They can describe the people their brand addresses in terms that go well beyond basic demographics and psychographics.* They understand and identify with people's functional, emotional, and social needs. Silvia Lagnado's insight into women's insecurities about their personal appearance was confirmed by surveys and academic studies.

☞ *They are passionate about their views, but don't try to impose them on others, working instead to win the commitment of their superiors and their team members.* They distribute customer data widely throughout the organization and make all decisions in the open rather than behind closed doors. "The mind-set behind our approach was Servant Leadership," says Dove's Alessandro Manfredi. "We had a duty to present a clear strategic direction for the brand, but at the same time we really had to listen and understand genuine concerns and practical needs so we could develop solutions that addressed them."

☞ *When they have sufficient support to take their ideas into the marketplace, they start small, testing and proving their concepts.* They let a track record of results build momentum. Their goal is to inspire both customers and team members. Dove's Real Beauty campaign started in only three small markets, but quickly built momentum on the results achieved.

☞ *They are not afraid to use nontraditional media, realizing that purpose brands benefit from targeted communications and are highly suited to social media.* But they are also careful to avoid anything that would undermine their brand's credibility. Dove's Real Beauty campaign stimulated online discussions by placing provocative videos on YouTube and through billboards that asked people to vote for their version of beauty via cell phone or online—"Is she wrinkled or wonderful?"—they asked of a ninety-six-year-old woman with a radiant smile.

☞ *They express their brand's meaning at every touch point, recognizing that it depends on the customer's total experience, not simply communications about it.* They enlist their distributors, dealers, and retailers in comarketing that expresses their brand's meaning and enriches the consumer's experience.

☞ *They make their marketing useful to customers in and of itself.* Dove established a Self-Esteem Fund to support workshops for young girls. Michelin started publishing its iconic series of road guides more than 100 years ago; Crocs created a *Cities By Foot* website travel guide in 2008. Nike started an online Bootcamp to teach young soccer players the finer points of the sport, promising to increase their speed and endurance by a third.

CHAPTER TEN

BE TRUE TO YOUR
BRAND'S MEANING

*"Authenticity is the benchmark
against which all brands are now judged."*

—JOHN GRANT, *THE NEW MARKETING
MANIFESTO*

Authenticity used to mean a product was made by the person whose name was on the label. Now it means the product is real, not as opposed to fake, but as the opposite of cynical. As author Bill Breen points out, "What's authentic is not always real, and what's real is not always what it seems."[1] Jon Stewart of *The Daily Show* is the host of a "fake" news program, yet he seems more authentic than many of the blow-dried anchors earnestly reading from a teleprompter on the "real" news programs.

To be authentic is to be true to one's meaning, to be consistent and predictable, to never say one thing and do another. In fact, truly authentic brands align every customer touch point with that meaning. Nick Vlahos, the vice president of customer development for Clorox, talks about creating a seamless experience across three "moments of truth"—from the marketing that creates a desire for the product, to the retail environment where a consumer decides to buy the product, to the delight a consumer experiences when he or she uses it.[2]

EXPERIENCE AS MARKETING

Experience is the new marketing, and authentic brands are careful to communicate the same message through all five senses—touch, taste, smell, sight, and sound. Folgers captured coffee's generic benefit in an advertising slogan—"the best part of wakin' up is Folgers in your cup"—and extended it to the product experience by strengthening the aromatic release of the beans it uses. It even developed a can with a resealable lid that preserved the coffee's aroma.

On the other hand, Starbucks lost its way when it began to automate the process of brewing its coffee to shorten lines at the counter and added egg sandwiches to its menu to goose revenue. Peoples' noses noticed the change before they did—the aroma of fresh-ground coffee beans gave way to the smell of frying eggs. One fragrance is not necessarily better than the other—but one was appropriate to a diner, the other to a coffeehouse. Things got so bad that Howard Schultz reinstalled himself as CEO and shut down all 7,100 stores nationwide for three hours so all 135,000 in-store employees could remind themselves what Starbucks is about, while they relearned how to pull the perfect shot, not burn coffee, and correctly steam milk. While Schultz is not the company's founder, he's the keeper of its meaning, of its authenticity.

Experiences should be tailored to a brand's target audience, while staying true to its heritage. Abercrombie & Fitch started in 1900 as a New York City store for genteel outdoorsmen. Today's stores retain some of the trappings of its original incarnation, including moose heads over the cash register and canoe paddles on the walls. But the overall scene is collegiate keg party, skewing slightly older than its largely teenage clientele. In fact, none of the 900 stores have window displays, preferring plantation shutters that are always half-closed on a dark interior, and music so loud that no one over age 30 would risk crossing the threshold. Ironically, the company's CEO is a sixty-three-year-old whose dyed-blond hair is in the "I-just-rolled-out-of-bed" style favored by his customers. Most days he can be found tooling around corporate headquarters in torn jeans and flip-flops. And, oh yes, he runs it all from the teen capital of New Albany, Ohio.

TRUE TO THE CORE

Sadly, the marketing world is littered with examples of brands that failed because they were not true to their meaning. Las Vegas tried to promote itself as a family destination in the 1990s, advertising kid-friendly roller coasters and water parks. The campaign was successful in attracting young families, but it turned off its core audience of gamblers, who liked the old "adults-only" atmosphere and didn't like it when the bare breasts they saw were attached to a nursing infant. The city quickly returned to its roots with two provocative campaigns— "What happens in Vegas, stays in Vegas" in 2002, supplemented by "Your Vegas is showing" in 2008. Rossi Ralenkotter, president and CEO of the Las Vegas Convention and Visitors Authority, reminds people that Las Vegas means "adult freedom." When it strays from that meaning it loses its neon, glitzy authenticity.

On the other hand, tourism officials in India credit the "Incredible India" promotion they launched in 2002 with doubling foreign tourist arrivals in just five years, after two years of declines. In 2008, the readers of *Condé Nast Traveler*[3] ranked India second only to New Zealand as their favorite vacation destination. The "Incredible India" campaign broadened the country's meaning by promising, in the words of one of the country's embassies, that "Practically everything about India surprises. Most are wonderful or amusing, some are wacky and weird." It promoted the country's heritage sites, its wildlife, its beaches, its deserts, and everything in between. But the campaign would have failed if it hadn't been in perfect sync with people's preconceptions of the slightly mysterious, exotic country of vast contrasts. (This was obviously before the November 2008 terror attacks in Mumbai revealed the deep inadequacy of the country's internal security forces.)

AUTHENTICITY FACTORY

Authenticity is in the eye of the beholder. Sometimes, being true to a brand's meaning requires careful fabrication and orchestration. The masters of marketing obsess about all the elements that support their authenticity. Kellogg's designed the mouthfeel and crunching sound of their cornflakes in the laboratory and patented it. Singapore Airlines sprays its cabins with Stefan Floridian Waters, based on the perfume worn by the original "Singapore Girls" cabin attendants, which has become the airline's olfactory trademark. Because aroma is lost in the process of making instant coffee, Nestlé adds a blast of "coffee smell" to each jar of Nescafé so it wafts out when the seal is broken. Faced with low-cost competitors, Crayola analyzed the scent of its original crayons and patented it. All of these experiences are manufactured. All of them are "real." In fact, just smelling a crayon will stimulate childhood memories in most American adults of a certain age.

Robert Stephens, founder of the Geek Squad, made dozens of such decisions when he came up with the idea for a mobile crew of technicians who could reanimate hard drives and solve other computer problems for people who couldn't afford full-time, in-house tech support, which is most of us. Now since his idea was fairly unique at the time, you might think "authenticity" wouldn't be an issue. But Stephens approached the project like a screenwriter—every frame has to move the viewer toward the big finish, in this case the joyous scene when his or her computer is back online. Stephens wanted everything about his new service to tell a story in which his customers got top billing. So he played into the stereotype of the nerd with the pocket protector who might not be able to get a date on Saturday night, but could debug code with one hand while playing video games with the other. He gave the company a very nontechnical name—the Geek Squad—to make it approachable. And then he followed through by modeling the squad's uniforms on the way NASA engineers dressed in Mission Control during the first moon shots, from short-sleeved white shirts to narrow black ties and laminated badges. The company car is a black-and-white Volkswagen, consistent with the company's motto, which sounds like something out of *Dragnet*—"Serving the Public, Policing Technology, and Protecting the World." The whole effect is part show business, part shared joke, and very authentic.

A REAL EXPERIENCE

The masters of marketing understand that the experience of a product—the process of buying and using it—is part of the product itself. When a brand delivers an experience in perfect sync with its meaning, it is capable of attaining the highest levels of authenticity. For example, when Howard Schultz got involved with Starbucks, it had been roasting and brewing world-class coffee for a solid decade. Its founders were fanatic about educating customers on the finer points of roasting and brewing coffee beans. What he brought to the company was the decision to re-create "the ritual and romance of coffee bars in Italy."[4] He didn't set out to make better coffee—Starbucks was already doing that. He set out to change the *experience* of drinking coffee away from home. He designed a "third place" somewhere between home and work, where people would feel comfortable just passing the time. Most successful restaurants are quasi-theatrical—their ambience contributes nearly as much to people's enjoyment as the food on their plate, in some cases more.

The importance of people's experience extends to other product categories as well. For example, fashion and cosmetics often express intimate aspects of people's self-identity. Their deeper meaning is often rooted in people's insecurities and aspirations, as well as their tastes and personal preferences. Most brands in these categories construct experiences that reinforce their appeal to these emotions. For example, everything about The Body Shop—from its retail storefronts to its product displays and packaging—communicates the natural wholesomeness that apothecaries used to dispense in simpler times.

At the other end of the continuum, Urban Outfitters' retail stores have the look of a particularly hip Goodwill outlet. Clothes hang on bare pipes, quirky merchandise is piled on tables and assorted bookcases, the signage looks as if the girl at the cash register scrawled it in magic marker moments before (which is probably the case). The loud music, the aroma of burning incense, and the intentionally shopworn fixtures all create an experience of discovery.

THE FIRST MOMENT OF TRUTH

Most marketers, who are at least one step removed from their product's end users, try to influence the product's presentation at point of sale through in-store marketing and promotional allowances. In fact, in recent years, marketing in stores has been growing faster than on the Web. Packaged-goods advertising now appears on supermarket floors, shelves, shopping carts, and at checkout counters. Since two-thirds of consumers don't know which brand they will buy until they are in the store, and they spend less than 2.5 seconds deciding, this makes a certain amount of sense. P&G alone spends an estimated $2 billion a year on it. But Jim Stengel had more than ads in mind when he was appointed the company's CMO. In addition to promoting his brands more effectively, he wanted to ensure they measured up to consumers' expectations at this "first moment of truth."

In P&G terminology, retailers had long been considered the company's "customers." Stengel decided to start treating them that way, greatly expanding comarketing programs to improve the shopping experience for the consumers they both depend on. For example, P&G worked with CVS to develop a merchandising unit that would help the retailer attract teen girls. The displays featured non–P&G products (though not those of competitors). Most significantly, the company shifted budget responsibility for in-store marketing from its sales organization to the marketing directors who controlled advertising decisions. Now if they find that a brand responds better to trade marketing than consumer marketing, they can shift more funds in-store. "We busted a lot of barriers to get better at in-store marketing," Stengel says, "but it was one of the key capabilities I was determined to improve." His goal, in the end, was to extend the meaning of every P&G brand to the very experience of buying it.

Apple has shown how mastering the user experience can trump being first to market. Apple didn't have the first MP3 player, but it made the process of buying music and getting it from your computer to your player so easy that it now commands more than 70 percent of the player market, and its iTunes website displaced Wal-Mart as the number-one outlet for recorded music in 2008. Not the number-one *online* outlet, the number-one outlet in the physical *and* online worlds. And it appears to be on track to accomplish the same feat in so-called "smart wireless phones," another product line where it was late to the party.

Many attribute Apple's success to its programming capabilities, and the company does produce elegant software. But what truly distinguishes the company is something every marketer can emulate, even in products free of silicon and software. Apple is obsessive about the user experience. In fact, the original Mac computer was the first to be ready to use out of the box. Before then—and for years after—most personal computers arrived in several boxes, requiring hours of assembly, installation, and time on hold, waiting for technical support. Apple's obsession with the user experience shows up in big things, such as the clean, elegant design of its products, websites, and retail stores. But it also shows up in small things, such as the logo on the cover of its laptops, which is upside down to the user, but not for those watching. Or the white Apple logo stickers that come with every product. Or the clean white color of the iPod earbuds. Or the tight seams that make Apple computers look as if they were carved from a single block of white plastic or silver titanium.

In fact, just taking an Apple product out of its box has become a vicarious pleasure for many people. In 2006, a fan named Josh Bancroft started a website that consisted solely of videos showing people "unbox" Apple products. As gearhead porn, it was incredibly successful. "It started as a whim," Bancroft says, "but it became so incredibly popular so fast that I didn't have time to keep updating it. I felt like I was disappointing people by starting something interesting that I couldn't sustain, so I sold it to Gear Live in July 2006." While coy about his precise take on the transaction, Bancroft says he received "more than a few hundred but less than a couple thousand." Dollars, one assumes. The site now features over fifty videos, about a quarter of which are of Apple products, which are downloaded more than 400,000 times a month.

Andru Edwards, Gear Live's editor, thinks there are two reasons for the site's popularity. "First, people like to know what they are buying. When you buy an iPod, you know you are getting an iPod. But you may not know if it includes a cable, or a dock, or a carrying case, etc. We give you all of that information by showing you exactly what is included when you purchase a given product. Second, people like to live vicariously through others. Some people can't afford to get every gadget that they want. Through Unboxing, they are able to be a part of the experience."

PERSONALIZATION

Experience is the new marketing—especially when buying and using a product expresses and reinforces its deeper meaning. Of course, in an era when people expect companies to offer products tailored to their specific preferences, the most satisfying experience is a personal one. Jones Soda comes in a simple bottle with a powerful label—the company solicits customers' photos to print on the label, as well as to post on its website. Lego created an online "factory" tool, which enables people to design their own creation and purchase just the Lego bricks needed to build it. Users can post photos of their creations and see those of others. The thrill of designing and building something original and sharing it with like-minded people is the essence of the experience, which perfectly reinforces Lego's deeper meaning of personal creativity.

It appears there are few limits to personalization. A simple swab of the saliva on the inside of a user's cheek (plus $120) is all My DNA Fragrance needs to produce four ounces of "biologically seductive" cologne or perfume that will "leave a memory of you in every room." But as enticing as that may seem, it does not guarantee a satisfying user experience. A peak experience is one that imparts a sense of identity and community. People are social animals, and even in an individualistic society like the United States, where rugged individuals are mythologized, most people derive their personal identity from the groups they join. And in a consumer society like ours that includes the goods and services we buy.

BOTTOM-UP MEANING

Sometimes the creation of meaning is a bottom-up process. For forty years, Timberland sold its rugged work boots largely to construction workers and had few illusions they would ever be fashionable. But then hip-hop artists began wearing them and Timberland boots became as much a part of the urban youth culture as slouchy jeans, exposed boxers, and lots of "bling." Similarly, Corona beer became "a vacation in a bottle" because it was the cheapest beer college students on spring break could afford when they descended on Southern California beaches in the 1960s and 1970s. The label rode that wave until 2007, when competitors introduced new products like the lime- and salt-flavored Miller Chill and Anheuser-Busch's BL Lime, a light beer with a touch of lime.

Certain products simply appeal to different "tribes." In one experiment, Dunkin' Donuts gave $100 to a group of its best customers, as well as to some Starbucks fans. The only condition was that each group had to spend the money in the other group's favorite coffee shop. When they were interviewed later, the company discovered that the Starbucks customers hated Dunkin' Donuts—they complained that the coffee was weak, the store itself reminded them of a high-school cafeteria, everything was rushed, and the seating was uncomfortable. The Dunkin' Donuts customers didn't consider Starbucks any better—the selection of coffees was overwhelming, the coffee tasted burnt, the lingo was bewildering, and if they wanted to sip coffee sitting on a sofa, they would have stayed home. Dunkin' Donuts and Starbucks had different meanings, each richly expressed in the experience they each created. At the core of that meaning was a sense of tribal identity or community. Ironically, Starbucks—which was built on a small community of coffee drinkers who enjoyed its club-like atmosphere—began to decline as it opened more stores and introduced caseloads of new products to broaden its appeal and attract a mass audience.

Marketers can sometimes ride the wave of strong cultural and social trends. For example, in the patriotic fervor following World War II, Coca-Cola exulted in Americana; in the divisiveness of the 1970s, it brought the world together on a hillside and bought it a Coke; in the racial strife of the 1980s, it showed that even Mean Joe Greene had a soft heart, just like the rest of us.

But the masters of marketing don't just ride the massive waves of popular sentiment; they look for the smaller, ill-defined swells that carry a particular subset of people. Then they try to understand the specific emotional and functional currents that brought them together. With that insight, they can prepare an offer that has sufficient meaning to bring those bobbing individuals together as a community. Defining a brand's user base is the most critical step in building a brand. Nurturing them as a community is the key to sustaining it.

Trader Joe's is a national chain of small stores with a funky South Pacific décor, an unusually large number of private label specialty foods, and daily blackboard specials. Everything about the store communicates a decidedly noncorporate passion for food and wine at a good value. Most faithful customers would be surprised to learn it's owned by the billionaire founder of a German discount supermarket chain.

BUILDING COMMUNITIES

User groups began in the early days of mainframe computing more or less as a self-defense mechanism. They enabled customers to share hard-won knowledge and useful software they had written independently of the factory-authorized sources. User groups became so influential within the technical community that many companies formed their own so they could operate from the inside, rather than simply observing and reacting to their own customers. Not surprisingly, with advances in social networking, many information technology companies took their user groups online.

Cisco's NetPro website, for example, has proven to be a useful tool for IT professionals. It not only helps them find the information they need among the millions of pages of online documentation, but it also provides a forum through which they can exchange tips, seek advice, and learn about new applications. Rob Huffman, a systems analyst at Mount Royal College in Calgary, Canada, is a typical member. He goes on the site so often, including on weekends, that his wife calls him part of the "nerd herd." But he credits the site with helping him learn to manage an extensive IP telephony system without formal training. "I've never experienced any forum or community that works together like NetPro does," he says. "People go out of their way to help each other, even building systems in the lab to verify proper configuration and operation."[5] And, of course, by extending their experience with Cisco products, NetPro has helped turn users into enthusiasts, which is the ultimate sign of authenticity.

As social networking caught on, company-sponsored online communities spread beyond technology products to categories ranging from cars to hot sauces. Harley-Davidson, for example, tries to enroll everyone who buys one of its motorcycles in the Harley Owners Group. Members are invited to special events, plan rides together, do charitable work, and share information. With over one million members in nearly 1,200 chapters worldwide, HOG is a living expression of Harley's deeper meaning—the thrill and freedom of the open road.

P&G's Tampax brand created beinggirl.com, an online community for teenage girls in forty countries. Tampax's sponsorship is clearly indicated on the site, which includes product sections and offers for free samples. But most of the site focuses on content of interest to young women, including music and discussions about everything from dating to losing weight. Forrester Research found that beinggirl.com is four times as effective as a similarly priced program using traditional media. That didn't surprise P&G, whose Home Made Simple site (homemadesimple.com), dedicated to solutions for the home, has around a million registered users. That puts it in the ranks of the leading women's service periodicals, but it also generates a gold mine of consumer insight that is entirely proprietary. The secret to both sites is that they provide content people can use in an environment that allows them to take control of the discussion.

However, no matter how carefully companies try to minimize the commercialization of their sponsored sites, they will always be open to criticism and, worse, skepticism, which is the opposite of authenticity. For example, some of the weight-loss tips on beinggirl.com struck some people as enabling eating-disorder behavior. And though some reviewers conceded that much of the health content on the site was useful and well presented, some complained about the number of product mentions.

Enthusiastic customers have a way of organizing themselves to spread the contagion of their interest. Rather than building their own websites—which will always be viewed skeptically by some—many marketers have learned how to harness their customers' enthusiasm, not only to promote their product, but as a means of adding value to it. "Communities already exist," Mark Zuckerberg, the founder of Facebook points out. "Think about how you can help that community do what it wants to do."[6] The first step is to get to know the boundary leaders, who are highly active, broker interactions, and have high authority. But you should also remember Jimmy Wales's caution. He founded Wikipedia, but acknowledges that the Wiki community is "one part anarchy, one part aristocracy, one part democracy, one part monarchy."[7]

The masters of marketing have learned that as they deepen the meaning of their product, it becomes a service to its users. Their brand is no longer self-contained, but part of a community, and its role is to help its customers navigate it. The masters of marketing are full participants in those communities, listening to the chatter, encouraging discussion, and acting on feedback. They understand what the communities are trying to do and they build tools to help them do it.

LETTING GO

Working with online communities requires marketers to learn a skill that does not come naturally to them—letting go. For decades, as marketing evolved from shilling products door-to-door to using sophisticated communications media to get into people's homes, one characteristic was constant—controlling every aspect of a product's presentation. Today, instead of intruding on people, the masters of marketing seek to engage them. They willingly trade control for influence.

"The story of Dove is one of a brand that progressively ceded control," Harvard Business School professor John Deighton says. "In the 1950s, Dove's advertising approach was similar to a World War II military campaign with a heavy bombardment of 30- and 60-second messages with very strong, functional content. It was all delivered with complete control over the message and the media."[8] Today, Dove has claimed new territory at the intersection of significant cultural trends and its own "best self." Instead of searching for advertising's proverbial "Big Idea," Dove targeted what Ogilvy creative director Steve Hayden calls "the Big Ideal." The sheer volume of viral media and user-generated content stimulated by the Dove Real Beauty campaign suggests it struck a chord. The depth and intensity of emotion in the word of mouth surrounding it indicate that Dove has made a strong connection with its customers.

In today's media-rich world, it's no longer possible to build "roadblocks" to capture people's attention. Hammering a message into their heads through sheer repetition isn't a viable option either. Instead, the masters of marketing make their customers' product experience so enriching and valuable that their enthusiasm becomes contagious. Advertising is not going away, but it is assuming forms no one could have imagined just a decade ago.

RELEVANCE

Two Stanford University students incorporated Google as a privately owned business at the beginning of the 1998–1999 school year. Today it controls one of the fastest-growing segments of advertising media. Google's secret is not its famous algorithm. That's just a means to the real secret, which the masters of marketing have known for centuries. The real secret is relevance. People don't dislike advertising that is relevant to their needs. In fact, they'll seek it out—many people buy *Vogue* magazine as much for the ads as for the editorial content. Google gave advertisers a way to infer people's state of mind from the content of their Web search so they could then serve up relevant advertising. That same capability is developing in television, radio, and other parts of the online world. GPS and Radio Frequency Identification technologies will bring it to in-store, outdoor, and mobile media. And the so-called semantic Web will not only deliver lists of Web pages in response to search queries, but also custom tables, charts, animations, databases, and summaries, all created on the fly.

The masters of marketing are using these capabilities to personalize not only their advertising, but also the entire product experience. Already, M&M's can be ordered in any of thirteen colors with a personal message on one side of the candy shell. Nike running shoes can be ordered in thousands of color combinations with a message embroidered on the side.

TRANSPARENCY

Social networking websites have been around since 1995, though they didn't achieve critical mass for about ten more years, when MySpace and Facebook could claim as many page views as Google. Now, social networking sites have become more than electronic Rolodexes; they are destinations in their own right, where the users are both suppliers and consumers of content. The sites derive their strength from the transparency of the participants' motives. Marketers gain entry only if they can facilitate the sites' functioning by contributing intellectual or cultural capital.

P&G posts its commercials on YouTube, where some—such as the "Talking Stain" spot that ran during the 2008 Super Bowl—have been viewed more than a million times and garnered a four-star rating (out of five). Going one step further, P&G invited customers to create their own commercial demonstrating how they "broke up" with traditional cleaning methods and fell in love with the company's Swiffer floor sweeper. Warner Music agreed to provide sixty-second snippets of fifteen "breakup" songs for use in the homemade videos, along with an "editor's tool kit." But before the contest was even officially launched, passionate consumers had already uploaded to YouTube some 600 user-generated videos featuring Swiffers.

Customer-generated content does not come without downside risks. When Chevy hosted a site where customers could edit clips to create their own commercials for the Chevy Tahoe, 30,000 people posted entries. Unfortunately, among them were activists whose spots dramatized the SUV's contribution to global warming. And YouTube helpfully "relates" videos that appear to be on the same subject. So when Delta Airlines posted an airline safety video there, one of the "related videos" was from a disgruntled passenger entitled "Delta Flight 6499, SEVEN HOURS on the tarmac." But even these risks are outweighed by the credibility that accrues to vaster amounts of positive content.

ENGAGEMENT

User-generated content has been around since the first electronic bulletin boards were launched in the late 1970s, but it didn't develop critical mass until Web browsers made using the Internet relatively easy in the mid-1990s. And it didn't begin to compete with prepackaged "professional" content until sometime between 2001, when Wikipedia was launched, and 2005, when YouTube began. Those two innovations represented the beginning of a new era—content is still king, but ordinary people are in control.

By 2008, YouTube was hosting more than eighty million videos on almost four million user channels with eight hours of new video uploaded every minute. The English-language edition of Wikipedia contained more than 2.2 million articles, which has been revised nearly 200 million times. Counting all 250 editions, Wikipedia recorded its ten millionth article in April of that year—it was about a sixteenth-century goldsmith named Nicholas Hilliard, posted in the

Hungarian version. Soon user-generated video content will be available on any screen—pocket-size or in living rooms.

The masters of marketing have learned to leverage user-generated content by inviting their customers to post content on product websites. JetBlue Airways and Starwood hotels invite customers to share their travel stories. Nearly all media sites post reader comments about stories. The venerable *Wall Street Journal*'s website gives nearly as much prominence to readers' comments as to the stories its reporters produce. Most online retailers post product reviews and recommendations. Bath & Body Works quotes user reviews in its e-mail campaigns and Wal-Mart prints them on hangtags in its brick-and-mortar stores. User-generated content represents an opportunity to nurture an even deeper level of engagement with a brand.

Salesforce.com, a maker of online applications for customer-relationship management, was drowning in customer suggestions for product upgrades. With 10,000 suggestions in 2005 alone, the company's marketing and development staffs couldn't agree on which features to add. Then, in 2006, the company launched its IdeaExchange, a website application that invites customers not only to suggest features but to vote on them. In time, the most popular ideas floated to the top of the list, while the less popular ones drifted away. The company's development cycle has been dramatically reduced. And since customers have vetted most of the features, developers and marketers have a common view of the product's evolutionary path.

Rather than pushing products, the masters of marketing are pulling customers in by offering them a more relevant, engaging, authentic experience. Of course, that requires a new way of thinking. But once you think of marketing that way, according to the ANA's Bob Liodice, "you're like the college kid who wakes up one morning and realizes he picked the wrong major. You have all kinds of new possibilities and none of the old rules apply."

Here's how the masters of marketing ensure that their brands stay real:

☞ *They align every customer touch point with the brand's meaning, not only in messaging but also through all five senses.* They realize that the brand experience may begin with advertising, but it continues in the brand's packaging, the process of buying it, using it, and, if necessary, servicing it. CMO Eva Ziegler is transforming Starwood's Le Méridien hotel chain into a brand that represents sophistication and modernism through careful attention to everything a guest encounters from lobby lighting to room décor. She commissioned special elevator music, a signature scent for public spaces, and card keys in limited-edition collectible designs that also give guests complimentary access to local art organizations. In all, she has hired a cast of twelve world-class artists—chefs, musicians, architects, painters, and designers—to transform fifty aspects of the hotel that customers experience.

☞ *They ensure that their brand evolves in step with their customers' changing needs and values.* They remain true to their brand heritage and values while tailoring its expression to customers' contemporary lifestyles. U.K. retailer Tesco's stores are virtually unrecognizable from country to country because Tesco so successfully adapts itself to local customers' needs and traditions. In Thailand, Tesco shops are like market stalls; in China, they sell live fish; in Korea, they're more like large department stores than supermarkets; and in the United States, they're small neighborhood convenience stores. Yet, in all these different formats, Tesco remains true to its heritage of giving customers a little more than they expect and rewarding them for coming back.

☞ *They invite customers to participate in their brand's development, trading their own absolute control for consumer influence over brand use.* They recognize that strong, authentic brands belong to their users, not to the companies that initially created them. Sheraton turned the lame "tell us what you think" card found in most hotel rooms into a multimedia feedback loop, inviting guests to e-mail photos as well as comments about their travel experience. It posts the most interesting guest stories on its website, organizing them by location on an interactive globe and by theme in a hyperlink sidebar (for example, beach, golf, romance, and so on). With the spread of camera phones, nearly every guest can be a travel writer, sharing discoveries with others—linked, of course, to relevant Sheraton properties.

☞ *They understand and reinforce the contribution their brand makes to their customers' sense of identity and community.* The couches and overstuffed chairs in most Starbucks send a loud signal that it's a place to sit and linger—a club of sorts. The "conversation starters," pithy sayings and observations, on its paper coffee cups reinforce the idea. And it turns that club into a community through a social networking site—Starbucks V2V—that enables customers and employees to recruit volunteers to work on worthy causes.

☞ *They don't make the mistake of assuming that "rational" and "emotional" considerations are at opposite ends of the same continuum.* They recognize that brands must meet functional and performance expectations, but they also understand that a brand's emotional and social benefits are the source of even deeper relevance. Campbell's sent anthropologists into the homes of Russian consumers to figure out why they weren't buying canned soup. When they discovered that making soup has deep emotional meaning to Russian homemakers, they abandoned plans to market their traditional line of heat-and-serve condensed soups there and introduced new "starter soups" and broths designed to help consumers save time while adding their own touches.

☞ *They conduct themselves responsibly, recognizing their ability to shape as well as to reflect society's mores.* For example, the alcoholic beverage industry refrains from advertising in media that reaches an audience predominantly under the legal drinking age. Fast-food, soft drink, and snack companies have voluntarily stopped advertising to children under twelve years old unless the products meet government nutritional standards (for example, less than 200 calories, no trans fat, low sodium, and low sugar other than from fruit).

CHAPTER ELEVEN

CULTIVATE POSITIVE "WORD OF MOUSE"

"Five years ago, we thought of the Web as a new medium, not a new economy."

—CLEMENT MOK

In the fall of 1993, Dan Pelson was just another twentysomething salesman, placing cold calls to chief technology officers who didn't really want to talk to him. Three years earlier, Pelson had talked his way into a job with Sun Microsystems. A liberal arts graduate from Colgate, he was given a typical entry-level job for nonengineers at the fast-growing high-tech company—driving a van from trade show to trade show. Within a year, he had wrangled a sales job and found himself trying to convince New York media companies to computerize their operations. He was good at it—companies like Sony Music, the Associated Press, and HBO bought servers and workstations from him. But they were using Sun's equipment for ancillary functions such as tracking royalty payments and tabulating election results. They didn't see its potential for expanding their reach and enriching their content. Computers were strictly backroom stuff. Few of his customers saw much value in "digitizing" their content beyond some uncertain production savings.

Then, in the fall of 1992, "I literally woke up in the middle of the night," Pelson recalls, "and I said, 'Why am I evangelizing to media companies when there's this huge revolution coming with digital content?'" Pelson quit Sun on December 31, 1993, and the next day he launched an online magazine that would eventually be called Word .com. It was a fairly simple website full of articles that he and a few friends wrote about coping with life after college. But there wasn't much on the Internet for mainstream users in those days and, along with Yahoo!, Pelson's site was one of the first places on the Web to accept advertising. He rode the Internet wave through several more successful Web start-ups, including Bolt, the first—and most successful—social network focused on teenagers. He cashed out just before the dot-com bubble burst in 2000.

Just thirty years old, Pelson ended up with enough money to buy a 4,000-square-foot loft apartment in SoHo, just a floor below rock star Lenny Kravitz. He could probably have spent the rest of his days on the golf course. Instead, he jumped back into the now shallower venture capital pool, starting a website that automatically connects teens and young adults, based on the music and videos they play. And to mollify one of his biggest investors, he accepted a job as senior vice president of consumer marketing for Warner Music. For two years, Pelson spent mornings at his start-up in SoHo and the rest of the day at Warner Music's headquarters in Rockefeller Center.

One lunch with Pelson in mid-2008 was all it took to conclude that his corporate gig was the source of endless frustration. He wasn't particularly bothered by the industry's notorious problems—piracy, declining sales, Apple iTunes' stranglehold on distribution, and so forth. But the music industry's hidebound culture drove him nuts. "First of all, we don't know who our customers are," he says. "I asked the marketing guys for one of our labels 'who buys Josh Groban CDs?' and the answer was 'Middle America.' Yeah, but I wanted to know how old they are, where they live, what their income is, what they watch on TV, how much time they spend on the Internet, who else they like. I wanted to know who these people *are*. The marketing guys wanted to throw me out of the room."

Nielsen SoundScan provides near real-time music sales figures based on cash register receipts of about 14,000 retail and online outlets. But the retailers themselves have much more detailed information. Apple's iTunes, for example, has access to information about more than sixty-five million credit card accounts. It not only knows what's selling, but who is buying, what else they've bought, and who knows what else. Unfortunately, retailers are shy about sharing data, which is ironic because the bulk of the music industry's marketing has traditionally been focused on them. What little consumer marketing the music labels do is basically designed to give retailers co-op allowances, which really amount to price discounts. Furthermore, each label operates as an independent duchy, doing its own marketing and building walls around its artists. Warner Music alone has about a thousand websites, at least one for each artist. Nothing ties them together.

What really rankled Pelson was the opportunity traditional music marketers were missing. He made his fortune creating "youth-focused" sites and he learned early on that "teens don't care what a bunch of twenty- or thirtysomethings have to say about sex, drugs, and rock 'n' roll. But they absolutely want to know what their peers are saying. And they want to chime in, without the risk of being beaten up for saying something uncool." Intense and focused, as you would expect of a serial entrepreneur, Pelson also likes to rattle cages. He punched up his presentations at recording industry conferences by screaming things like "Content as we know it is DEAD! DEAD I TELL YOU!!" Or "Content may be King, but CONTEXT is Queen, and we all know who runs the house."

Such provocative pronouncements from a senior record company executive may seem blasphemous, but Pelson's goal was to shake up the culture. On the other hand, he knew that people found him abrasive and brusque so he surrounded himself with managers "who play nicer than me." But his message never changed, whether shouted across the room or slipped into the corporatese of a neatly organized memo—Warner Music's real value may not come so much from selling CDs as from capturing information about the people buying them. And building relationships with those people may depend more on engaging their interest than in getting an imprint of their credit card—or their dad's.

"One of the things I learned early on," Pelson says, "is that people don't only want to control their content, they want to *be* content." Social networking media satisfy that need and Warner Music is sitting on a mother lode of content around which such networks can be built.

Warner's content reaches one billion people a day through CDs, radio, the Internet, and other media. And fifteen million people a month visit its artists' websites. Pelson's vision is of a global platform that will give Warner's individual labels plenty of autonomy but relieve them of the commercial transactions, including capturing customer data. "Once you have five million unique visitors, advertisers get interested," he points out. "We have that—they're just all in different places and we don't know who they are. Once we do, it would be easy to say the equivalent of 'I see you're buying cereal. You want milk with that?'"

In mid-2008, Pelson quietly left Warner to concentrate on his start-up, but in an ironic turn, he also found himself juggling calls from other record companies that wanted him to get them plugged in to a new way of doing business.

Entertainment and information are natural candidates for online distribution. As Pelson learned early in his career, digitizing content is a relatively easy exercise. Creating content that takes full advantage of the online world is a little more complicated. But the real stumbling block for most media companies has been erasing the functional boundaries between their "real" and "virtual" worlds. And most hard goods marketers face precisely the same problem. They treat online media as supplementary forms of promotion and order taking. But the masters of marketing have integrated their virtual and real worlds. Buy a sweater at Macys.com and you can return it to any of their brick-and-mortar stores. See a refrigerator on the sales floor of a Best Buy and you can order it online from any of the kiosks scattered around the store. Savvy retailers are discovering that their physical stores have become showrooms and customer service centers for their online storefronts. And many of the customers entering those virtual stores are directed there from online communities.

BORN DIGITAL

In strictly demographic terms, Pelson is a "digital immigrant." He didn't grow up with computers, MP3 players, texting, e-mail, IMing, blogs, chat rooms, or any of the other devices and applications that are commonplace to his own children. But he is perfectly in tune with people who were "born digital" and have never known life without the Internet. "Today's teens are the first demographic to come of age online," he says. "They have made the Internet part of the fabric of their culture." One might expect a music marketer to be sensitive to the teenage market, but Pelson is making a larger point—because they are technologically savvy, today's teenagers will drive the digital economy as they grow up. And because the digital economy will dominate the larger economy, they will literally define that too.

Some marketing masters have already tumbled to that fact, even though teenagers are only incidental to their overall marketing effort. Microsoft, for example, employs anthropologists to observe teens around the world in their "natural habitats" from Seattle shopping malls to Seoul street corners. "Kids drive technology today," says Microsoft anthropologist Anne Cohen Kiel. "By meeting their needs, we meet everyone's needs."[1]

Marketers are already feeling some of the implications. The "born-digital" generation is more culturally diverse than other generations—one out of three members is non-Caucasian. They are more tightly connected to each other—more than eight out of ten send text, e-mail, or instant messages; more than half use social networks of some kind. They're media savvy and trust their friends more than ads or third parties. They're socially conscious and more aware of the world around them than previous generations. They don't draw bright lines between commerce, content, and communication in their everyday life. They were brought up in a world of interactions, rather than transactions.

To Pelson's way of thinking, this should deeply color the way marketers look at technology. For example, he believes that the digital world is all about communication and communities of interest. "Traditional content will become the context for dialogue," he says. "Instead of focusing on broadband downloads and other things that look a lot like television to us older folks, marketers should provide utility that enables better customer communications."

That's the idea behind his latest online venture—an application called uPlayMe. Once downloaded, uPlayMe tracks its members' online content usage in real time so it can connect them to other members who like the same music and videos. Of course, in the process, the service also compiles meta-data (artist, song title, genre, and so forth) from which it can create a detailed psychographic profile of its members. "There's no better way to get into people's brains than to watch what music they play at different times of the day," Pelson says. He's quick to add that the service only tracks usage data: It doesn't wander into other files on people's computers, doesn't access personal information, doesn't compile individually identifiable information, and allows members to disable the service if they want to watch a video in privacy. "The key to privacy is to give people control," he says. "People will give you some information about themselves if you give them something of value for it. In uPlayMe's case, that's the opportunity to hook up with people of similar interests."

Marketers learned to predict relevance by tracking where people go online (behavior) and capturing keywords on the sites they visit (context). But the masters of marketing have discovered that "people of similar interests" are the key to triangulating relevance. Amazon, Netflix, TiVo, and a host of dating services develop their recommendations by matching an individual's preferences to those of a larger group. Reed Hastings, the cofounder of Netflix, calls this "harnessing the power of the community to generate better results for the individual."[2] In that sense, social media are not mere advertising vehicles, but a new form of marketing.

TAILORING

From a marketer's perspective, services like uPlayMe offer the opportunity to tailor offers to ever more precise segments of people who are more likely to find meaning and relevance in their offers. "The goal is one-to-one marketing," Pelson says. "Segment to the point of inaction. That is, keep segmenting your audience on the basis of their behavior and values until the cost of segmentation exceeds the value of doing it."

Maurice Lévy, the urbane CEO of Publicis, one of the world's leading marketing networks, takes a historical perspective. "Just as the Renaissance broke down the distinctions between sacred and profane art forms and between individual and community," he says, "so we are seeing a similar exciting blurring today—and this will only intensify."[3] People are no longer willing to put up with commercial interruptions during entertainment, but they don't necessarily think of content, commerce, and communication as isolated islands. The masters of marketing build bridges between those islands by engaging people in genuine and honest ways.

Even the venerable *New York Times* began experimenting in social media when it launched the beta version of "TimesPeople" in mid-2008. Readers were invited to download software that would keep track of all the articles they recommended, comments they posted, and movies or restaurants they rated. Their so-called "public activity" would be compiled on their personal TimesPeople page and would also show up in a special toolbar at the top of every *New York Times* Web page where those in their personal TimesPeople network could view it in real time. The paper billed it as "a great way to discover things on NYTimes.com that you might not otherwise have found and to share your discoveries with people you know and trust." A search feature also made it easier to "connect with other *Times* readers whose recommendations interest you," though the nation's paper of record went out of its way to caution that it wasn't proposing to "get you *Times* dates." Of course, in addition to making the website "stickier," it made possible a range of customized advertising buys, for example, for people who went to the movies a lot, ate out frequently, or were interested in politics.

WORD OF MOUSE

If the first wave of the Internet consisted of shoveling corporate content online, the second wave put the shovel in users' hands. They used it to collaborate with each other on a range of activities, from advising on purchases (TripAdvisor, Epinions), to selling and trading goods (eBay, Craigslist), sharing their own creativity (YouTube, blogs), and simply socializing with each other (Facebook, MySpace).

According to a 2007 study by accounting firm Deloitte & Touche, about two-thirds of Internet users (62 percent) read consumer-written product reviews online before making a purchase.[4] And of those, eight out of ten (82 percent) say what they read either confirmed their original intention or influenced them to buy another product. Surprisingly, while younger people tend to be more avid readers of online product reviews, even their grandparents pay attention to them—42 percent of people over seventy-five years of age consult online reviews before making a purchase.

Consumers are not just reading about big-ticket items. Nearly half report consulting online reviews before purchasing home electronic equipment and nearly 20 percent go online before buying kitchen appliances, food, apparel, or cleaning products. Word of mouse, it seems, is just as powerful as word of mouth. In fact, it *becomes* word of mouth—seven out of ten readers of online reviews (69 percent) say they share them with family and friends. Reporters and financial analysts often quote online reviews. And, of course, reviews live forever in a brand's search results.

Communities of enthusiasts have sprouted within social media networks, such as Facebook's 40,000-member Southwest Airlines group and its nearly 70,000-member "Addicted to Starbucks" group. Of course, this being a free country, the blistering emotion of disloyalty has also erupted on thousands of sites across the Web, from personal blogs to podcasts to YouTube. Third-party feedback sites such as PlanetFeedback.com, Complaints.com, and My3cents.com are dedicated to spreading the bad word. Mobile-enabled blogs let users post photos or videos from anywhere, tagging them with labels like "BadMcDonaldsExperience," so search engines can find them more easily.

For anyone who believes markets have morphed from faceless transactions to ongoing conversations, this negative feedback is a little alarming. Consumer-generated content has rebalanced the power between marketer and customer. Search engines amplify the power of an individual customer's opinion by putting it in front of a highly motivated target—someone seeking information about a specific brand. And opinions that originate with someone like the reader are inherently more trusted, more engaging, and stickier than anything a brand might say about itself.

The Pew Research Center estimates that more than a third of adult Internet users (35 percent) have created online "content."[5] While brand reviews constituted only a small portion of that content, Nielsen Online estimated that, as of 2005, more than 1.4 billion consumer-generated brand comments had been archived on the Web and the volume was growing 30 percent a year. Furthermore, Nielsen estimated that 70 percent of consumers who provide feedback through company websites are active across other sites, including social networks, special interest groups, and blogs.[6]

The net present value of a blogger's complaint is not only the revenue he or she represents over a lifetime of purchases, but the "viral power" of his or her circle of influence, which could easily be a hefty multiple. Researchers have learned that influence is largely a function of identity. Someone you know will have more influence on you than a stranger. But three researchers in the United Kingdom studied word of mouth in online social networks and discovered that "online communities can act as a social proxy for individual identification."[7] In other words, the influence of a product review can come from the website itself rather than from the person who wrote it. So, in an extrapolation of Metcalfe's famous law, the net present value of an online rating could be proportional to the square of the number of people who regularly view the website on which it appears.[8]

Every marketer worth his or her pinstripes has set up a system to track brand mentions online and to respond quickly and honestly to any complaints. According to research by the Aberdeen Group, 65 percent of best-in-class companies have formal processes for monitoring consumer social media.[9] Few marketers pretend it's not worth worrying about the small number of people who notice an online slam. But the masters of marketing minimize the number of complaints that go viral by making sure people have an easy-to-use company-sponsored forum in which to lodge their grievance. They make sure everyone with a complaint gets an answer from someone knowledgeable, who uses his or her real name and acts like a human being, acknowledging when complainers are justified even if they're strident, and always making things right. Most importantly, the masters of marketing use the information gathered from complaints to ensure the problem doesn't happen again.

When problems do break into the blogosphere, the masters of marketing join the conversation early, knowing that the rhetoric will only get more heated and more negative if they wait. Again, they act like human beings, not corporate tools. For example, here's how Geek Squad founder Robert Stephens responded to a blogger with a service complaint:

Tom—Saw the issue on the laptop—I wanted you to know that we are on the case to resolve. Not every dish is cooked to perfection, but we try our hardest. If you or any of your other readers ever experience less than perfect service from The Geek Squad, feel free to put them directly in touch with me.
Regards,
Robert Stephens
Founder and Chief Inspector
The Geek Squad

Accustomed to automated responses and a wee skeptical, the blogger replied to the e-mail but refused to play along with any pretense that he had actually heard from the Geek-in-Chief, whom he assumed was on some beach in Aruba, blissfully unaware of his little laptop problem. Within an hour, he received a phone call from someone claiming to be calling at Stephen's request. Still, he assumed the whole charade was the product of a well-oiled squad of geeks scouring the Web for mention of problems with their service and responding in the name of their boss of bosses. But when he hung up the phone, he found this in his e-mail:

It is me. I am far from a beach in Aruba—in a chillier region in Minneapolis. I hope that by taking care of all of our customers, they will beg for me one day to retire there. We shall not rest until your problem is addressed.

—R[10]

SOCIAL MEDIA

Traffic to social networking sites grew twice as fast as to other websites in the summer of 2008, representing a tectonic shift in the Internet's center of gravity.[11] Search-related advertising has been the principal funding mechanism for most websites, but social networks are "gated communities" beyond the reach of the "spiders" that crawl the Internet indexing content and serving it up to the highest bidder. Brands can buy their way into social media, but relevance isn't for sale so cheaply. Indeed, the masters of marketing don't try to seed messages on social networks; they use them to build stronger relationships, whether they are guests on someone else's site or hosting a network of their own customers.

The seeds of those online relationships are increasingly sown in the form of "widgets," that is, small computer programs that sit quietly as a desktop icon until activated by a user or by an unseen force deep in the Internet. Media pundit Bob Garfield calls them "the perfect expression of the Post-Advertising Age" and he can't understand why they aren't even more ubiquitous.[12] They're relatively cheap to produce, but since users have to make a conscious decision to download and install a widget, its ubiquity is a function of its utility. And its cost-effectiveness is in direct proportion to its virulence. If a widget is useful enough—or has enough entertainment value—people will want to share it, absorbing the distribution costs.

So Southwest Airlines's Ding widget notifies you when there are cheap fares to your favorite destinations. American Express's account widget helps you stay up to date with your credit card balance without logging in to the corporate website, right from your desktop. UPS's widget lets you schedule and track shipments from your desktop. And, in a triumph of social value over utility, Schick Quattro's Trim Flixx widget lets you superimpose your face (or a friend's) onto a bare-chested hunk pillow-fighting on a rumpled bed with a couple of nubile girls.

PLATFORMS FOR COLLABORATION

Steve Rubel has helped hundreds of companies wade into the digital world from his perch at the world's largest independent public relations agency. To his mind, the term "social media" is a vestige of an earlier era when there was something special about people organizing themselves into online communities of interest.[13] Today, he says, social networking is a prominent feature of almost any website worth its bandwidth, including those of leading marketers. Indeed, the masters of marketing treat social media as a platform for collaboration. Within their own sites, they set rules for civil discourse and moderate discussions, but they don't get heavy-handed about it. If an unanticipated crisis—think Mattel and lead paint—generates negative spikes in the conversation, they listen and react appropriately, refusing to engage with ranters who don't really want to have a civil conversation.

By building trust over time—acknowledging mistakes, even linking to critics when it's helpful to the community—they can count on their fans to support them if a critic gets abusive.

Many companies put their toe in these waters by hosting blogs that allow reader comments. But a blog is really only a precursor to a true social network. Computer purveyor Dell started there—it publishes seven blogs in five languages. But it has also taken a cannonball dive into a full-frontal social network called Dell Community. On the very first page, customers are invited to "tell us about it—discuss, review, suggest, compliment, complain, comment." Customers can join discussions on everything from small-business applications to gaming, and the company's responsiveness convinced one influential blogger that Dell had "leapt from worst to first" in listening to customers.[14] Dell's support forum has grown to four million posts, of which about a quarter answer questions about the company's products, saving Dell the cost of customer-support calls. In all, the company counts more than 100 million online customer "touches" a year.

CEO Michael Dell considers the customer network essential to innovation. "I'm sure there's a lot of things that I can't even imagine, but our customers can imagine," he says. "A company this size is not going to be about a couple of people coming up with ideas. It's going to be about millions of people and harnessing the power of those ideas."[15] It may not be sheer coincidence that Dell was the only Windows PC maker to improve in the 2008 American Customer Satisfaction Index published by the University of Michigan.

Similarly, Cisco's NetPro Community bills itself as "a forum for peer and expert wisdom to get answers you need." Once registered, customers are free to ask questions, seek advice, and resolve concerns—among themselves, not just the company. Cisco's site even includes a wiki where customers can collaborate. Intuit's QuickBooksGroup is a users' community, organized by industry, where the moderators lurk in the background, only popping up when necessary to facilitate discussion.

The secret to these customer social networks is that they were built from the ground up to help customers connect with each other, not as Trojan horses containing company promotional messages. Dell, Cisco, and QuickBooks all offer products that are so complex social networks constitute a sort of self-help group. Cynics may argue that the companies set up their customer networks as a way of relieving pressure on their service staffs and that any goodwill they accumulate is only a happy by-product.

But the same principles apply to everyday consumer goods as well—create a community around your customers' interests, empowering them to help each other or simply to share their enthusiasm, and you will deepen your relationship with them. You will convert them from satisfied customers to brand enthusiasts. Scissors maker Fiskars dipped its toe into social networks in December 2006 when it started a site for scrapbookers to share their passion, projects, and tips. It hoped to increase overall online discussion about the Fiskars brand by 10 percent and to eventually recruit 200 additional unpaid "brand ambassadors" who would talk the brand up in craft stores. But the company underestimated the enthusiasm of crafters, who, as one put it, don't consider crafting "a matter of life and death; it's much more important than that." In just five months, the online discussion of Fiskars products had surged 400 percent and more than 1,400 people had applied to be "Fiskateer" ambassadors. (That number now exceeds 3,000, and when a Fiskateer visits a craft store, sales triple.)

A social network is not the same thing as a company website, though the former may hang off the latter. For example, Johnson & Johnson, the U.S. company known for its baby products (though they represent a miniscule portion of its revenue), operates Baby Center.com as a separate subsidiary with a presence in twelve countries and Latin America. BabyCenter, and its companion sites, Pregnancy .com and ParentCenter.com, can take a couple from pregnancy through a child's eighth year of life with e-mailed newsletters, expert developmental advice, user product reviews, and an active community through which new moms and dads can get practical answers to their questions from other parents, as well as medical professionals. Furthermore, members can create profiles, upload content from other social-media sites like Flickr or blogs, and create private groups. The content of all three sites rivals most print publications dedicated to the subject, but Johnson & Johnson has done more than shovel information onto the Web. It has built a community and earned its members' trust.

Social networks are a brand's ultimate competitive weapon because the biggest competitor any brand faces is not another brand, but indifference and inertia. The good news is that most people are willing to have a relationship with brands they trust, as long as they can control the conversation and get something in return—useful information, entertainment, savings, or advice. For example, according to Prospectiv, a Massachusetts-based lead-generation company, three out of four consumers would like to receive e-mail regarding savings offers and nearly half say they'd like to receive an online newsletter. In fact, about a quarter say their favorite way to find what they're looking for is from e-newsletters they've subscribed to, whether sent by a brand, an online community, or a retailer. That's a bigger percentage of consumers than those that use search engines, newspaper and magazine sites, or comparison-shopping sites comprise. On the other hand, eight out of ten consumers don't visit branded sites, largely because they don't know they exist. And the minority who are aware of branded sites claim they aren't very helpful and can't be trusted.[16]

TAP ENTHUSIASTS

The key to building a social network is to tap into your customers' existing enthusiasms. Some lucky marketers represent brands people are naturally bonkers about—Porsche drivers are an enthusiastic lot, as are Scotch drinkers. But most brands are in low-interest categories. Even then, there is almost always a closely related enthusiasm or concern that brand and customer can share. Dove, for example, is about real beauty; it's not just soap or body lotion. It's hard to get excited about baby shampoo, but babies are another matter—especially to new or expectant mothers. Enthusiasm is not something you deliver in a Web page; it's something you provoke in people. Once ignited, it takes on a life of its own and it's contagious.

The masters of marketing cultivate good "word of mouse" in these ways:

☞ *Whether "born digital" or recent "immigrants," they study the digital world closely and surround themselves with native guides.* They make a point of personally using new applications and staying current with new technologies. But most importantly, they try to understand the culture. *Business Week Online* editor Patricia O'Connell wasn't too bashful to admit in a post headlined "Wanted: Reverse Tech Mentor" that she needed "some sweet, patient Gen Y-er" to help her figure out the ways of the digital world.[17] That's exactly what the Warner Music Group did, on a slightly grander scale, when it convinced Dan Pelson to give them half his time for a couple of years.

☞ *They think in terms of interactions rather than transactions.* They don't use social networks to send messages, but to build stronger relationships with and to better understand their customers. Coca-Cola brought World Cup fans together online to talk about soccer; Pepsi did the same for European football. Sprite set up a cell phone–based social network where members can set up profiles, post pictures, and meet new friends. Members can download free music and videos by typing a PIN found under bottle lids.

☞ *They engage people in a genuine way wherever their interests overlap.* They look for topics their customers will find relevant and authentic. If communities have already formed around those topics, they nurture their development, careful to assume the role of facilitator, not leader. Reebok's GoRunEasy.com lets runners discuss their workouts and share photos. MarthaStewart.com sets members up with their own page, including their profile and favorite recipes. Saturn enables the car's fans to share stories with each other and exchange ideas. Think.MTV.com is all about social activism, from the environment to politics to fighting poverty.

☞ *They respond quickly and honestly to any complaints or questions.* But they don't try to control or dominate online discussions, even when it's uncomfortable to restrain themselves. They recognize that social media are about customers helping each other. Dell, Cisco, and Sun not only allow readers to comment on company blog postings, they provide online forums for customer product reviews, suggestions, and questions.

CHAPTER TWELVE

CULTIVATE POSITIVE
WORD OF MOUTH

*"People don't want to be 'marketed TO';
they want to be 'communicated WITH.'"*
—FLINT McGLAUGHLIN

A s Gilbert and Sullivan might put it, Steve Knox looks every inch a modern-day "marketeer"—tall, confident, enough gray in his hair to suggest experience, yet plenty of youthful exuberance. He was one of the high-potential P&G managers A.G. Lafley interviewed to take the company's pulse when he became CEO in 2000.

After more than two decades at the company in various sales and marketing positions, Knox had more than a few opinions. When his conversation with the CEO got around to new ways of connecting with consumers, Knox said that, in his view, the most powerful medium by far was what a trusted friend told you. That didn't surprise Lafley, but what intrigued him was Knox's belief that creating word of mouth could be systematized and scaled. Lafley gave Knox the assignment to try to do just that and, in 2001, P&G began an initiative that would later be christened "Tremor," a word-of-mouth marketing agency that works not only for P&G, but also for a range of noncompeting companies, including Toyota, Verizon, Sony, and Coca-Cola.

Many people think word of mouth is guerrilla advertising like the stunt that ignited a terror scare in Boston by seeding mysterious black boxes with blinking lights all over town to promote a Cartoon Network TV show. But at its best, word of mouth is more than a buzzworthy exploit; it's a community of people who are so enthusiastic about your brand they feel good about spreading the word further.

As cartoonist and blogger Hugh MacLeod says, "People will only spread your virus if there is something in it for them."[1] Sometimes, word of mouth is propelled forward by something with entertainment value. So-called "branded content" ranges from video games and short films to complete television series. For example, Burger King reportedly sold two million video games featuring their advertising icons, the Subservient Chicken and the King, in just four weeks for $3.99 with the purchase of a value meal. IBM produced a series of short documentaries on its involvement in everything from tracking avian flu to fighting street crime in New York City. Unilever's Axe deodorant sold MTV on a series titled *The Gamekillers*, based on a popular ad campaign that showed how the annoying characters young people often have to deal with can leave a date in shambles. Branded content only works when both sides of the equation are in balance— the brand fits so well with the content it isn't a distraction, and the story line emanates directly from the brand's core promise.

Other times, the propellant can be something of social value. The president of North American operations for Gap combs the celebrity magazines like *Us Weekly* and *In Style* to see if her company's products are being worn by any boldface names. She's looking for more than visibility; she knows that her core customers take many of their fashion cues from celebrities. Seeing Reese Witherspoon in one of the Gap's signature tank tops can turn it into an essential element of the season's fashion uniform. And since it's available in twelve unique colors, which is an innovation Gap invented, it won't seem boring. Similarly, when Michelle Obama mentioned she was wearing a J.Crew outfit on *The Tonight Show*, the company created an entire Web page devoted to the outfit and used it as a landing page for sponsored links in searches and on the Gmail website.

For word of mouth to work, it also has to be relevant—to both the brand and the intended audience. You can always generate "buzz" by doing something so outrageous everyone is talking about it. But if isn't relevant to customers, it won't affect their behavior. Paris Hilton's TV commercial for the Carl's Jr. restaurant chain was nearly as explicit as her well-circulated sex tape, except in this case she was making love to an automobile as she slathered it with soap suds and purred "That's hot." It was the single most-viewed video on the Internet for three weeks. But it bombed as decisively as her singing career. Same-store sales declined 6 percent. To be fair, Ms. Hilton's performance may not have been the stunt's only problem. When Oprah Winfrey gave a Pontiac G6 to everyone in her studio audience, it dominated the evening news and many newspapers. General Motors estimated the new model received $110 million in publicity. Everyone seemed to be talking about it, but it didn't move cars off the lot. Six months later, the *Detroit Free Press* reported that the automaker had to "dramatically ramp up rebates on the car just to get it selling at modest levels."[2]

STEALTH MARKETING

You can hire ordinary-looking people to advocate on behalf of your brand. So-called "buzz marketing" agencies have hired people to ride commuter trains reading new magazines; they've paid doormen in luxury apartment buildings to put "packages" from catalogue merchants in their lobbies, as if tenants had not picked them up yet. Sony Ericsson hired sixty actors to pose as tourists in ten cities across the United States to promote its camera-equipped cell phones by asking bystanders to take their picture in front of landmarks like the Empire State Building in New York or the Space Needle in Seattle. Wal-Mart paid a couple to travel across the country in a recreational vehicle and blog about their visits to the company's stores, even camping out in the parking lots. And when Julie Roehm worked for Ford, she loaned Focus automobiles for six months to 120 young people she considered trendsetters in five key markets. They were assistants to celebrities, local disk jockeys, and party planners, and all they had to do was be seen with the car and hand out Focus-themed trinkets to anyone who expressed interest in it.

The results from these scripted playlets are hard to nail down. Sony Ericsson's cell phones never really took off, but that may be because camera phones quickly became common. The Ford Focus was on *Car and Driver*'s 10Best list for five consecutive years between 2000 and 2004, which one assumes was not influenced by the car's marketing.

Furthermore, the "loaners" were just one element of an ambitious marketing plan that was so well targeted at the young drivers who were in the model's crosshairs that it won Roehm a higher-level job at Chrysler and, eventually, at Wal-Mart.

Both the Sony Ericsson and Wal-Mart campaigns were exposed by the *Wall Street Journal* and *BusinessWeek*, respectively. Sony Ericsson's marketing people expressed no apologies or regrets about the stunt, but the public relations agency that conceived the coast-to-coast RV trip for Wal-Mart fell on its sword in the face of unrelenting criticism from the giant retailer's usual opponents. "I want to acknowledge our error in failing to be transparent about the identity of the two bloggers from the outset," the agency's CEO said. "This is 100% our responsibility and our error; not the client's."[3]

Stealth marketing assumes that deception is a key to building buzz. The marketer's invisibility may create the illusion of authenticity, but at some point, people will find a real customer—or become one themselves—and learn the truth about a product. In the "gotcha" ethic of today's media, that's increasingly likely.

The Word of Mouth Association, in fact, has established standards of honesty and transparency to ensure that "the voice of the consumer . . . is never polluted in any way."[4] Neither Sony Ericsson, Ford, nor Wal-Mart were members at the time of these incidents. And to be fair, such tactics are not exactly new. To counter a social taboo against women smoking in public for his tobacco client, the so-called "father of PR," Edward Bernays, organized a group of young socialites to march down New York's Fifth Avenue smoking cigarettes on Easter Sunday 1929, at the height of the suffragettes' efforts to win the right for women to vote. A *New York Times* story reported that "groups of girls puffed cigarettes as a gesture of freedom." Other newspapers called it the "Torches of Freedom" march and made no mention of Bernays's role, nor did the papers in other cities where the demonstration spread. Bernays had little interest in the suffragettes' goals—his client was a tobacco company—but he leveraged their news value to his own purposes.

Critics accuse stealth marketers of intrusion, dishonesty, and exploitation. No one likes to be fooled unless they're in on the gag as in a magic show or an over-the-top "mockumentary" such as the one

BMW produced in 2008 purporting to report on efforts to literally catapult a sedan from Germany to the United States.

Paying actors to ask bystanders to snap their photo with a camera phone is a trivial deception, the marketing equivalent of a fib. But if people become really invested in the deception, their reaction to being deceived will be more than annoyance. They will consider it a breach of trust. And no matter how trivial, if a company is already under attack for other reasons, any deception becomes confirming evidence of its basic perfidy, another nail in its coffin. Perhaps because they are more sophisticated about media, people today place a higher value than ever on products and messages that seem sincere and genuine.

The Federal Trade Commission has looked into the practices of "stealth marketers" who disguise their involvement while paying people to endorse their products. But most reputable marketers have been aboveboard in their word-of-mouth efforts. Hebrew National, for example, hired 250 PTA presidents, Hispanic community leaders, and, yes, Jewish mothers to serve on "mom squads" that drove around in sport-utility vehicles emblazoned with a Hebrew National logo, hosted backyard hot dog barbecues, and passed out discount coupons at community events. The signs on the SUV and on their aprons made it clear who was sponsoring the effort. If people invited a member of the "mom squad" into their backyard, it was probably because they thought they'd get something out of it. Hebrew National's interest in spreading the word about their wieners wasn't an issue.

Promoting hot dogs at a barbecue is not exactly rocket science. It's almost as obvious as giving away free ice cream on a hot summer day in sunny California. That's what Umpqua Bank did to break into the bank-saturated California market. It gave prospective customers free ice cream in summer and hot chocolate in winter from the back of two Umpqua trucks. The bank also gave loans of $10 to young lemonade-stand entrepreneurs as part of a "Lemonaire" program that had parents talking about the bank. The Lemonaire promotion alone picked up 1,500 new small- to medium-size business customers for the bank.

TIPPING POINT OR FOREST FIRE?

The academic literature has been littered with theories on how ideas, trends, and opinions spread through society ever since 1955 when

Paul Lazarsfeld floated the idea that people are influenced by so-called "opinion leaders."[5] Recently, in his best-selling book *The Tipping Point*, Malcolm Gladwell termed these people "connectors," "mavens," and "salesmen." Each plays a different role in the spread of something new, but they are all supposed to have a rare set of social skills that invest them with outsized influence over other people. Some believe as little as 15 percent of the population can literally "tip" the momentum for change until it becomes unstoppable. Recently, new academic research, using mathematical modeling as well as experimentation, has suggested that the process is not quite so straightforward.

Duncan Watts, a Columbia University sociology professor and principal research scientist for Yahoo!, thinks the whole theory of influencers is baloney. Watts believes a trend depends less on the "influence" of the people who start it than on the "susceptibility" of the rest of us. He has no doubt that word of mouth is important. "People almost never make decisions independently," he wrote in the *New York Times*, "in part because the world abounds with so many choices that we have little hope of ever finding what we want on our own; in part because we are never really sure what we want anyway; and in part because what we often want is . . . to experience the same things as other people and thereby also experience the benefits of sharing."[6] This last factor, the social value of choices, has been generally underappreciated

Watts designed an ingenious real-world experiment to test this theory, recruiting 14,000 people to test a new online music service by ranking forty-eight songs by unknown bands based on their personal tastes. Some of the recruits were put into groups that could see how others were rating the songs and, as Watts predicted, word of mouth took over.

In the groups where people could see the ratings of other people, a small number of songs became enormously popular, rated way above average, while another small number were rated way below average. Surprisingly, in each of the groups where people could not see each other's ratings, the top songs were completely different, as were the ones at the bottom. It seems that the first songs to get good ratings when people could observe each other's voting tended to get many more good ratings. Whether one song or another benefited from those early votes was mostly a matter of chance. When recruits didn't know how others were ranking the songs, their ratings tended to average out, with a very small number getting slightly better or worse scores. It seems that people like to like what other people like. We like to share experiences.

"If society is ready to embrace a trend, almost anyone can start one—and if it isn't, then almost no one can," Watts concludes. "To succeed with a new product, it's less a matter of finding the perfect hipster to infect and more a matter of gauging the public's mood."[7] He thinks the epidemic analogy, in which a virus spreads through a large population in the excretions of a few carriers, is misleading. It's really more like a forest fire, in which any old spark can ignite a blaze if the woods are dry enough. The trick, according to Watts, is to stop obsessing about "magic people" with outsized influence and instead build networks that can spread messages that people care about.

TREMOR

Steve Knox believes that Tremor, the company he started after several years of research, represents such a network. He built Tremor around two consumer panels: 600,000 women who have children under nineteen years old and 250,000 teenagers thirteen to nineteen years old. All of these people are volunteers, who are carefully screened to ensure that they are what he calls "connectors," people who thrive on keeping in touch with a large circle of friends. The only physical compensation they receive in return for their participation is occasional free samples or coupons.

Knox brags that his panel members have social networks that are five to six times larger than average. "If the average mom talks to five or six people a day," he says, "the Tremor members talk to twenty or thirty a day. They have a psychological need to share information and to nurture relationships." A typical teenage girl on the Tremor panel will have 150 to 200 names on her instant messaging buddy list. Tremor seldom sends messages to its full list of members, but if it did, some simple math demonstrates the potential impact—600,000 moms times an average of twenty-five connections comes to 15,000,000 contacts.

Knox claims to have a secret battery of psychological tests—administered through an innocuous online survey—to screen for "connectors." He's cagey about the precise criteria, but admits that among the desirable traits are inquisitiveness, connectedness, and persuasiveness. Only about 15 percent of the people who apply for membership pass muster. Even then, the first assignment they are given is actually a test to see if they have as many connections as they claim, which usually leads to another third being dropped. So in the end only 8 to 10 percent of applicants become panel members. But one suspects that's not the real secret to Tremor's success. Even Knox admits, "Connectors are not more influential than other people, they're just more connected so their impact is larger. They're viewed positively by their social network only if they deliver useful information."[8]

Other practitioners of so-called "WOM" (word-of-mouth) marketing have noticed the same thing. BzzAgent has built a nice business on the fact that some people are just natural-born sharers. For example, it found 2,000 people willing to pass out free Al Fresco sausages at July 4 parties and collect feedback. For Lee jeans, it recruited 1,000 people to wear a new pair of One True Fit Jeans and hand out promotional material to friends who asked about them. And it gave 2,000 Spanish-speaking people 32-ounce bottles of Clamato juice to share with friends. BzzAgent taps into some people's need to know about the latest new thing before everyone else. They get stuff for free, but that's beside the point. They really get off on the buzz of having had the product first. They may not be trendsetters, but they sure are trend sharers.

Meanwhile, 80 percent of Tremor's work comes from outside the company and the demand is so great it struggles to send no more than twenty campaigns a year to individual panel members.

ADVOCACY AND AMPLIFICATION

Tremor trades on the trendsetter's need to know first, but its real secret is the way it crafts the messages it puts into the network. According to Steve Knox, word of mouth depends on two factors: having a message with "high advocacy" as well as "high amplification."[9] "Advocacy" is a measure of the degree to which someone *cares* about a product or a message. "Amplification" refers to how much he or she wants to spread the word and how easy it is to do. The reason to care and the reason to share are seldom the same.

"Women care about Tampax sanitary tampons," Knox points out, "but they're not very interested in talking about it. People love how Crest Whitestrips brighten their teeth, but it's hard to talk about." Similarly, some advertising catchphrases enter the popular culture and come out of everybody's mouth. They have lots of amplitude, but if they don't have advocacy—people who really care—they don't amount to much more than background noise. For example, a popular Budweiser TV campaign had lots of people saying "Wassup?" when they ran into friends on the train platform or in the office. But beer sales were flat. Lots of amplitude; no advocacy.

The message consumers want to hear and the message they want to communicate to their friends are always different. A company's advertising is usually focused on the former; its word-of-mouth efforts need to uncover the latter. "If you think you are going to go create word of mouth in the marketplace by getting the consumer to talk about your advertising message, you are wrong," Knox warns. If consumers do parrot ad slogans or catchphrases, it won't have any impact because they don't necessarily care about the underlying message, assuming there is one. They talk about something related, but different. "It's our job to figure out what that is," Knox says. "What is it they want to share with their friends?"

Knox talks about "disruptive equilibrium" being at word of mouth's core. In layman's language, that's "surprise." The idea is that everyone has a mental model of how the world works—for example, in the United Kingdom, people drive on the left. "The human mind is prewired to want to talk when the equilibrium gets disrupted," Knox says. "Consumers get back to equilibrium by talking about the situation with their friends." That's why telephone traffic spikes following an unexpected event such as an earthquake. Even people outside the damage zone have a need to talk about it. On the other hand, Knox cautions that surprise by itself is not sufficient.

For word of mouth to serve marketing, any disruption must be connected to a brand's foundational truth. "What does your brand mean in the gut of the consumer?" Knox asks. "Failing to connect the disruption to the foundational truth will result in amplification without the necessary advocacy to drive your business." For example, Las Vegas's campaign in the 1990s to portray the city as "family friendly" was disruptive, but it rang false to people who still thought of it as "Sin City." The campaign that replaced it—"What happens here, stays here"—was both disruptive and related to its foundational truth.

To ensure that the messages passed along to one of Tremor's panels have a high "reason to share" connected to a brand's fundamental meaning, Knox's team tests every word-of-mouth campaign with a smaller group of about 500 members. For example, when P&G launched a new version of its Dawn dishwashing liquid, the advertising focused on its grease-cutting power. Tremor tested that message with its sample of connectors, but it also experimented with alternatives that might have the right combination of advocacy ("reason to care") and amplitude ("reason to share").

The message that won had little to do with grease cutting—it suggested that all the foam the new formulation created would make dishwashing fun for kids. Tremor delivered the pitch to some of the 600,000 moms on its panel in the form of coupons and talking points. It apparently worked, because Dawn sales increased by 50 percent in test markets.

Indeed, the *Journal of Marketing* recently published the results of a study that showed that word of mouth creates nearly twice as much long-term value as traditional marketing tactics.[10] And a Roper Survey in 2004 indicated that 92 percent of Americans consider their friends, family, and other people as the best source of information on everything from restaurants to investments and the best buys (up from 67 percent in 1977).[11] The purchase decisions of African American, Hispanic, and Asian American consumers are especially influenced by people they know and trust.

KNOWLEDGE LEADERSHIP

P&G's Tremor doesn't handle business-to-business assignments—its panels are strictly consumer focused. But the principles of "advocacy" (reason to care) and "amplitude" (reason to share) also apply in the world of industrial marketing. At the end of the day, after all, enterprise clients are consumers and have the same emotional needs. In fact, a 2007 survey of U.S. and British executives indicates that word of mouth has more influence on business purchase decisions than any other factor, cited by more than half of respondents.[12] The study also suggests that business executives are active connectors, engaging in 118 conversations about products and services every week.

The masters of marketing have discovered how to create both advocacy and amplitude around their products and services. Donovan Neale-May, executive director of the CMO Council, has termed the technique "intelligent market engagement," which sounds more businesslike than "word of mouth." The public relations agency he leads in his day job has trademarked the term, and the CMO Council itself may be one of its most visible applications. The Council, which Neale-May founded, claims a by-invitation-only membership of more than 3,000 marketers across North America, Europe, and Asia. Members meet annually, usually in the comfortable surroundings of a resort, to share knowledge and insights with each other and with sponsors who have paid anywhere from $5,000 to $50,000 for the privilege. (The $5,000 gets your company's name on the lanyard from which the attendees' name tag swings.)

Neale-May, a native of South Africa, played professional rugby in Italy for three years and has lost neither his accent nor his scrappiness. After hanging up his cleats, he turned to a series of public relations and marketing jobs in London, New York, Silicon Valley, and Los Angeles, including five years as head of Ogilvy's West Coast public relations operations. Along the way, he developed a low opinion of the "random acts of marketing" that characterize most industrial firms. "Marketing in most companies doesn't have enough credibility and respect to initiate meaningful strategies," he says. "The mid tier of the organization is tactically oriented, risk averse, and loyal to its current vendors. Little penetrates into the sales organization and distribution channels. What does get pushed in gets thrown out."

Intelligent market engagement, Neale-May says, is more than "thought leadership," which usually consists of publishing bylined articles in the trade media, giving speeches at industry meetings, and reprinting copies of both with enough lamination that they can be read in the shower. "Thought leadership is all about presenting your point of view on something," he says. "Intelligent market engagement is a process of defining the problems and opportunities at the intersection of your customers' needs and your own capabilities. It integrates fragmented marketing tactics into a cohesive strategy." Thought leadership is "spouting off"; intelligent market engagement is "taking in and reassembling."

Neale-May's own analysis of his PR firm's potential customers—company marketing officers—suggested that one of their biggest challenges was the sheer loneliness of the job. "Where do marketers get objective advice and counsel?" he asked himself. The answer, at the time, was either from books, the trade media, or industry conferences. But when asked what source they would value most highly, many marketers cited their peers. Thus, the CMO Council was born and began issuing a steady stream of research reports and white papers in addition to a monthly newsletter and periodic special-interest meetings.

Neale-May hardly has a corner on the market. Various universities, management consultants, and recruiting firms have all sponsored "CMO Summits" at one time or another. Senior marketers can shell out $50,000 a year to hobnob with their peers at the exclusive Marketing 50 or cough up a mere $295 to join the more quotidian CMO Club.[13]

INTELLECTUAL CAPITAL

Intellectual capital, in fact, is the great differentiator in a business-to-business market where proprietary advantage is measured in days rather than years. The masters of marketing set their products and services apart by wrapping them in relevant knowledge that isn't available elsewhere. GE Commercial Finance, for example, shares its knowledge of Six Sigma quality techniques with customers eager to learn how to better operate, manage, and grow their businesses. Under such circumstances, marketing becomes less about promoting your company and more about giving customers innovative knowledge that will help their businesses prosper. The source of such knowledge might be experience or original research. But it must be centered on your customer's big-picture problems and opportunities, even if the link to your offering is at best tangential, as in the case of GE Commercial Finance. If your customers care—and if you have given them a reason to share—intellectual capital will become market capital.

Constellation Wines, for example, launched one of the largest research projects ever undertaken in the wine industry, collecting data on more than 10,000 on- and off-premise purchases of premium wine. Based on the data, Constellation identified six distinct segments with different wants and needs. Through zip code analysis, it was even able to identify the relative mix of customer types for every off- and on-premise retailer. What's more, the company classified all premium brands—its competitors' as well as its own—by segment, so it could evaluate an account's product assortment. So it might tell a restaurant that its wine list was skewed toward one segment while its actual customers were largely from another. Or it might show retailers whether their promotions and displays addressed the needs of customers in their trading area. By sharing its knowledge of premium wine drinkers, Constellation helped its customers grow by improving their product balance and promotions.[14]

The dynamics of change are different in every industry, and every company has its own internal challenges, but all businesses exist to create value for their customers. Focusing on your customer's customer, as Constellation did, can open a rich vein of knowledge leadership.

New York Times columnist David Brooks has pointed out that the central force driving economic change is not the fact that information can now travel around the world in an instant, but the challenge of moving it the last few inches—the space between a person's eyes or ears and the various regions of the brain. "We're moving into a more demanding cognitive age," he writes. "In order to thrive, people are compelled to become better at absorbing, processing, and combining information."[15]

E-BUSINESS

The masters of B2B marketing help their customers cope with the change around them by making sense of it, creating meaning out of confusion. That was the genius behind IBM's e-business campaign of the late 1990s. The idea had been around since 1995, when it was called "network computing," but the emphasis then was wrong—it focused on IBM's business rather than its customers'. The company's initial effort to refocus the strategy by calling it "electronic commerce" was a little better, but it sounded like something the purchasing department came up with. When the company's ad agency showed IBM Chairman Lou Gerstner some ideas they had been "fooling around with," he was initially a little irritated. "I thought we agreed to call it 'e-commerce,'" he said. But he quickly warmed to the new nomenclature as a bigger idea—e-commerce is about selling stuff, e-business is about the whole company.

When the e-business campaign launched in October 1997, the Internet was the Big New Thing that threatened to change everything. E-business gave companies a roadmap through that changing landscape to the future. It was more than an ad campaign; it was every company's business strategy. And because IBM defined and branded it, the company "owned" it. "E-business" gave IBM a credible platform from which to exercise its knowledge leadership.

Ironically, at the time, only a small (some say insignificant) proportion of IBM's sales had much to do with the Internet. And some of the people behind the e-business campaign sheepishly admit they weren't sure they themselves knew just what e-business was. But they did know that associating IBM with the advent of digital business was critical. It worked. By sheer force of will the company convinced its customers—and its own employees—that it was the world leader in what it had christened "e-business."

No detail was too small. The "e" in "e-business," for example, was stylized to suggest the "@" in Internet addresses. The company implemented a comprehensive internal communication program so every IBM employee, in every division, knew what e-business meant for them and for their customers. Television commercials set the stage for case histories and product-specific print ads. Executive speeches discussed the e-business revolution. The company's website became a portal into the world of e-business. And IBM salespeople were armed with tailored communication packages to show customers in different industries how e-business would help them grow and become more efficient.

More than a decade later, IBM's website still has a special section on e-business. It no longer owns the term, which it never tried to trademark, and competitors from Oracle to HP and Sun have adopted it. A Google search turns up more than thirty-four million uses online. And it spawned a host of derivative terms, from "e-tailing" to "e-loans." But because the initial idea had advocacy (a reason to care) and amplitude (a reason to share), it spread like wildfire, and IBM will always own the concept.

In effect, e-business moved IBM from the information technology business to the knowledge business. Today, services are IBM's fastest-growing business segment, accounting for 60 percent of sales versus 25 percent before launching e-business.

The masters of marketing know how to generate and sustain word of mouth:

☞ *They never confuse word of mouth with buzz.* The former is relevant to their brand and to their customers; the latter is little more than noise someone has paid the equivalent of a disk jockey to generate. To affect behavior, word of mouth has to be relevant.

☞ *They understand that word of mouth must be cocreated and that people will only participate if there's something in it for them.* The strongest word of mouth carries something of cultural or social value.

☞ *They stimulate word of mouth by developing messages that people care about and want to share with others.* Their messages are easy to share and are of value to both sender and recipient. The messages that travel the furthest are those that consumers create themselves.

☞ *They are completely aboveboard in their efforts to stimulate word of mouth, disclosing their interests from the very beginning.* They don't pretend to be disinterested third parties and, when they hire others to represent them, they disclose their relationship without waiting to be asked.

☞ *They become a source of intellectual capital for their business customers, wrapping their products and services in relevant knowledge that is not available elsewhere.* They integrate that knowledge into all their marketing programs and communicate internally as aggressively as externally, equipping anyone who touches a customer to reinforce their platform of intellectual capital.

☞ *They don't get seduced by the reach of their messages; they focus on impact.* It's nice to produce something that gets repeated over and over, but the ability of a message to ring the cash register is the true measure of success.

CHAPTER THIRTEEN

WIN PEOPLE'S TRUST

"The biggest thing going on with U.S. consumers is that they want to trust something. They want to be understood; they want to be respected; they want to be listened to. It's trust in the largest sense of the word."

—JIM STENGEL, GLOBAL MARKETING
OFFICER, P&G

At the end of the first decade of the twenty-first century, one of the country's leading marketers tells us the biggest thing going on with U.S. consumers is that "they want to trust something."[1] Maybe public events in their lifetimes have made baby boomers and their Gen X children skeptical, if not cynical, about authority. Maybe they're more media savvy and take less at face value. Maybe a culture that worships celebrity has made credibility harder to discern. Whatever the reason, peoples' search for something, or someone, to trust does not mean they feel like victims. On the contrary, they are very aware of their new power. The transfer of control from marketer to consumer may be as significant as the shift from a product to a market orientation at the beginning of the twentieth century. It has certainly changed the role of marketing in ways we are just beginning to understand.

People today care about the people behind the brand. They care about the maker's values and behavior. They no longer make their purchase decisions in a vacuum. And they won't fall for the old brand magic of borrowed interest and misdirection. They want authenticity and relevance, brands that make straightforward promises and keep them. And people no longer separate the marketing experience from the product experience. When Commerce Bank (now TD Bank) decided to open on Sundays, it demonstrated how far it is willing to go to meet customers' needs. Google, iPhone, Wal-Mart, and Target are full expressions of their brand meaning, separate from any of their marketing efforts. Similarly, a graphic designer's Macintosh workstation is a full expression of the Apple brand. Business executives and recruiters feel the same way about Harvard Business School, as do mechanics about Snap-on tools and construction foremen about Caterpillar. Consumers and businesspeople have strong feelings about brands based on their judgment of the brand's competency and sincerity. Can it do what it promises, and will it? Those are two separate questions with answers based as much on emotion—gut feel—as careful analysis. The answers to those questions add up to a judgment of trust.

MARKETING'S VISION

Executive recruiter Jane Stevenson says, "Five or six years ago, advertising was 80 percent of the marketing job because it was the easiest, cleanest way to communicate with people. Now advertising is only a small part of connecting with people. In general, the CMO role has become more strategic. CEOs expect more from their chief marketer than good ads—they want to see growth." They also want someone with peripheral vision—preferably wide enough to see around corners, so the company is not on the wrong side of emerging trends. Most MBA programs have yet to catch up with that demand, which may be why the tenure of many traditionally trained CMOs is not much longer than the MBA program itself. On the other hand, Phil Kotler, the Northwestern University professor who wrote the most widely used college textbook on marketing, has a more expansive view of the practice than most. "Authentic marketing is not the art of selling what you make, but knowing what to make," he says. "It is the art of . . . creating solutions that deliver satisfaction to the customers, profits to the producers and benefits for the stakeholders."[2] Marketing's role is broader than commonly believed, not only in function, but also in perspective.

The top marketing people at three of America's leading companies came to the role directly from public relations—Beth Comstock at GE, Jon Iwata at IBM, and Mich Mathews at Microsoft. All three companies are sprawling enterprises, often in the public eye, and closely watched from Capitol Hill to Wall Street and Main Street. They're also companies that are often on the leading edge of new management trends. Is combining PR and marketing a trend or is this just a coincidence?

None of the three think it's a coincidence. Mich Mathews says the skills she developed in a twenty-year career in PR prepared her well to take on a broadened marketing role. Jon Iwata, senior vice president of marketing and communications at IBM, also began his career in public relations. But he cautions that it isn't a case of PR knowing something marketing doesn't. "The kinds of skills needed for *both* marketing and communications are changing in profound ways," he says. "Is it important that a company think about its relationships and reputation across all of its many constituencies? Definitely. Does marketing involve a lot more than pushing products? To be sure. But the reality of global integration, the digital network revolution, and the rise of myriad empowered stakeholders are every bit as challenging for traditional corporate communications as they are for marketing."

Researcher John Gilfeather, who has studied many companies under attack, notes that "In a crisis, the brand doesn't respond, the company does." He points out that Johnson & Johnson's name didn't appear anywhere on the Tylenol package when product tampering led to several deaths back in 1982. But it was the company, not the brand, that was expected to respond. More recently, the same principle applied with Merck's Vioxx. Apparently CEOs are beginning to realize that one downside of instant communications and empowered consumers is that crises are no longer an occasional possibility, but a constant threat.

Brand managers—who typically change jobs every two years—are notoriously focused on short-term issues. But McKinsey consultants suggested as long ago as 1999 that "relationship benefits seem to have growing importance for customers; indeed relationship building (through loyalty programs, better service, and a better understanding of customers) may now count for more than functional benefits."[3] Combined with a growing conviction that brands are a company's most valuable intangible asset, it's no wonder many CEOs want one person to help navigate the shifting currents of public opinion and to keep all the boats in the company fleet sailing in the same direction.

BETH COMSTOCK

Beth Comstock is on her second tour as General Electric's chief marketing officer, after spending two years as president of NBC Universal Integrated Media. And she's certain one of the reasons she was first plucked out of corporate communications for the position is because "marketing these days has to deal with customers as stakeholders." Companies need to draw from one core message in speaking to every constituency. "Customers today look at a company's reputation in addition to the merits of any product they might be considering," she says. "These days no one can get away with saying one thing and doing another, or saying one thing here and another there." Public relations people are used to connecting the dots for different constituencies and building mutually beneficial relationships. Most of all they need to help the CEO make sense of the company's business, creating meaning on an enterprise scale.

Two years into her first tour as GE's chief marketing officer, Beth Comstock told *Business Week* she was "a little bit of the crazy, wacky one"[4] at corporate headquarters. When Jeffrey Immelt became GE's CEO in September 2001, just days before the attacks of 9/11, he had already decided growth through acquisitions would be too expensive and uncertain—his predecessor's last hurrah had been an attempt to acquire Honeywell that was foiled by European regulators. Besides, the environment had changed far too much to expect the same strategy to deliver the same results.

The only alternative was to dramatically increase the company's rate of innovation to fuel organic growth. "[Traditional] professional management isn't going to give you the kind of growth you need in a slow-growth world," he told *Business Week*.[5] That meant changing a culture that was world famous for wringing cost out of its operations, but hadn't seen game-changing innovation since Edison hung up his lab coat. Immelt had begun his GE career in sales and still had the instincts of a marketer. He believed his predecessor's emphasis on "Six Sigma" operating efficiency had caused the company to become too internally focused. He wanted to turn GE's attention outward toward the marketplace and customers. "In the late 1990s, we became business traders not business growers," he wrote in the *Harvard Business Review*. "Today, organic growth is absolutely the biggest task in every one of our companies."[6]

In a company with fabled bench strength, Immelt made his top public relations executive the company's first chief marketing officer since Jack Welch had abolished the position twenty years before. Immelt charged her with driving innovation throughout the company's ranks. At first, her appointment as CMO had people outside the company, as well as some GE lifers, scratching their heads. *Advertising Age* noted that she was "the rare breed" of marketing chief who has never worked in marketing.[7] The fast-talking forty-two-year-old had begun her career covering the Virginia state legislature for a local news service, and later moved to GE's NBC, working in media relations in Washington and New York. In 1990, she joined Turner Broadcasting, where she promoted CNN, TNT, and TBS programs before moving to CBS as director of entertainment publicity. By 1996, Comstock was NBC's chief spokesperson, before becoming senior vice president of NBC corporate communications. The deft way she handled the launch of MSNBC—in which both Jack Welch and Bill Gates participated— put her on Welch's radar screen. About two years later, in August 1998, perhaps thinking about the imminent launch of his successor, Welch personally appointed her the company's vice president of corporate communications.

When Immelt broadened Comstock's responsibilities to include marketing, she gave herself ninety days to figure out what she was supposed to do. She studied best practices at companies from Procter & Gamble to FedEx and 3M. She brought in a raft of marketing gurus and peppered them with questions. And, most importantly, she spent time with the company's business leaders.

GENERAL ELECTRIC

GE's structure was the other reason people wondered why the company needed a chief marketing officer. Each of the conglomerate's divisions handled its own marketing and was fiercely independent. Their mantra was "if you tell me what to do, you can also take responsibility for my numbers." That's what had led Welch to eliminate the position in the first place. What would a chief marketing officer do at GE, other than preside over quarterly show-and-tell sessions that led nowhere?

But Immelt had a little more than that in mind. And Comstock had already been a big part of it. In January 2003, the company had replaced its twenty-four-year-old tagline "We bring good things to life" with "Imagination at Work." Though not widely publicized at the time, Comstock had had a major role in the new campaign's development, ensuring that it reflected the direction in which Immelt was taking the company. "We did a ton of research and unearthed a lot," she says. "We discovered that GE employees, customers, and investors all expected us to be innovative, whatever business we were in. But the organization also told us something that seemed like the opposite of innovation, that the company is very process-oriented. To move the company where it needed to go, we needed to do both." That was the idea behind "Imagination at Work," and Immelt wanted her to make the campaign's promise real *inside* GE—not just as a happy-talk slogan that gave people warm and fuzzy feelings, but as a hard-core, metrics-driven strategy that changed how they worked.

People who had worked with the hard-driving executive thought the choice made sense. "I've seen Beth and how she deals with senior management at GE," one of the CEOs of a GE PR agency told *Advertising Age*. "She influences branding, advertising, and she reaches out to many constituencies. Beth is clearly seen as a senior strategic part of the decision-making process."[8] Now with the CMO title, and the CEO's backing, she was in a position to use that influence to make the advertising real.

IMAGINATION BREAKTHROUGHS

Comstock had already begun a series of internal programs to educate employees on the need for organic growth, and division leaders were including "stretch targets" in their long-term strategies, but the effort was still ad hoc. And some of her initiatives, such as workshops to encourage creativity through play, raised a few eyebrows in the executive suites, if not outright guffaws. But in September 2003, Immelt made it clear he was serious when he challenged the business leaders at GE to come up with "Imagination Breakthroughs," innovative new projects that would serve as the centerpiece of GE's organic growth initiative. "IBs," as they became known in the company's acronym-happy culture, were supposed to have the potential to generate $100 million in new business within two to three years. Immelt and a small group of Comstock's corporate marketing people reviewed fifty projects initially and approved thirty-five of them, each of which Immelt promised to personally review every six months.

At around the same time, in the fall of 2003, Immelt emerged from a series of long-range strategy sessions with his division leaders and told Comstock he was struck by how often the environment and climate change had come up in their discussions of emerging trends that would impact their businesses over the next five to ten years. "I think there's something there," he told her, "but I don't know what. See what you can do with it." To Comstock, taking on environmental issues seemed like a big leap for a company that had spent much of the previous decade refusing to excavate toxic chemicals it had dumped into the Hudson River (which was legal when GE did it). What was widely perceived as the company's "arrogance" had made it one of the environmental movement's favorite targets.

But she dutifully began an eighteen-month investigation of the issue, bringing in some of GE's biggest customers for what she billed as "discovery sessions" with the company's top leaders. In the course of the two-day sessions, thirty-five customers at a time in industries such as energy, aviation, or water debated market and technology trends with senior GE executives, including Immelt. In effect, they were asked to imagine life in 2015—and the products they would need from GE. Comstock and the other GE executives took away a clear message: Rising fuel costs, ever tighter environmental regulations, and growing consumer expectations would translate into demand for cleaner technologies across all of the company's infrastructure businesses, which represented nearly 90 percent of revenue.

Immelt described one session to *Fast Company* magazine: "We had the railroad CEOs in . . . grounding ourselves on where the industry is, where we are, what their [and] said, 'Okay, here are some things to think about: higher fuel, more West-East shipments because of imports from China. . . . If you had $200 million to $400 million to spend on R&D at GE, how would you prioritize it?' "[9]

ECOMAGINATION

The company's "ecomagination" campaign grew out of half a dozen of these sessions. But Comstock hesitated to move too quickly. Instead, she began a yearlong "listening tour" among employees, customers, investors, activists, and public officials. The basic idea had come from customers, but they cautioned the company not to get too far ahead of them, especially in talking to public officials. Not too surprisingly, the other constituencies were all somewhat skeptical, especially the company's own employees.

"Our internal audience was the toughest," Comstock remembers. "They were worried it was just a PR campaign, that it wasn't real. Some doubted we could deliver. And they were all aware of the company's very public battle to keep from removing PCBs from the Hudson River." To Comstock, this was a make-or-break issue. "If employees don't buy in, customers won't either," she says. "Marketing is all about culture—internally and externally. You can't create something that sticks unless you get into the culture."

Skepticism was not limited to lunch-box-toting rank-and-file employees. Immelt told *Vanity Fair* magazine that, by his count, eight out of ten of the company's senior executives "were against the plan" when they first heard about it in December 2004.[10] Comstock remembers an audience of frowns that got deeper with every PowerPoint slide in her boardroom presentation. Over the following months, Immelt and Comstock laid out the argument for the program.

The company had already invested in the environment. As the number-one producer of power-plant equipment, airplane engines, and locomotives, it had little choice. Years of R&D had already given it the most efficient large-scale energy technologies on the market. In 2002, GE had bought a wind turbine business from Enron, the largest manufacturer in the country. In 2004, GE had bought AstroPower, the nation's biggest solar producer, and had increased its investment in clean-coal technologies.

With the exception of the Hudson River controversy, GE actually has a good record on environmental performance. Yale University's

Center for Environmental Law and Policy gave the company plaudits for setting high standards and for holding managers accountable for meeting them. Finally, clean energy was vital in the overseas markets GE had already targeted for 60 percent of its growth and where major customers were subject to the Kyoto Protocol on global warming.

GREEN IS GREEN

Immelt summed up his pitch in a slogan that may have sealed the deal internally, as well as among other skeptical constituencies—"green is green." One thing GE employees do understand is the company's relentless focus on revenue and profit. "Ecomagination" was not being adopted because it was trendy, or even the moral thing to do. It was about making money by giving customers what they need.

Immelt himself launched the "ecomagination" campaign in mid-2005, repeating his "green is green" slogan during simultaneous news conferences in Washington, D.C., Brussels, and Tokyo. Comstock says it resonated even more powerfully than she expected. There were a few critics who sniffed "greenwash," but by and large the environmental community took a wait-and-see attitude. Immelt's decision to negotiate an agreement with the Environmental Protection Agency to clean up the Hudson River obviously contributed to the ceasefire. But the campaign also rang true to most people. The case histories were modest and believable. GE salespeople were armed with "scorecards" that told customers in dollars and cents exactly what the lower emissions and higher fuel efficiency of a new GE product meant to them in fuel savings. And, in typical GE fashion, the company integrated the campaign into its business processes, including the now famous Imagination Breakthroughs, with targets and metrics to track progress. Overall, GE set a very public goal to increase revenue from clean energy products from about $10 billion in 2005 to $20 billion in 2010.

By mid-2008, GE had increased its ecomagination portfolio to sixty products from seventeen in 2005. Revenue in 2007 reached $14 billion, with $70 billion in orders and commitments. Based on those early successes, the company increased the 2010 target to $25 billion. Comstock says that the campaign's impact on GE's reputation was totally out of proportion to its budget, estimated at $100 million in its launch year. *BusinessWeek* and Interbrand, for example, credited GE with increasing its brand value by 13 percent—$6 billion—between

2005 and 2008, at a time when the company's stock price was at best flat. Comstock admits that she wouldn't be vouching for the Interbrand data's validity if the scores showed a decline in brand value. And while she's confident the company will achieve its goals by 2010, she also volunteers that she's "frickin' impatient."

WHOM DO YOU TRUST?

When P&G studied fifteen product categories in fifteen countries, it discovered that the brands with the highest market share also had the highest level of trust among consumers. That begs two questions: Which came first, market share or trust? And if people buy brands they trust, who says you have to do more than make a product that does what it promises to win their trust?

Steve Jobs for one. When Apple introduced the iPhone in July 2007 and priced it at as much as $500, early adopters around the country gulped and then lined up, credit cards in hand, to buy one. The iPhone clearly did what it promised. But then, just two months later, Jobs dropped the price to $399. People who had reveled in the minor celebrity of having the first iPhone on the block suddenly felt duped. At first, Apple said falling prices were simply the way of the high-tech industry, but in the wake of a few scathing blogs and plenty of nasty e-mail, Jobs relented and, in an open letter posted on Apple's website, admitted that the company needed "to do a better job taking care of our early iPhone customers. . . . Our early customers trusted us, and we must live up to that trust with our actions in moments like these."[11] Jobs then offered $100 worth of Apple coupons to anyone who had bought an iPhone at the higher price.

Jobs understood that his customers' trust depended on more than the quality of Apple products. It depended on the quality of their relationship with the company. As Nike and Wal-Mart discovered, customers include how a company treats its employees—on the payroll or contracted—in that equation. A company's environmental record, its governance, and the conduct of its executives, among other factors, all figure in the equation. Indeed, as Beth Comstock points out, companies need to treat their customers as stakeholders, that is, people who are affected by—and can affect—a company's behavior in ways beyond their commercial transactions.

The masters of marketing don't have a transactional view of the world. They realize that the secret weapon of twentieth-century marketing—intrusiveness—has lost in throw weight in a world of digital video recorders, on-demand entertainment, and portable media. Weapons of mass disturbance are less effective in a world of fragmented media. The new metaphor is not "engagement" as in a battle but as in a relationship. Such relationships are built, not on borrowed interest, but on a deep understanding of people's needs, desires, and values, as well as the trends that will shape them. As GE's ecomagination campaign demonstrates, such relationships are not limited to the interpersonal world, but apply between institutions as well.

In a flat, always-connected world, marketers can't compartmentalize their messages. When Mattel had to recall twenty million toys in August of 2007 because they were contaminated with lead paint, its CEO said Chinese suppliers had betrayed the company.[12] Not surprisingly, that didn't go over well in China. Worse, the company later discovered that 85 percent of the products were recalled not for lead paint, but because of a faulty Mattel design. When the company apologized to the Chinese government, saying "the vast majority of these products that we recalled were the result of a flaw in Mattel's design, not through a manufacturing flaw in Chinese manufacturers,"[13] the U.S. media and consumer advocates smelled a backroom deal. New York Senator Charles Schumer likened the company's apology to a "bank robber apologizing to his accomplice rather than the person who was robbed."[14] Now the company's sincerity, as well as its competency, was in question.

A brand's strength comes not from the breadth of its promise, but from the depth of people's trust that its promise will be kept. And trust is rooted largely in emotions, not the intellect. That distinction can make all the difference. Yale University economics professor Robert Shiller wrote a best seller, *Irrational Exuberance*, around the idea that economics today is largely a matter of emotion and psychology.

Brands are empty words into which marketers pour meaning and feelings. For example, McDonald's classic "You deserve a break today" advertising campaign gave moms permission to take the kids to a fast-food restaurant. It not only made them feel good about McDonald's, it made them feel better about themselves. The Nike swoosh is a badge that identifies the wearer as energetic and a bit of a rebel, whether roll-erblading or lying in a hammock. And a Whole Foods reusable shopping bag says you're not just buying groceries, you're taking care of your family while helping to save the planet. As strong as those brands may be, though, allegations of serving hormone-laden meat, exploiting children in third-world sweatshops, or a nasty labor dispute can undermine their meaning and poison people's feelings toward them.

Global brands are especially vulnerable to left-field attack both because their operations are more dispersed and because they make higher-profile targets. People are more inclined to give a brand with which they have a strong relationship the benefit of the doubt. But their relationship has to be built on actions—not words—that are relevant to people and credible coming from the brand. Relevance flows both ways. If the program isn't relevant to a company, it won't have meaning, and any association its customers make will be by happenstance. GE is unapologetic in explaining the self-interest behind its ecomagination program: "Ecomagination is a business initiative to help meet customers' demand for more energy-efficient products and to drive reliable growth for GE—growth that delivers for investors long term."[15] In other words, green is green.

Finally, the brand promise on which such relationships are built can't simply be something stuck at the end of an ad or on a conference room wall. It has to be the "golden thread" that runs through every internal process and through every interaction with customers. GE's ecomagination initiative is reflected in every important business process, from the way it evaluates and trains managers to the way it develops its business plans and sets budgets.

THE ROAD TO TRUST

At GE, the road to profitable growth converges with the road to trust. And the company never forgets that the customers who travel that road are people. As Comstock says, "People at work don't only think about work. Business is also about stories and emotions." Indeed, anyone who thinks otherwise has never been in a corporate board meeting.

So the voyage to trust begins in discovery—listening to customers, understanding not only their current needs but also major trends. Most of all, it means finding a neutral area where customer and company interests intersect. Out of that inquiry, a story begins to form whose hallmarks are authenticity and relevance. "You can't tell one story to some people and another to others," Comstock says. "You have to have one core message that you can translate to different constituencies. And your story has to match your capabilities—you have to give people a reason to believe. Ecomagination had to be about making money or it wouldn't have been taken seriously—inside or outside the company."

Marketing's role on that journey is to connect the dots across the company, to act as a catalyst for change, and to create platforms for customer and employee collaboration. "We all understand that human resources is very much in touch with a company's culture," Comstock says. "But marketing has to be too. That was a big surprise for me in the beginning, but we really focused on the notion of employees as brand ambassadors. And we did a lot of work with sales-force training and getting them to embody the story." Marketing needs to embed the brand story into the company culture.

But it's not all touchy-feely. A voyage of such complexity requires a sophisticated navigation system. "Change without process is chaos," Comstock warns. Corporate finance ensured that the ecomagination initiative built environmental benefits and value metrics into a pipeline of Imagination Breakthroughs. GE marketing created a common language across the company and engaged other organizations in institutionalizing the processes to make ecomagination real. For example, the company's fabled Six Sigma quality leaders created "net promoter scores" for every GE business. The net promoter scores are a measure of customers' willingness to recommend the company to others minus those who wouldn't. "In the end, we had a triumvirate of sales, quality, and marketing rallying around the customer," Comstock says.

Connecting emotionally with customers is not about generating warm and fuzzy feelings. It's about connecting with them on a fundamental level about issues they really care about. It's about building trust. That's where the masters of marketing excel.

☞ *They don't have a transactional view of the world.* They realize the days of one-way, intrusive communication have passed and the new paradigm is one of relationships. Sometimes the first step in building a relationship is to do something unexpected. Charmin outfitted restrooms at fifteen state fairs with products and cleaning people one summer; during the holiday shopping season, it did the same thing in busy Times Square. Pantene shampoo has a website—BeautifulLengths.com—to encourage women to donate their hair to cancer victims. Goldfish crackers sponsors Fishful Thinking.com to help parents teach kids to be optimistic.

☞ *They begin by listening to all their stakeholders, defined as anyone who contributes to the success—and bears the risks—of the company's operations.* They try to understand not only their current needs, but also major trends where their interests intersect with the company's. They heed adman Keith Reinhard's admonition that "consumers shouldn't be viewed as 'targets' but as 'guests.' And the way to do that is to start by letting consumers know that you understand them and what's important to them."

☞ *They understand that a brand's strength comes not from the breadth of its promise, but from the depth of people's trust that their promise will be kept.* They know that they live in a world of instant communication where it is impossible to compartmentalize their activities and messages. So they always say what they mean and do what they say. When they make missteps, they admit them quickly and correct them. When Apple's Me.com network went down because traffic exceeded projections, it acknowledged the problem, fixed it, and added thirty days' free service to customers' contracts.

☞ *They build their relationships on actions—not words—that are relevant to both the company and its communities.* They are unapologetic about their motives, not pretending that their actions are entirely selfless, but pointing out areas of mutual interest.

CHAPTER   FOURTEEN

INVEST IN RELATIONSHIPS

"Marketing is a tax you pay for not being remarkable."

—ROBERT STEPHENS, FOUNDER AND CHIEF
INSPECTOR, THE GEEK SQUAD

In the end, the masters of marketing leave us with a question: If marketing is a tax companies pay for not being remarkable, is it better to pay it up front in the development of better products or downstream in their promotion through advertising, trade allowances, and discounts?

This book suggests that, for most companies, whether their customers are individuals or institutions, the smart investment is one that supports the development of insight and foresight, because their real goal is to build enduring relationships, and you can't build a relationship with someone you don't know. You can, of course, become well known; you can buy the trappings of celebrity and attract paparazzi. Some people will even be drawn by the flashbulb's burst. But when the spotlight dims, as it eventually will, so will their interest.

Most people think of marketing as promoting a product or communicating with customers and prospects. These are obviously important functions, but they occur downstream from a product's conception. What happens before the product exists—upstream, as it were—is even more critical. That's where the product is conceived; its target customer, defined; its competitive advantage, determined; and the price it has to command, set. When both upstream and downstream marketing are in sync, the result is a product that surprises people in a meaningful way. That's what being "remarkable" means.

For Bank of America, that meant walking in the shoes of recent Mexican immigrants to understand their banking needs. As a result, it began accepting Mexican Consular ID cards in all its branch offices to make it easier for recent immigrants to open accounts and cash checks. And it developed a new service that allows them to send money to family back home safely and inexpensively through more than 20,000 ATM machines in Mexico. Which may be one reason three out of four Mexican immigrants living in California are Bank of America customers.

People will talk about you if you're outrageous, but that quickly gets old. If you fulfill people's genuine needs, desires, and values, however, you can begin to build an emotional connection that endures. Intangible, emotional connections are hard to copy. Once a brand makes an emotional attachment, it's very hard to dislodge. "You can say the right thing about a product and no one will listen," ad great Bill Bernbach used to admonish young copywriters. "You've got to say it in such a way that people feel it in their gut, because if they don't feel it, nothing will happen." Bob Liodice, the president of the Association of National Advertisers, calls marketing "a platform for creating connections" and points to American Express's John Hayes as a master of the art.

JOHN HAYES

Hayes has been the chief marketing officer of American Express since 1994, and ironically it was a job he almost didn't take. When approached by a headhunter, Hayes was president of a New York ad agency, Lowe & Partners, and didn't know how he would like moving to the client side. In fact, he admits that he "wasn't entirely comfortable with the idea at first." In senior positions at Ammirati & Puris and Saatchi & Saatchi Compton, he had worked on global campaigns for Citibank, Aetna, Procter & Gamble, Prudential Insurance, RJR Nabisco, Mercedes-Benz, and Reebok. Even as an agency president, he stayed involved with clients. He liked the variety and challenge of working in different categories and on different brands.

But he was flattered to be asked by American Express, and he agreed to a series of interviews with the company's top executives. On the second round of interviews, pretty sure he would be offered the job, but still not certain he would take it, he asked one veteran executive "What's the one thing I would need to succeed in this job if I took it?" Without missing a beat, the executive said, "Don't become one of us." With those marching orders, Hayes took the job and has never looked back.

THE REWARDS OF MEMBERSHIP

As Hayes discovered, American Express is not only unafraid of change, it embraces it. What should logically be a 150-year-old freight forwarding company has morphed into one of the world's leading financial institutions by continually reinventing itself around its customers' evolving needs. Hayes took the same tack as the company's chief marketing officer. At the very beginning, he shifted the company's marketing focus from building awareness (which was becoming a nonissue for the company) to creating relationships through such initiatives as giving members access to exclusive dining and entertainment offers. The result was more than a decade of double-digit income growth.

Hayes builds surprise into member relationships by figuring out what will appeal to them before they know themselves. He keeps his hand on the pulse of popular culture through a broad network of contacts in the creative community, such as Robert De Niro, Jerry Seinfeld, and Annie Leibovitz. But he leaves himself open to inspiration from any source. The Seinfeld "webisodes" that ran on the Internet in 2004 grew out of a long car trip when he ferried his son and friends to Boston College. They were sitting in the back cracking up at clips of the old *Seinfeld* TV show on a portable DVD player.

Hayes convinced Jerry Seinfeld to reprise a supposed friendship with Superman that first debuted in a 1998 Super Bowl commercial. Two four-minute "webisodes," cowritten by Seinfeld and directed by acclaimed film director Barry Levinson, followed Superman and Seinfeld through their day as they discussed their views on reality television, visited a local diner under a reservation for "Man of Steel," caught a Broadway show, and, of course, fought for truth, justice, and the American Way.

The webisodes were little entertainment gems that attracted thousands of young card prospects to the company's website, which of course was the whole idea. Driving consumers to the site is hugely more valuable than running ads on television, because a good proportion of the TV audience won't qualify for a card. Furthermore, a TV spot must prod qualified prospects to call an 800 number or apply online. But if they're already online at the American Express site watching the Seinfeld webisode, they're just a single, hard-to-miss click away from signing up right then and there. Plus, you've given them something they wanted to see, probably enjoyed, and can share with their friends.

The brief mentions of the card in the webisodes seemed integral to the story line. But Hayes admits the company has sometimes pushed its presence a little too much. One episode of a network TV series that tracked the travails of opening a new restaurant included a scene where the harried owner said, "I think we better get Open, the Small Business Network, on the phone." "I think the kitchen was on fire at the time," Hayes remembers. "I just went, 'Eeesh!'" Thankfully, most of the time, the company's sensibilities are flawless. And when that's the case, delivering valuable, relevant, and compelling content to customers and prospects can be integral to building a deeper customer relationship.

EXPERIMENTATION

To help fuel a constant flow of new ideas and approaches, Hayes sets aside about 10 percent of his annual marketing budget to fund the equivalent of an "R&D laboratory" dedicated to exploring innovative marketing approaches. Separate groups create platform-neutral content, figure out how to extract as much value as possible from the company's entertainment and media partnerships, and institutionalize the learning from these experiments. The results have ranged from an exhibit of photographs by Annie Leibovitz to an outdoor concert by Sheryl Crow in Central Park.

The Crow concert was designed to introduce the company's new Blue card in 1999, and the company took the unusual risk of producing it itself. Crow agreed to do the concert for a flat fee and invited friends like Eric Clapton and the Dixie Chicks to join her on stage.

The whole thing cost less than a single Super Bowl commercial, which seemed like a bargain, until it started to rain. By showtime, the sun came out, Hayes's stomach dropped back into his abdominal cavity, and all the blue rain ponchos he had ordered went back into the trucks. The concert was a success—the resulting album went platinum and garnered three Grammies. American Express owned all the rights.

Not everything associated with the launch of the Blue card went as well. To set the card apart from its competitors, and to make it appear more contemporary, Hayes had recommended that it be transparent. Two days before the launch, someone discovered that a clear card would get stuck in ATM machines because lasers couldn't read them. Eventually, someone came up with the idea of sandwiching foil in the middle of the card so it would appear transparent but not frustrate the lasers.

With all the ups and downs, Hayes is committed to experimentation. "We learn a lot every time we try something new," he says. For example, the Seinfeld and Superman webisodes changed the way the company goes to market with promotions. "We learned that if we get the content right, consumers will seek us out," he says. "They'll literally spend more than ten minutes on our website and pass the word along to their friends." As the pace of change increases, Hayes believes it's more important than ever to keep experimenting and learning. "When times get tough and budgets are squeezed, it's important to get more efficient," he says, "but you should fight the temptation to quit experimenting. You have to try new things to learn what works and what doesn't." Management consulting firm McKinsey seems to agree. In fact, its consultants suggest that "One of the best ways to diagnose a marketing organization's ROI discipline is to assess the extent and quality of the media and messaging tests in progress at any given time."[1]

REINVENTION

"American Express was 108 years old before it launched its first charge card," John Hayes explains. "This is a company that constantly reinvents itself. You have to reinvent. Consumers are reinventing their lives. They used to come home and go to the mailbox first thing. Now, they come home and go to the electronic mailbox. We're constantly trying to stay where the consumer is."

Anticipating where consumers are going is what sets the masters of marketing apart. "We have sociologists and anthropologists to help us understand trends," Hayes says, "but ultimately it comes down to a few people here in marketing, information management, and operations who had to absorb all the data and say 'I think this is how all these pieces come together.'"

The company's decision in the 1990s to aggressively expand beyond its traditional travel and entertainment franchise to everyday purchases was just one example of understanding the intersection of social trends and the company's business. "Once a decision is made," Hayes says, "the key thing is to leave the smallest possible space between the brand and operations."

Under Hayes's direction, the iconic card shifted its meaning so deftly that hardly anyone noticed, certainly not the millions of people it considers "members." When Hayes joined the company, the American Express card virtually defined "prestige." People filled out the application wondering if they would measure up to its undefined, but assumed demanding, standards. If they somehow passed muster, they looked forward to all the "privileges" that came with "membership," as the company's advertising promised.

"The card had Gordon Gekko written all over it," Hayes says, citing the character in the film *Wall Street* who rose at a public meeting to praise greed. And in the hyper-consuming 1980s, that was not necessarily a bad association for a charge card, particularly one that commanded the respect of the haughtiest waiter.

But times change and "the exclusivity that fit so well with the 1980s dissipated in the 1990s," Hayes remembers. Worse, members may have hesitated to leave home without the card, but they were unlikely to use it at the hardware store. In its own research, the company discovered increasingly large numbers of people who said "it's not the card for me." "When a lot of people say 'you're not for me,' it's time to ask yourself who you are," Hayes says. That became one of the first jobs he tackled at the company. He discovered that the American Express card had some admirable attributes, including a high level of trust and a stellar reputation for service. But what defined—and limited—it was a sense of prestige or elitism.

SPECIAL BUT INCLUSIVE

"We wanted the card to be considered special, but inclusive," Hayes remembers. "To grow, we had to bring more people into the franchise and encourage our existing members to use the card for everyday purchases in addition to a big night out at a fancy restaurant." Doing that required more than advertising, and Hayes is candid that some of his early efforts, such as a campaign exhorting members to "Do More" with their AmEx card, fell short in their initial iterations. The big breakthrough came when he decided to implement an idea he had had in the back of his mind for years—getting the top 1 percent of the world's best creative minds thinking about his brand.

"I wanted the American Express brand to be relevant in popular culture," he says. "What better way than to engage the people who were helping shape that culture." People like Tiger Woods, Jerry Seinfeld, Ellen DeGeneres, Wes Anderson, and M. Night Shyamalan. But instead of trying to turn them into shills for the card, Hayes briefed them on his business goals and challenges as thoroughly as he would one of his ad agencies. Then he asked for their suggestions. "Sometimes we had to rework things," he says. "But most of the time, what they did was really impressive."

So were the results. In 1990, 64 percent of American Express card billings came from travel and entertainment charges and 36 percent came from retail. That proportion has now been more than reversed. In 2007, nontravel and entertainment billings represented over 69 percent of charges. What's most impressive is that the company says this came about because "the types of merchants that began to accept" the card grew "in response to consumers' increased desire to use these cards for more of their purchases."[2] In Hayes's own words, "our customers played the biggest part in defining who American Express is."

Sometimes living up to that brand meaning requires changes in operating policies. For example, at one point Hayes discovered that only the primary card member could move reward points to an airline frequent flier account. That meant some members were asked to have their spouses call to complete a transaction. A quick meeting with the

210 SECRETS OF THE MARKETING MASTERS

company's chief financial officer had that policy changed. In marketing, as in evolution, the brands that survive are not necessarily the biggest or the strongest, but those that are most responsive to change. The marketing boneyard is littered with once-mighty brands such as Oldsmobile, DeSoto, Digital Equipment, Wang, and *Mademoiselle* and *Saturday Evening Post* magazines. Each died from multiple causes, but what they all had in common was that they lost touch with their customers' changing needs, desires, and values.

Investments in customer insight should spit out more than ads; they should result in new products and changes to existing ones. Hayes has participated in the creation of over 200 new products based on such insight. One new card—the all-black Centurion card—has a $5,000 initiation fee in addition to an annual membership fee of $2,500. Still, the demand exceeds the supply. Even with no advertising. As of mid-2008, it wasn't even mentioned on the company website.

Better customer acuity can also help translate what's special about the brand into relevant customer experiences across all points of customer contact. American Express, for example, offers its card members specially produced episodes of popular television series such as *Lost*, *Prison Break*, and *24*. During the holiday shopping season it provides "member lounges" at major malls where cardholders can relax, away from the madding crowds, with a cup of coffee or a soft drink. An online "wish list" gives card members the chance to buy limited-supply, high-end items or experiences at unheard-of prices at different times during the day. A BMW might go on sale for $5,000 and the first person to order it, gets it. Members could ask to be put on the list for e-mail reminders when the next "deal" was posted, but there was always something unusual or special on the site, from a week at a Rock 'n' Roll Camp to courtside tickets to the U.S. Open tennis matches. In the first year, more than seven million people visited the site and bought everything in inventory within three and a half weeks. The following year, when card members were asked what items they would like to see on the "wish list," more than 150,000 replied.

Hayes thinks of American Express's marketing as its distribution network and as an extension of the core product. The card, the website, the bills, the special promotions are all of a piece—everything is designed to engage the customer in a deeper relationship whether or not a particular transaction rings the cash register. As a credit card company, American Express has access to its customers' most intimate financial information and compiles reams of data on their purchases, giving it keen insight into their interests and values. That provides the critical context necessary to design personalized, relevant offers and rewards that can be key to deepening customer relationships.

RELATIONSHIP MANAGEMENT

But you don't have to be in financial services to gather relevant customer information. U.K. retailer Tesco has offered its grocery customers a Clubcard since 1995. Every quarter, based on the amount they've spent, cardholders receive vouchers that they can spend in the store. And every time customers use their Clubcard, Tesco tracks which store they shopped in, what products they purchased, and how much they paid. Based on that information, Tesco periodically sends them special offers and surprise rewards. Similarly, Virgin Entertainment offers a V.I.P. loyalty card that not only accumulates points, but tracks customer purchases, so a Jay-Z fan won't get a backstage pass to a Mariah Carey concert. In fact, Virgin married its loyalty program to the 300 celebrity events it stages every year so its best customers get invitations to meet with their favorite performers.

Marketers from Coca-Cola and JCPenney to HP and General Electric are investing heavily in Customer Relationship Management (CRM) software to compile, integrate, and analyze all the streams of customer data flowing through their companies. A few masters of marketing have flipped the model, giving customers themselves greater control over the relationship. This is not simply to assuage customers' privacy concerns, but to deepen the relationship itself. They are turning customer relationship management from a one-way data-collection exercise into a two-way conversation.

P&G's Tremor initiative is an example of "customer-managed relationships." Once moms or teenagers sign up to participate in the company's panels, they are in charge. Tremor may send them product samples or coupons, but whether they pass them on to their friends or provide any feedback is entirely up to them. The only compensation they get, other than the product itself, is the emotional satisfaction of sharing something they believe has value. In return, Tremor's clients get invaluable information they can use to shape their marketing strategies or the products themselves.

As we have seen, consumer companies of every size are using online media to deepen customer relationships, as well as sources of insight and intelligence. Amazon built its business model on giving customers unprecedented control over every aspect of their relationship. Disney Destinations gives customers all the online tools they need to plan their vacation, from location, to travel options, accommodations, dining reservations, and extras like guided tours. Consumer websites from Amazon to Zappos make room for customer product reviews. Zappos goes even further by sponsoring a moderated discussion called the "Daily Shoe Digest" for dedicated "shoe lovers."

At the other end of the scale, companies like HP, Cisco, Sun Microsystems, and AT&T's enterprise division give their customers all the online tools they need to select, order, and maintain their products and services, including access to experts and the larger community of users. They also support active user communities within their websites, including customer support forums, blogs, and message boards. That level of control and participation deepens the consumer's relationship with a brand and increases his or her loyalty.

RELATIONSHIP REHAB

Sometimes, relationships need to be rebuilt, either because they have been neglected or because they have been seriously damaged. The secret in both cases is to begin by listening and to respond, not with words, but with action.

Gary Loveman built Harrah's into one of the world's largest gaming corporations by figuring out who its best customers were and focusing his energy on their needs. To his surprise, Harrah's best customers were "emphatically not the limousine-riding high-rollers we and our competitors had fawned over for many years," he admits, but middle-aged and senior adults with discretionary time and income who enjoy playing slot machines on their way home from work or on a night out. Those retired teachers, doctors, bankers, and machinists produced 80 percent of Harrah's revenue.

Loveman mined data on those customers' past visits to design offers and loyalty rewards tailored to their preferences, from special events and free meals to complimentary casino chips. He awarded tiered loyalty cards based on a customer's theoretical annual value. The very visible rewards of the higher-tier cards—such as shorter lines at hotel registration and restaurants—appealed to customers' aspirations and rewarded exactly the behavior that Loveman wanted to encourage. When he discovered that customers who were very happy with their Harrah's experience spent 24 percent more, he tied employee bonuses, not to financial results, but to customer satisfaction with the speed and friendliness of service. And he tracks the business's overall performance against three metrics that are directly linked to customer behavior—its share of customers' annual gambling expenditures, the percentage of customers qualifying for higher tiers in its loyalty program, and the percentage of customers visiting more than one of its thirty properties.[3]

Wal-Mart knows who its customers are, but they were becoming increasingly suspicious of the company because of the battering it took in the media for allegedly exploiting its workers and driving neighborhood stores out of business. After a few years of trying to punch back out of a political campaign-like "war room," with its own front groups, Wal-Mart woke up and realized that actions spoke louder than words. Ironically, it took a hurricane to point the way. When Wal-Mart was quicker than the government and many charitable organizations to get relief supplies to Hurricane Katrina's victims along the Gulf Coast, it not only won public praise, it realized that it had the power to positively influence communities.

Wal-Mart's CEO, Lee Scott, set out to regain people's trust by taking credible action on two burning issues—sustainability and health care. The retailer offered lower-cost health insurance to its own employees, started selling generic drugs for $4, and opened in-store health clinics, which offer low-priced services from vaccinations to cholesterol screening. It set aggressive targets for energy conservation and reducing waste, became the world's largest buyer of organic cotton, sold more organic milk and produce than any other retailer, sold more green-friendly products like energy-saving fluorescent bulbs, and made selling local produce a priority. Jim Prevor, a longtime Wal-Mart observer who publishes a newsletter called *The Perishable Pundit*, found the secret behind the company's greening. "Helping the environment is an area where Wal-Mart felt culturally comfortable," he said. "It could maintain its core values of eliminating waste and driving costs down while reducing packaging and creating energy-efficient stores."[4] Plus, he might have added, it was good for the bottom line.

ORCHESTRATION

What's remarkable about many of these examples—from American Express to Wal-Mart—is the relatively narrow role advertising agencies played. Ever since 1869, when the first "full-service" ad agency opened its doors, most of a company's "marketing tax" went to ad agencies. That's where all the marketing know-how was. For most companies, marketing and advertising were once practically synonymous. Mary Lou Quinlan, who has been on both the agency and client side, says that most agencies are still focused on the creative department as their engine and ads as their product. "When agencies talk about Big Ideas," she says, "they usually mean an ad, not a business strategy." Clients still like good ads, but in today's hypercompetitive world, what they really value is counsel across the full spectrum of marketing.

Ben Machtiger used to be an ad agency executive and is now the chief marketing officer of executive search firm Spencer Stuart, which gives him an interesting perspective on the issue. "My impression is that, over time, most agencies have allowed themselves to become more like vendors," he says. "They tend to trade in ads more than in strategy." Part of the reason, he believes, is because financially squeezed clients have turned the screws on their agency "suppliers" in turn. Since an agency's principal cost is human talent, they had little choice but to cut back there and, over time, they stopped attracting the kind of people who can be strategic counselors. For example, in 1958, ad agencies hired eight members of the graduating class at Harvard Business School. In 2008, not one did. Indeed, Burtch Drake, former president of the American Association of Advertising Agencies, calls entry-level salaries in advertising "a disgrace," making it very hard to attract really bright people. Of course, in his view, the root cause is the "margin pressure" agencies are experiencing.[5]

While American Express's John Hayes doesn't agree that ad agencies have lost their intellectual capital, he does admit that a number of agencies have evolved from the "persuasion business to the TV commercial business." And he's quick to point out that the explosion in communications channels has caused agencies to diversify. As a result, there are simply more *kinds* of agencies than when he led one. The job of orchestrating the different channels has become more significant and, in many cases, there's no one to do it but the client. In fact, Hayes himself may be Exhibit A of the shift in know-how from agency to client. Instead of an agency of record, he works with a consortium of best-in-class marketing communications companies, which he supplements with the "top one percent of creative minds" he dreamed of putting to work on behalf of his brand.

In today's environment, "orchestration" has become another of the marketing masters' secrets. But it has a much broader meaning—and greater strategic significance—than ensuring communications have a similar look and feel or carry the proper logo. Orchestration today means working across media to build and nurture enduring customer relationships. Some companies, like American Express and P&G, accomplish this by finding the very best providers across a range of services and organizing them into a "virtual agency" with the client as CEO. Other companies, like IBM and Dell, consolidate the bulk of their marketing services at a single agency, which they treat as an extension of their own staff, not only in terms of information sharing, but also in terms of compensation and competency building.

But whatever model they follow, the masters of marketing focus all their resources on building enduring customer relationships:

☞ *They think of marketing as a platform for creating connections, mining customer data for new points of access and affiliation.* And once they connect with customers, they give them the tools necessary to manage important aspects of their relationship, including the opportunity to interact with other customers.

☞ *They work hard to keep in touch with popular culture and trends that impact their customers.* They set aside a significant portion of their budget for experimentation to fuel a constant flow of new ideas and approaches. And they are

rigorous in documenting the results so everyone in the organization learns from them.

☞ *They create customer experiences that reinforce brand values and deepen relationships, even if they don't ring the cash
register every time.* They reward the behavior they want to
encourage, taking a long view of customer value, but rigorously quantifying it over a reasonable period.

☞ *They don't make "customer loyalty" a program, but a way
of doing business.* They know that customer loyalty flows
from superior product performance and from treating customers in a way that demonstrates they know and value
them as individuals.

THE OBAMA EFFECT

"If you keep doing what you always did,
you'll keep getting what you always got."

—TEXAS PROVERB

When historian Daniel Boorstin studied the 1960 presidential campaign, he concluded that television had fundamentally changed the nature of campaigning. The medium's insatiable appetite for "images" had put a premium on manufactured events, such as photo ops, debates, and news conferences, at the expense of a sober discussion of issues. In fact, that shift had begun with the introduction of the wire photo back in the 1920s, but newspapers operated on a daily schedule and had limited space for images. Television, which in 1960 reached eight out of ten homes, was built on images and operated around the clock. Feeding television's maw became the national candidates' daily preoccupation.

PSEUDO-EVENTS

Boorstin called these manufactured events "pseudo-events" and worried they would lead to pseudo-qualifications.[1] Partisans debate whether they have produced pseudo-presidents. But most observers will agree that they have led to the dumbing down of public discourse as politicians trimmed their messages to the tight time requirements of network television and dealt in slogans and imagery rather than substance.

Many blame these developments on marketers who, they say, peddle candidates like so many bars of soap. And certainly it is true that political candidates have adopted many of the techniques and processes of marketing, from focus group research to message development and market segmentation. In fact, Karl Rove took George W. Bush to victory in the 2000 and 2004 presidential elections largely through exquisitely targeted, pinpoint marketing that fired up potential supporters and got them to the polls.

Candidates speak of their "brand" and their campaigns execute media buys that would be the envy of the largest packaged-goods companies. In some instances—microtargeting and rapid response, for example—the candidates' campaigns have actually exceeded the capabilities of most commercial marketers. But in some respects, political marketers are failing our democratic system, and the reason may lie in their obsession with technique over purpose.

Political marketers are less interested in building relationships than in securing votes; their perspective is largely transactional. Their research is not focused on understanding people's needs, but on figuring out how to get their vote by pushing issue-buttons that will attract them and avoiding issues that will drive them away. And in recent elections, "opposition research" has fed attack ads, both by the candidates and their surrogates.

"Swift boating" has entered the lexicon as a technique for undermining an opponent's character through charges that are difficult to disprove, but will linger in people's minds long after they have forgotten the original source. Ironically, if commercial marketers were to attempt to "swift boat" a competitor, they would face harsh questioning by the Federal Trade Commission, as well as a skeptical public. Political marketers say they dislike "negative campaigning" but confess, "it works." One of the reasons it works is because television—and now the blogosphere—considers negative ads a juicy pseudo-event with ready-to-use footage and, if the person attacked responds, a dollop of emotion and conflict. Eighty percent of the media coverage of the 1960 presidential campaign was favorable in tone; since 1980, more than half of campaign coverage has been negative.[2] Boorstin was right in his analysis, but he may have been too modest in his prognosis.

Pseudo-events have not only cheapened the candidates we get, they've made the electorate more cynical and apathetic.

MARKETING AND DEMOCRACY

Harvard Business School professor John Quelch proposes not to eliminate marketing from politics, but to improve it, suggesting, "The two major parties should focus on learning current and emerging citizen needs, developing policy and program solutions, informing interested citizens about themselves, and making themselves easily accessible."[3] In other words, politicians should think of people not as voters they need to cultivate every few years, but as customers whose loyalty they'd like to keep forever.

They should take a tip from the masters of marketing, who are focused on creating and keeping customers. They build enduring relationships by developing products that fulfill people's needs. At their best, they appeal to people's higher values. They don't pander to top-of-mind obvious desires, but dig for the unarticulated needs, even anticipating how they will be shaped by events outside people's current perspective.

If the presidential election of 1960 marked a shift in political campaigning toward staged events and carefully packaged candidates, the campaign of 2008 may be turning the clock back to greater citizen participation. And this time it may be marketers who have a few lessons to learn.

THE ELECTION OF 2008

When the Internet first caught on, many marketers thought its biggest and best use would be as a turbocharged, wallet-seeking form of direct marketing, depositing highly tailored offers into people's electronic inboxes without the cost of paper and postage. At minimum, marketers imagined they could shovel their catalogues onto the Web and open expansive electronic storefronts, free, in most cases, of sales tax. But with the development of computer-to-computer networking, the Internet became less about marketers communicating with people than about people communicating among themselves. Marketers found themselves on the outside trying to earn their way in.

Furthermore, many marketers are discovering that control over a brand's very meaning has shifted to the broader community of users. Intrusion and hype are out; participation and authenticity are in. Search engines and website cookies[4] can give marketers real-time hints to a person's interests, but capitalizing on that knowledge requires coming up with something of value and relevance. Social media allow people to form communities of interest, but marketers can only participate if they're invited as a facilitator or ally. To leverage "word of mouse," marketers have to offer something of cultural or social value. Even more alarming to marketers used to having a firm grip on all the big levers, they have to cede a certain degree of control to prosper in this new world.

OBAMA

A skinny guy with big ears and a funny name demonstrated that giving up control online, in the right way, unleashes its own power. More than any brand to date, Barack Hussein Obama has tapped into the power of social media. It took him from negligible national name recognition in 2004 to the presidency just four years later. To be sure, Obama had a few offline successes too—beginning with his opposition to the war in Iraq when he was still a little-known Illinois state senator, which supporters say demonstrated his good judgment, to a well-received address at the convention that nominated John Kerry, which gave him national exposure.

Obama has remarkable strengths—there are few better public speakers, he has a sharp intellect, and his personal story is a living example of the American Dream fulfilled. As adman Keith Reinhard has noted, "Barack Obama is three things you want in a brand: new, different, and attractive. That's as good as it gets." But, most of all, his success in winning the presidency, as in securing the Democratic nomination, demonstrates how the sun may be setting on the days of top-down, broadcast-based marketing.

Obama refined the online strategy developed by Howard Dean in his unsuccessful run for the Democratic nomination in 2004. Dean proved that it is possible to raise large sums of money in very small donations over the Internet. Obama, without benefit of a national organization and facing opponents with long-standing ties to major donors, had little choice but to follow in Dean's web tracks. He even hired the people who built Dean's Internet operations. But he also brought in one of the founders of Facebook, Chris Hughes. Just twenty-four years old when he left Facebook to join the Obama campaign, Hughes is unassuming and looks like any other college-aged kid who likes to fool around with computers, though he holds options that are potentially worth tens of millions.

What Hughes brought to the campaign was a strategy based less on connecting with potential supporters than on connecting them with each other. Initially, the website he developed, MyObama.com, was dedicated to a single state—Iowa. But it was the connective tissue that gave people the sense they were part of something important. And it was the engine that mobilized people to call their friends, set up neighborhood meetings, and attend the all-important caucuses.

When Obama won in Iowa, people in other states flocked to the MyObama website, which was then ready to organize them into "virtual precincts," based on where they lived, what issues interested them most, or their social connections. The Internet became the engine of a sophisticated "microtargeting" program, which used powerful analytical tools to identify potential supporters. But the key was always to facilitate their involvement, not to push anything on them. Obama's online strategy was guided by three principles: keep it real, keep it local, and keep it moving.

KEEP IT REAL

Few experiences are as artificial as running for president. Candidates are surrounded by Secret Service agents, handlers, and advisers. Every gesture, every utterance, every wardrobe choice is recorded and analyzed. For most people, the candidate is a photo in the paper, an image on television, a body hurtling along a rope line, or a small speck at the front of a huge crowd. Distance and celebrity seem to be baked into the process.

The Obama campaign went through the ritual moves to "humanize" the candidate, to make him seem like the better choice to share a beer with. Obama and his family appeared on the cover of *People* and *Us Weekly* magazines and submitted to an interview with *Access Hollywood*. The candidate danced on *Ellen* and traded wisecracks on *The Colbert Report*. His wife helped cohost *The View* in a sundress that could have come off a rack at Macy's. The strategy seemed to work—an Associated Press–Yahoo! News poll timed for Fourth of July newspapers in 2008 reported that 52 percent of Americans would like to invite Barack Obama to their summer barbecue versus the 45 percent who would extend the invite to John McCain.[5]

But what kept the Obama campaign real was not so much the carefully orchestrated "he's a celebrity just like us" campaign as the candidate's unerring ear for the dominant pitch of current discourse. After 9/11, many pundits opined, "Irony is dead." It seemed we would never laugh again. But in the years since, not taking ourselves too seriously gained new currency. People tend to trust those who acknowledge that they are in on the joke. Fake newsman Jon Stewart and phony bloviator Stephen Colbert are the current champions of the technique. Obama's sense of humor can be just as sardonic, whether participating in a *Saturday Night Live* Halloween sketch in an Obama mask or chiding John McCain for not remembering how many homes he owns. One early campaign video showed him warning reporters trailing him on a door-to-door meet-and-greet to "stay off people's grass" just after a solemn-voiced announcer promised a strong environmental policy. He knows how to use language that echoes off marble walls, but he also knows it can be just as valuable to poke fun at himself. Most of all, his cool, unruffled demeanor is perfectly attuned to the screens on which most people see him.

KEEP IT LOCAL

Keeping things local means that the Obama campaign does not have a single website, but a family of coordinated sites that move together like the arms on a starfish. Keeping it real means the websites speak in the voices of regular people with regular concerns. The sites are friendly and accessible to everybody. And major announcements, such as the name of his running mate, were released via text message to supporters before being sent to national media. (Of course, the choice had also leaked before the roughly ten million people on Obama's e-mail list received the message.)

The main site—BarackObama.com—featured a blog by campaign workers, constant news updates, position papers on every conceivable issue, videos, photos, downloadable ringtones and widgets, and a calendar of upcoming events, not only of the candidate but of seemingly all his supporters. The site added material so often there was always a reason to come back. And much of the material came from the sister sites. On MyBarack, Obama supporters could create their own blogs around platform issues, send policy recommendations directly to the campaign, set up their own mini-fund-raising site, organize an event, even use a phone-bank widget to get call lists and scripts to make calls from home. In addition, there were Obama microsites for people with particular interests, such as Asian Americans, environmentalists, people of faith, and veterans. Not to mention a microsite for every U.S. state and territory, some of which couldn't even vote in the presidential election.

But in addition to creating a community for its supporters, the Obama campaign also tapped into social networks people had set up for other reasons. It participated in online communities such as Facebook, MySpace, YouTube, BlackPlanet, AsianAve, and FaithBase. The Obama profile on BlackPlanet had nearly 500,000 "friends." The campaign also took advantage of messages created by others. The "Yes We Can" mash-up by will.i.am of Black Eyed Peas cost the campaign nothing and became an online hit, with more than twenty million plays on YouTube.

On the other hand, the campaign demonstrated remarkable restraint and a deep understanding of the Internet, when an actress and self-styled "Obama Girl" posted a video of herself seductively singing "I've got a crush on Obama" to a montage of the candidate's photos. The video turned out to be the brainchild of an ad exec not connected to either presidential campaign. It was so successful that he produced a whole series of "Obama Girl" videos. When asked about the video by the *Des Moines Register*, Obama said, "It's just one more example of the fertile imagination of the Internet. More stuff like this will be popping up all the time."[6] While the candidate later admitted that the video upset his two young daughters and he wished people would consider such ramifications, *People, Newsweek*, the Associated Press, and AOL all picked it as the Web video of 2007.

"Obama Girl" joined a long list of videos produced by Obama's own staff. He had fifty people producing videos, sometimes in as little as fifteen minutes from shooting to posting online. Obama's campaign posted 1,165 videos online during the Democratic primaries alone, with 14.8 million views on YouTube. The goal was to keep supporters in touch with the candidate through their own medium of choice. So online videos took their place alongside Facebook (where Obama had 1.3 million friends) and Twitter (60,000 followers in mid-2008).[7] But surprisingly, the average age of the videos' viewers was forty-five to fifty-five years old, not the born digital millennials one might expect.

KEEP IT MOVING

Some critics worry that social media can become an end in itself. "At some point doesn't this need to communicate everything anywhere need to translate into doing something somewhere?" asks brand consultant Jonathan Salem Baskin.[8] The "doing" he has in mind is selling something. He pines for the days when "consumers blithely obeyed our commands to buy." Those days probably didn't even exist in the hard-drinking, womanizing, nicotine-stained days depicted in the *Mad Men* television series. But that doesn't mean marketing is no longer about moving people to action.

Obama's social media was entirely directed at turning all that online energy into action offline. Keeping supporters informed gave them the confidence necessary to take action. The campaign constantly reinforced their "reasons to care" and "reasons to share." Daily e-mail blasts addressed the issues most likely on people's minds and read like they came from someone who respected both their intelligence and their time. The campaign encouraged people to sign up for regular text updates on their cell phone. People could even text "health," "education," "Iraq," "jobs," or "reform" to 62263 (O-b-a-m-a) to get specific policy updates. A microsite, FightTheSmear.com, gave supporters the documentation they needed to refute rumors emanating from opposition websites. The campaign also gave supporters practical tools, from lawn signs to schedules of local events and phone banks. The aim of the websites was to get people to take some kind of action, either raising money, making calls, writing letters, or hosting house parties. At campaign events, Obama's staff gave people waiting in line call lists and asked them to dial undecided voters from their cell phones.

Henry Jenkins, codirector of the MIT Comparative Media Studies program, noted that "Obama has constructed not so much a campaign as a movement."[9] The difference is significant—campaigns are top-down, time-bound, and focused on short-term goals; movements are bottom-up, of indeterminate duration, and have long-term goals. Campaigns try to establish connections with the electorate (or customers). Movements capitalize on the connections people already have with each other.

Of course, all the Obama websites included a red "Donate Now" button. But the real point isn't so much the money raised—though the Obama campaign's fund-raising was of historic levels. It's the engagement that followed the smallest donations. The campaign learned that donating online, even in small amounts, created a community of Obama ambassadors. Small donors felt personally connected to a candidate and more likely to volunteer, knock on doors, or make phone calls. In fact, many small donors challenged their friends to contribute. Some challenged friends to donate $10 for every foot of their height plus $1 for every inch. Others went on diets and asked friends to contribute money for every pound they took off. Plus, small contributors could be tapped several times, deepening their relationship with the candidate every time they wrote a check or charged a donation to their credit card.

Even Karl Rove expressed grudging admiration for the way Obama "harnessed the Internet for persuasion, communication and self-directed organization."[10] But Obama's use of social media was more than a campaign tactic; it was an extension of his brand strategy. As a candidate, Obama understood that a brand is more than logos and slogans. It is an empty word into which one pours meaning. It's attaching an idea to something, whether a product, a place, or a person, and then making sure that people's experience of it lives up to that meaning. Logos, slogans, advertising, websites—and everything else that passes for "marketing"—are just tools that reinforce that meaning. Taking a cue from his campaign slogan—which Obama reportedly wasn't crazy about initially—most observers assume that the idea he tried to attach to himself was "change." That idea certainly differentiated him from his two biggest competitors—first Hillary Clinton in the Democratic primaries, then John McCain in the general election.

But the change Obama represents is more than a change in political party. It is a change in political par*ties*. He is perhaps the first postpartisan candidate, and his actions after the election demonstrated that he doesn't consider citizen participation only a campaign tactic. His style of problem solving is to involve people at every level, not only because he's open to new ideas (which he is), but also because he knows the solution to the thorniest problems will require broad consensus and participation. So after the election, his website not only kept supporters up-to-date on his cabinet appointments, it solicited their ideas for change, including an invitation to thousands of mid-December local house meetings. The Obama transition team launched a Change.gov website that encouraged online discussions about issues such as the economy and health care.

In all of this, Obama appeals to voters who have grown tired of ideological posturing and political gridlock. As one of Rudy Giuliani's speechwriters once wrote, probably intending it neither as a compliment nor a prediction, "Obama speaks the language of our contemporary culture and he looks like what's next—the first high-tech, hip-hop president."[11] Obama may have to give up his BlackBerry in the White House, but he is unlikely to abandon the source of his real technological edge. His use of social media wasn't simply an accommodation to what was initially a slim organization with meager funding. It is an expression of the candidate's political philosophy and his brand. His campaign's unofficial slogan captured it best—"Yes we can."

SECRETS OF THE MARKETING MASTERS

Obama probably never took a marketing course, but he instinctively understood the secrets of the marketing masters.

- ☞ *Think Inside Out.* Obama was both product and CMO. He began his campaign by ensuring that everyone on his small, close-knit team had the same understanding of their brand promise and was pulling in the same direction. His only request beyond that was "No drama."

- ☞ *Think Outside In.* Obama and his key lieutenants instituted a customer service model, staffing their headquarters with people who would ensure that requests were fulfilled and questions were answered, not only from the media but also from the supporters they were organizing into a living, functioning community. Their goal was build long-lasting relationships.

☞ *Connect Emotionally.* Obama's very candidacy carried deep and powerful meaning. It represented change, reconciliation, the achievement of the dreams, not just of one man, but also of a country. Through his speeches, writings, and most of all through his use of social media, Obama transformed himself into a symbol of possibilities that lie beyond political parties, ideologies, and shopworn grievances.

The election of 2008 tells us something important about the future direction of marketing. If, as Boorstin suggested, "image" was the dominant marketing paradigm of the last fifty years, perhaps "community" is the new model. The primary function of marketing is still to create meaning, but marketers now share that responsibility with the very people whose needs, desires, and values they seek to serve. Rather than waging "campaigns," they need to start thinking in terms of participating in "movements." And that means they need to find their higher purpose.

That's the ultimate secret of the marketing masters.

THE SECRETS

THINK INSIDE OUT

Run marketing like a professional service.

- Get C-suite agreement on your role and authority.
- Ensure you have the organizational capabilities to fulfill your role.
- Make whatever internal changes you're going to make as quickly as possible.
- Treat C-suite colleagues as internal customers.
- Focus your team on concrete goals to grow revenue and profits.
- Measure everything, including internal customer satisfaction.

Build a marketing culture.

- Spend time to understand the company's existing culture.
- Make sure you're empowered to make the necessary changes.
- Develop C-suite allies.
- Anticipate a multiyear journey if you need to make major changes.
- Look at change from the key players' points of view.
- Build systems to institutionalize the marketing culture.

Become known as the voice of the customer.

- Learn more about the company's customers and prospects than anyone else.
- Identify the core customer with whom you can build an exclusive relationship.
- Bring the voice of your core customer to strategic business discussions.

- Find ways to amplify the customer's voice within the company.
- Ensure your brand promise is reflected in every customer touch point.

Share results that matter—good and bad.

- Speak the language of business.
- Define success in terms that matter to the business.
- Measure the return on marketing investment rigorously.
  - —Focus on three or four metrics that can cascade through the organization.
  - —Use metrics that are particular to your brands.
  - —Track metrics that reflect your impact on customer behavior.
  - —Measure your relative performance against competitors.
  - —Review the appropriateness of metrics annually.
- Invest time in your personal development.
- Build a strong team of creative and analytical professionals.
- Spend time with business colleagues.
- Tie everything to the company's financial results.

THINK OUTSIDE IN

Develop insight into people's needs.

- Define the customer and task to be studied.
- Schedule multiple face-to-face visits in your customer's "natural habitat."
- Reach out especially to customers you wouldn't normally meet.
- Send cross-functional teams equipped with appropriate training and support.
- Capture functional, social, and emotional aspects of the task.
- Be open to unexpected results and input.
- Watch for local tastes and customs relevant to your product.
- Share new insights and information broadly.
- Schedule a debriefing for participants; include others.

Develop insight into businesses' needs.

- Visit customers who use your product in different ways.
- Bring people from a variety of levels and functions.
- Give team members appropriate training and support beforehand.
- Don't turn the visit into a sales call.
- Get into the environment where your product is actually used.
- Schedule multiple visits with customers of different sizes.
- Include people who didn't visit customer in final debriefing.

Turn insight into foresight.

- Assume that customers' needs, desires, and values will evolve.
- Develop forward-sensing mechanisms to spot new trends.
- Schedule personal time to sample popular culture firsthand.
- Engage all employees in spotting trends and opportunities.
- Put R&D staff in direct contact with customers.
- Make multicultural marketing a mainstream activity.
- Involve customers in innovation process.
- Use external R&D resources to supplement and stimulate internal staff.

Build customer listening posts.

- Make it easy for customers to ask questions or make complaints.
- Build dialogue into everything you do.
- Pay special attention to category enthusiasts.
- Monitor third-party channels for comments about your brands.
- Tap your own employees for customer intelligence.
- Consolidate all customer comments and questions for analysis.
- Confirm your firsthand experience with data.

CONNECT EMOTIONALLY

Find your brand's higher purpose.

- Identify your category's generic customer benefit.
- Understand your brand from your customers' perspective.

- Identify your customers' functional, social, and emotional needs.
- Ask how your brand improves people's lives.
- Find your purpose in customers' higher-level needs.
- Make sure your promise is meaningful to customers and credible coming from your brand.
- Earn the commitment of superiors, colleagues, and team members.
- Start small, testing and refining your concepts.
- Use social media to enlist allies.
- Express your brand's higher purpose across every touch point.

Be true to your brand's meaning.

- Align every customer touch point with your brand's meaning.
- Reinforce the emotional and social aspects of your brand's meaning.
- Ensure your brand evolves with your customers' changing needs and values.
- Invite customers to participate in your brand's development.
- Give customers a relevant, engaging, authentic experience.
- Act responsibly, recognizing your power to shape mores.

Cultivate positive "word of mouse" online.

- Learn the ways of the digital world.
- Tightly integrate your company's virtual and real worlds.
- Think in terms of interactions and relationships rather than transactions.
- Engage people wherever their interests overlap with yours.
- Respond quickly to questions and complaints.
- Recognize that social media belongs to customers. You are only a guest.

Cultivate positive word of mouth offline.

- Define specific goals in terms of customer behavior.
- Give people a reason to care and a reason to share.

- Never hide your involvement in word-of-mouth efforts.
- Become a source of intellectual capital for your enterprise customers.
- Use your intellectual capital to integrate your marketing effort.
- Equip customer-contact people to reinforce your intellectual capital platform.

Win people's trust.

- Begin by identifying your brand's stakeholders in addition to customers.
- Listen to stakeholders and to the people they listen to.
- Identify areas where stakeholders' interests intersect with yours.
- Select a neutral area of highest meaning to you and your stakeholders.
- Build a new relationship in that area based on actions, not words.
- Admit missteps quickly, correct them, and give something back.
- Be candid about your self-interest.

Invest in relationships.

- Think of marketing as a platform for creating connections with people.
- Focus significant marketing effort downstream in customer understanding.
- Set aside significant funds for experimentation.
- Reward customer behavior you want to encourage.
- Give customers the tools to manage their relationship with you.
- Create relevant customer experiences that reinforce brand values.
- Take a long view of customer value, but measure it.
- Focus all resources on building enduring customer relationships.

ACKNOWLEDGMENTS

A number of people were extremely generous with their time and insights as they helped me in the research for this book. However, I recognize that naming them might create the impression that they endorse the opinions expressed in the previous pages or somehow share responsibility for any factual errors that evaded my corrective actions. So allow me to make the customary safe harbor declaration: Any errors in these pages are entirely my own, as are the opinions expressed.

With that out of the way, I would like to express my deep appreciation to Bob Liodice, CEO of the Association of National Advertisers, and Burtch Drake, retired CEO of the American Association of Advertising Agencies. Both gentlemen have long been among the marketing industry's most visionary leaders, and they are effective advocates for their respective constituencies.

David Bell, retired CEO of Interpublic, David Kenny, formerly CEO of Digitas and now chief digital officer of parent Publicis; Shelly Lazarus, chair of Ogilvy & Mather Worldwide, and Keith Reinhard, chariman emeritus of DDB Worldwide were among the advertising agency leaders I interviewed. Their perspective on the changing face of marketing was invaluable, as was their advice and guidance.

Beth Comstock of GE, Lauren Flaherty of Nortel, John Hayes of American Express, Tony Hsieh of Zappos, Jon Iwata of IBM, Ben Machtiger of Spencer Stuart, Rob Malcolm of Diageo, Alessandro Monfredi of Unilever, Mich Mathews of Microsoft, Dan Pelson of uPlayMe and formerly of Warner Music, Mary Lou Quinlan of Just Ask a Woman, Jim Speros of Fidelity Investments, and Jim Stengel of P&G were among the senior marketing executives who shared their experiences and wisdom with me. Greg Green of Digitas gave me a firsthand tour of exciting new digital marketing applications. Julie Roehm understandably wouldn't rehash the story of her time at Wal-Mart, but she was generous with her time in discussing larger marketing and career issues. Each of these leaders could be the subject of a whole book. I hope I accurately reported their perspectives.

As two of the leading executive recruiters serving the marketing community, Jane Stevenson of Heidrick & Struggles and Greg Welch of Spencer Stuart have unique perspectives on the state of the practice. I benefited greatly from their suggestions and deep knowledge of best practices and trends.

Gail McGovern, formerly of the Harvard Business School and now CEO of the American Red Cross, was one of the first people I consulted before undertaking my research for this book. Her encouragement and guidance set me on the right path. Michael Goodman of Baruch College is a good friend whose comments on an early draft of this book contributed greatly to its content and organization. Jonathan Struthers, a good friend and vice president of Communications Consulting Worldwide, made a number of helpful suggestions. Similarly, several long conversations with my friend and marketing consultant Bill Feuss helped me organize my approach to several topics.

Abe Jones of AdMedia Partners is a longtime friend who made the transition from advertising to investment banking even more seamlessly than my transition to writing. His extensive experience on nearly all sides of the media landscape provided essential perspective. Similarly, Donovan Neale-May is a new friend who has not only worked closely with many of the marketing masters but has become one himself. His views of marketing and its practitioners are always provocative, perceptive, and wise.

I benefited greatly from the work of a number of marketing consultants, many of whom were generous with their time, especially Ed Landry of Booz Allen Hamilton, Nigel Hollis of Millard Brown, Kevin Clancy of Copernicus Marketing, and John Gilfeather of TNS Research. Esther Novak, founder and CEO of VanguardComm, provided especially helpful guidance on multicultural marketing.

A number of other people rendered invaluable assistance, including Charlotte Otto and Tami Jones of P&G, Gary Sheffer and Renata Hopkins of GE, Mona Williams of Wal-Mart, Mike O'Neill and Joanna Lambert of American Express, Cecilia Coogan of Diageo, Mike Guadagnoli and Karen Zech of Zappos, Josh Bancroft of TinyScreenfuls.com, and Andru Edwards, editor of GearLive.com.

Finally, my wife and partner, Ginny, and my children, Chris, Liz, and Juli, were a source of encouragement and practical advice throughout this project.

—Dick Martin
August 2008

NOTES

Most of the direct quotes in this book were taken from interviews I conducted during 2007 and 2008 with marketing executives at a number of companies and advertising agencies. I also had the benefit of discussions with some of the marketing industry's leading executive recruiters, association leaders, academics, and consultants. And I did independent research on each of the marketers and companies profiled. Some of the source material I consulted is provided below for readers who want to follow up on their own.

INTRODUCTION

1. Some species of fruit flies can live as long as two years, though most have a life span measured in weeks. For information on fruit flies, see the University of Kentucky's entomology website, http://www.ca.uky.edu/entomology/entfacts/ef621.asp (accessed June 23, 2008).

2. William D. Witnauer, Richard G. Rogers, and Jarron Saint Onge wrote an interesting article on the length of Major League Baseball careers in the twentieth century. See "Major League Baseball Career Length in the 20th Century," *Population Research and Policy Review* 26, no. 4 (August 2007): 371–86.

3. Once CMOs started appearing in the "Who's News" column of the *Wall Street Journal*, marketers of every stripe coveted the title. And not just at companies. Nonprofits like the Girl Scouts have CMOs. So does the North Atlantic Treaty Organization, the state of Vermont, and so, once, did the City of New York. By the time Harvard Business School completed a 256-page case study on the position, it was eliminated amidst political infighting. Nevertheless, in the decade the title has been around, other "chiefs" have jumped on the bandwagon, including chief communications officers, chief people officers, and chief information officers. Not to mention chief privacy officers, chief innovation officers, and chief happiness officers.

4. See, for example, Ashok Gupta, et al., "A Model for Studying R&D—Marketing Interface in the Product Innovation Process," *Journal of Marketing* (April 1986).

5. Yankelovich uncovered people's weariness of advertising in a study conducted for the American Association of Advertising Agencies and

presented at its annual conference in 2004. A number of publications covered the meeting. See, for example, Stuart Elliott, "A Survey of Consumer Attitudes Reveals the Depth of the Challenge that the Agencies Face," *New York Times*, April 14, 2004.

6. The estimate of 5,000 commercial messages a day was used in consulting firm Booz Allen Hamilton's report *Beyond the Mass Mailing,* March 2008. Most experts consider this a somewhat inflated estimate based on a loose definition of "commercial messages" to include not only ads (including individual newspaper classified ads), but also packaging, signage, and company logos. Using more conservative criteria, others suggest people are exposed to as few as 500 to 600 commercial messages a day. By any measure, there is little question that Americans at least are exposed to a very high level of advertising, which helps fund almost every source of information, entertainment, and, increasingly, transportation and communications.

7. Bob Gilbreath, the chief marketing strategist for Bridge, a digital unit of direct-marketing agency Wunderman, made the comment in the preamble to a discussion organized by ad agency DDB Worldwide.

8. The accusation of "self-loathing" appeared in an article by Jack Neff, "Top Advertisers Add Meaning to Marketing," *Advertising Age*, May 26, 2008.

9. Seagate's CEO, Bill Watkins, was quoted by Don Clark, "Can a Hard Drive Make a Fashion Statement?" *Wall Street Journal*, January 4, 2008. Watkins was replaced as Seagate CEO in January 2009.

10. Quelch and his colleague Gail McGovern argued that corporate boards should pay more attention to marketing effectiveness in an article for *Directors & Boards*, Spring 2006.

11. Mark Jarvis, CMO of Dell Computer, was quoted by David Kiley and Burt Helm in "The Short Life of the Chief Marketing Officer," *BusinessWeek*, November 29, 2007. Jarvis was replaced as Dell's CMO in January 2009, just twenty months into his tenure.

12. A 2008 survey by the Association of National Advertisers estimated the number of times marketing departments had been reorganized in a seven-year period. See "The Continuously Changing Role of Marketing," published by the ANA in March 2008.

13. "A Modest Proposal: Put CMO Role Out of Its Misery," *Advertising Age*, October 29, 2007.

14. The Institute of International Research surveyed senior U.S. business executives to identify key areas of expertise required by the next generation of business leaders. Marketing was the clear choice, with 31 percent of votes, followed by 20 percent for operations, and 16 percent for financial expertise, 11 percent for sales, and 6 percent for engineering. See www.marketingtoday .com/research/0305/marketing_leaders.htm (accessed August 8, 2008).

CHAPTER 1

1. Flaherty was quoted by Rob Gerlsbeck in "Nortel's Brand Fixer-Upper," *Marketing*, December 10, 2007.

2. "Find Who, Then What" is the title of the second chapter in Jim Collins's best-selling book, *Good to Great* (New York: HarperCollins, 2001). When Anderson Analytics surveyed members of the exclusive Marketing Executives Networking Group in 2007, Collins's book was cited as the book they would most recommend to fellow marketers, followed by Al Ries and Jack Trout's *Positioning* and Steven Covey's *Seven Habits of Highly Effective People*. Collins also appeared on their list of the "top marketing gurus." The others were Seth Godin, Steve Jobs, Peter Drucker, Warren Buffet, David Aaker, Tom Peters, Jack Welch, Malcolm Gladwell, Al Ries, and Phil Kotler.

3. Castro-Wright was interviewed by Ann Zimmerman in "Engineering a Change at Wal-Mart," *Wall Street Journal*, August 12, 2008.

CHAPTER 2

1. Sam Walton is quoted saying this on page 164 of his autobiography, *Made in America,* written with John Huey (New York: Doubleday, 1992).

2. Julie Roehm was quoted by Stuart Eliott and Michael Barbaro in "Rocky Return to the Roots at Wal-Mart," *New York Times*, December 9, 2006.

3. See, for example, a posting in the blog Jezebel, "Wal-Tart Julie Roehm's Sad, Slutty Fight with Wal-Mart Is Over," http://jezebel.com/gossip/publicity-whores/wal+tart-julie-roehms-sad-slutty-fight-with-wal+mart-is-over-319239.php (accessed July 10, 2008).

4. The question of Roehm's possible clash with Wal-Mart's "old boys' network" was posed in the Right Pundits blog. See www.rightpundits.com/?p=239 (accessed July 10, 2008).

5. Roehm was named one of the "distinguished young alumni" of the Chicago Graduate School of Business in 2006. In connection with the recognition, the school's alumni magazine published an interview with her under the title "Pushing Boundaries in Marketing." See www.chicagogsb.edu/news/daa2006/04-roehm.aspx (accessed July 10, 2008).

6. Roehm was interviewed by Robert Berner for his *BusinessWeek* story, "My Year at Wal-Mart" (February 12, 2007) before a financial settlement with the company forbade discussion of her experiences there.

7. For more on Wal-Mart's sales training and development, see the company's website, http://Wal-Martstores.com/Careers/7740.aspx (accessed July 10, 2008).

8. O'Hare was quoted by Matthew Creamer, "Death of the Rock Star CMO," *Ad Age,* January 22, 2007.

9. See "What You Need to Know about Exchange 12," *Windows IT Pro*, May 2005, http://windowsitpro.com/article/articleid/45880/what-you-need-to-know-about-ex change-12-e12.html (accessed August 11, 2008).

CHAPTER 3

1. Sinha was quoted in Johannes Bussmann, Gregor Harter, and Evan Hirsh, "Results-Driven Marketing: A Guide to Growth and Profits," *Business + Strategy*, January 1, 2006. Sinha became the CMO of Zurich Financial Services Group in April 2007.

2. All data are from *The Evolved CMO*, a report prepared by Forrester Research and the Heidrick & Struggles executive search firm. The full report is available at www.heidrick.com/NR/rdonlyres/AC86DF4D-DA48-41A4-97E4-637B3E92253E/0/TheEvolvedCMO.pdf (accessed August 11, 2008).

3. Conklyn was quoted in "USAA: Soldiering On in Insurance," *Business Week*, March 5, 2007.

4. Hansen was quoted by Jennifer Saranow, "Gap Reorders Its Priorities," *Wall Street Journal*, July 9, 2008.

5. Klein described his strategy in an address to the Harvard Business School Marketing Club in May 2004. See Wendy Swearingen's report in HBS's *Working Knowledge, for Business Leaders*, "Can Burger King Rekindle the Sizzle," http://hbswk.hbs.edu/archive/4105.html (accessed May 31, 2008).

6. Chidsey was quoted by Janet Adamy in "Boss Talk," *Wall Street Journal*, April 2, 2008.

7. Donald Calne, *Within Reason: Rationality and Human Behavior* (New York: Pantheon, 1999), 236.

8. The meaning of the "golden thread" here is from the Total Quality Movement, where it means aligning internal processes to achieve customer satisfaction.

CHAPTER 4

1. "Bollocks" is a word of Anglo-Saxon origin, meaning "testicles." The word is often used figuratively in English, as a noun to mean "nonsense" or conversely to mean "top quality" or "perfection." Malcolm clearly intended it in its original meaning as an expletive.

2. See Lloyd Trufelman, "Death by Data," *Advertising Age*, June 18, 2007.

3. Christopher Vollmer, *Always On: Advertising, Marketing, and Media in an Era of Consumer Control* (New York: McGraw-Hill, 2008), 116.

4. For more on Diageo's approach to marketing, see an interview by Rob O'Rehan and Samar Farah for *CMO* magazine that was never published, but is available on the Internet at http://magnostic.wordpress.com/best-of-cmo/

interview-rob-malcolm-president-of-global-marketing-sales-and-innovation-at-diageo/ (accessed August 11, 2008).

5. Diageo's "Dogs and Stars" chart owes much to the Boston Consulting Group's famous "Growth-Share Chart." In fact, it was originally proposed by a BCG alumnus working within the company's United Kingdom marketing group.

6. Explaining how to build a marketing dashboard is beyond the scope of this book, not to mention the author's capabilities. However, there are a number of consultants who specialize in leading companies through the process. A good place to start is the website for Marketing NPV, an advisory firm that specializes in this work. See www.marketingnpv.com.

7. Tim Calkins and Derek D. Rucker, "Don't Overemphasize ROI as Single Measure of Success," *Advertising Age*, February 4, 2008.

8. Paul W. Farris, Neil T. Bendle, Phillip E. Pfeifer, and David Reibstein, *Marketing Metrics: 50+ Metrics Every Executive Should Master* (Upper Saddle River, NJ: Wharton School Publishing, 2006).

9. The Net Promoter Score is a registered trademark of Satmetrix Systems, Bain & Company, and Fred Reichheld. The concept was first described in an article Reichheld wrote for the December 2003 issue of the *Harvard Business Review*, "The One Number You Need To Grow," and in his subsequent book, *The Ultimate Question* (Boston: Harvard Business School Press, 2006). Despite its popularity, it is controversial among researchers and academics, who have critiqued the concept and questioned the research on which it is based. See, for example, Keiningham, Cooil, Andreassen, and Aksoy, "A Longitudinal Examination of Net Promoter and Firm Revenue Growth," *Journal of Marketing* (July 2007).

10. In a recent joint study of CMOs by Forrester Research and Heidrick & Struggles, more than half the respondents said building a strong relationship with the CFO was very important to them, second only to the head of sales among all their peers. Unfortunately, they also rated it as the second worst relationship. See Jennifer Rooney, "It's about the Bottom Line for CMOs," *Advertising Age*, May 5, 2008.

11. See Spencer Stuart, "Isolating the Marketing DNA: The Essential Skills and Qualities of the New CMO," May 2008, available at http://content .spencerstuart.com/sswebsite/pdf/lib/cmoSumm_08.pdf.

CHAPTER 5

1. Anthony Bianco, "The Vanishing Mass Market," *BusinessWeek*, July 12, 2004.

2. Ibid.

3. The single-use packets of Tide Clean White were more than just a packaging

gimmick. According to an analysis by *Chemical and Engineering News*, Tide Clean White includes "a hardness-tolerant balance of surfactants and polymers, increased nonionic-to-cationic surfactant ratio, and boosted soil suspension polymer and brightener levels." See "Soaps and Detergents," *Chemical and Engineering News* 83, no. 4 (January 24, 2005): 15–20.

4. James Stengel, Andrea Dixon, and Chris Allen, "Listening Begins at Home," *Harvard Business Review* (November 2003). For more on P&G's approach to customer immersion and innovations, see also Geofrey Precourt, ed., *CMO Thought Leaders* (Booz Allen Hamilton, 2007); an interview with Chief Technical Officer Gilbert Coyd, "360 Degree Innovation," *BusinessWeek*, October, 11, 2004; an interview with CMO James Stengel, "It's All About Targeting," *BusinessWeek*, July 12, 2004; an article on P&G's CEO A.G. Lafley, "Teaching an Old Dog New Tricks," *Fortune*, May 31, 2004; "Selling P&G," *Fortune*, September 5, 2007; and Larry Huston and Nabil Sakaab, "P&G's New Innovation Model," *Harvard Business School Working Knowledge* (March 20, 2006).

5. Buck Weaver was quoted in "Thought Starter," *Time,* November 14, 1938.

6. Peter Drucker, *Management Tasks, Responsibilities and Practices* (New York: Harper and Row, 1974), 61.

7. Many of these practices, at use at P&G and other consumer companies, owe much to a concept called "empathic design" first described in the *Harvard Business Review* in 1997. See Dorothy Leonard and Jeffrey F. Rayport, "Spark Innovation through Empathic Design," *Harvard Business Review* (November–December 1997).

8. McCracken writes the blog "This Blog Sits at the Intersection of Anthropology and Economics," which is full of astute observations on marketing and contemporary culture. See www.cultureby.com/trilogy/. This quote is from a posting on September 18, 2008.

9. McQuillen founded and runs the customer experience team for Credit Suisse. His work has been featured in publications such as *Fast Company*, the *International Herald Tribune,* and many others. He is also a frequent speaker on the topic of usability and customer experience. For links and more, see his blog, http://davidmcquillen.com/articles-speaking/ (accessed August 11, 2008).

10. These five principles are drawn from an excellent description of IDEO's approach to "design thinking," *The Art of Innovation* by Tom Kelley and Jonathan Littman (New York: Doubleday, 2001).

CHAPTER 6

1. Clayton M. Christensen, Scott Cook, and Taddy Hall, "Marketing Malpractice: The Cause and the Cure," *Harvard Business Review* (December 2005).

2. Becton, Dickinson later reentered the medical systems field with more success. This particular episode, which took place in the 1980s, is entertainingly described in a magazine article one of the participants wrote years later. See Ralph Grabowsko, "The Board's Fiduciary Responsibility To Market Research," *Corporate Board*, May/June 1998.

3. See Hueston's blog, "Tactical Leadership," http://blogs.sun.com/tacticalleadership/entry/breaking_the_fourth_wall (accessed May 10, 2008).

4. Watkins was interviewed by Don Clark in "Can a Hard Drive Make a Fashion Statement?" *Wall Street Journal*, January 4, 2008.

5. The story of HP's operating room observations is told in Dorothy Leonard and Jeffrey Rayport's seminal *Harvard Business Review* article on empathic design.

6. Schiech told his story to Booz Allen Hamilton consultants. See Barry Jaruzelski and Kevin Dehoff, "The Customer Connection: The Global Innovation 1000," *Strategy + Business*, December 2007, www.strategy-business.com/press/article/07407.

7. Hill-Rom has provided Clayton Christensen fodder for articles and classroom discussions. This particular anecdote appears in an article he co-wrote for MIT's *Sloan Management Review*. See Christensen, Anthony, Berstell, and Nitterhouse, "Finding the Right Job For Your Product," *MIT Sloan Management Review*, Spring 2007.

8. For more on the *gemba* concept and other aspects of customer research, visit Glenn Mazur's website, www.mazur.net.

9. DuPont's marketing has been the subject of numerous articles and even books. Interested readers will find the following works of particular interest: Regina Lee Blaszczyk, "Selling Synthetics: DuPont's Marketing of Fabrics and Fashions in Postwar America," in the October 2006 issue of *Business History Review*. Susannah Hadley's *Nylon: The Story of a Fashion Revolution* (John Hopkins University Press, 2000).

10. Homlish was interviewed by Jennifer Rooney in "Why CMOs Don't Last," *Advertising Age*, April 7, 2008.

11. Marketing professor Edward F. McQuarrie has written broadly on the subject of "customer visits." See, for example, *Customer Visits: Building a Better Market Focus*, third ed. (Armonk, NY: M.E. Sharpe, 2008).

12. Jim Guerard is vice president of product management and product marketing for the tools business at Macromedia, which includes the Studio, Flash, Dreamweaver, Fireworks, and FreeHand products. In his blog, Guerard described the customer-focused process Macromedia used in developing the Studio 8 software tools for interactive design. It involved visiting nearly 100 customer sites, talking to over 500 users, and logging at least 1,500

Macromedia employee hours with users. See http://www.adobe.com/devnet/
logged_in/jguerard_studio8.html (accessed July 23, 2008).

CHAPTER 7

1. Drucker was interviewed by George Gendron in "Flashes of Genius," *Inc.*,
   May 1996, http://www.inc.com/magazine/19960515/2083_pagen_2.html
   (accessed June 1, 2008).

2. The research was described in an Association of National Advertisers (ANA)
   White Paper, "The Continuously Changing Role of Marketing," published in
   March 2008.

3. For more on the marketing-R&D interface, see Ashok Gupta, et al., "A
   Model for Studying R&D-Marketing Interface in the Product Innovation
   Process," *Journal of Marketing* (April 1986).

4. Levitt made this observation in his now classic article "Marketing Myopia,"
   Harvard Business Review, July 2004.

5. Sara Lee's CEO, Brenda Barnes, was quoted by Julie Jargon in "Kiwi Goes
   Beyond Shine," *Wall Street Journal*, December 20, 2007.

6. Huston was interviewed at the University of Pennsylvania's Wharton School
   in June 2007. Listen to the podcast, which is available at http://knowledge
   .wharton.upenn.edu/article.cfm?articleid=1765 (accessed August 11, 2008).

7. Ibid.

8. Larry Huston and Nabil Sakaab, "P&G's New Innovation Model," *Harvard
   Business School Working Knowledge*, March 20, 2006.

9. Quoted in Geoffrey Precourt, ed., *CMO Thought Leaders: The Rise of the
   Strategic Marketer* (Booz Allen Hamilton, 2007), 257.

10. For more on how Xerox is involving customers in product development, see
    "Xerox Refocuses On Its Customers," by Nanette Byrnes in *Business Week*,
    April 18, 2007, l.

11. See, for example, "Del Monte To Take Its Cues From Moms," by Abbey
    Klassen, *Advertising Age*, July 2, 2007.

12. Target's CMO, Michael Francis, was profiled by Jennifer Reingold in
    "Target's Inner Circle," *Fortune*, March 18, 2008.

13. Michael Francis's role in recreating a Paris flea market within Marshall
    Field's Chicago store is described in Laura Rowley, *On Target: How the
    World's Hottest Retailer Hit a Bullseye* (Hoboken, NJ: John Wiley and Sons,
    2003), 26.

14. Waters wrote a book on trends entitled *The Hummer and the Mini:
    Navigating the Contradictions of the New Trend Landscape* (New York:
    Penguin, 2006), but this quote was printed on a Starbucks grande cup as the

110th conversation starter in its series of pithy sayings and opinions titled "The Way I See It."

15. Francis described the hermit crab race to Ann Zimmerman in "Staying on Target," *Wall Street Journal*, May 7, 2007.

16. Method's breakthrough with Target was described by Bridget Finn, "Selling Cool in a Bottle of Soap," *Business 2.0*, December 2003.

17. Francis was quoted by Ann Zimmerman, "Staying on Target," *Wall Street Journal*, May 7, 2007.

18. "The Growing Complexity of America's Racial Mosaic" is one in a series of the Rand Corporation's Policy Briefs on Population Matters. See the complete series on the Rand website: www.rand.org/labor/popmatters/publications.html#immigrate (accessed August 11, 2008).

19. The Center for Hispanic Marketing Communication at Florida State University has done groundbreaking work in multicultural studies. See, for example, "Hispanic Marketing Communication: A Cultural Perspective," by Felipe Korzenny and Betty Ann Korzenny, 2005.

20. For example, Spanish-language television network Univision was the most-watched network in prime time during the last week of July 2008 among adults eighteen to thirty-four years of age, beating ABC, CBS, NBC, FOX, and the CW. It aired ten of the top twenty programs, regardless of language, among adults eighteen to thirty-four and seven of the top twenty among adults eighteen to forty-nine.

21. The full story of Pepsi's groundbreaking multicultural effort is told by Stephanie Capperral in *The Real Pepsi Challenge* (New York: Free Press, 2007). It's probably not coincidental that the company's current CEO is a woman of Indian descent.

22. The Lego Mindstorms story has been told in numerous newspaper and magazine articles. Among the best is "Lego Mindstorm: The Structure of an Engineering (R)evolution," by David Mindell of the MIT Media Lab. See web.mit.edu/6.933/www/Fall2000/LegoMindstorms.pdf. For more on the Mindstorm User Panel, see *Wired* magazine, "Geeks in Toyland," by Brian Koerner, February 2006, and the company's website for the expanded and renamed "Developers Panel," http://mindstorms.lego.com/MeetMDP/.

CHAPTER 8

1. Kirby Drysen, "Cisco's Customer-Centric Corporate Culture," Creating Loyalty Library, http://www.creatingloyalty.com/story.cfm?article_id=561 &searchtext=listen (accessed May 31, 2008).

2. Transversal's 2008 study evaluated 100 leading U.K. companies in the banking, telecoms, insurance, travel, consumer electronics, grocery retail,

fashion retail, CD/DVD retail, consumer electronics retail, and utilities sectors for their ability to answer simple routine questions, For more, see Transversal's website: www.transversal.com/html/news/viewpress.php? article = 81.

3. Kevin Hillstrom, president of MineThatData, actually projected that Zappos would beat their $1 billion sales goal by $60 million. Of course, that was in the spring before the financial crisis rattled the stock market, the banking system, and personal budgets across the country. Nevertheless, Zappos's revenue growth has been impressive. For more on Hillstrom's analysis, see his website: www.minethatdata.blogspot.com/2008/04/zappos-sales-trajectory-and-customer.html.

4. Scott Broetzmann was quoted by Jenna McGregor in "Consumer Vigilantes," *Business Week*, February 21, 2008.

5. Cabela's was profiled in *Business Week*'s first ranking of "customer service champions" in March 2007. See: www.businessweek.com/magazine/content/07_10/b4024001.htm.

6. Deborah Meyer was quoted by Dale Buss in "Chrysler Opens Online Post for Listening to Customers," *Edmunds Auto Observer*, May 6, 2008, http://www.autoobserver.com/2008/05/chrysler-opens-online-post-for-listening-to-customers.html (accessed on June 3, 2008).

7. From the Forrester Research CMO Group research project "The Marketing of Marketing," available at www.forrester.com/role_based/pdfs/Marketing_Of_Marketing_ReportBrief.pdf (accessed August 11, 2008).

8. FairWinds published a white paper on the topic, "The Power of Internet Gripe Sites," as part of their *Perspectives* series on August 13, 2008. See www.fairwindspartners.com/en/newsroom/perspectives/vol-3-issue-6/background-on-direct-navigation (accessed August 25, 2008).

9. Anderson was quoted by Beth Snyder Bullik in "What All That Chatter Is Really Saying," *Advertising Age*, March 8, 2008.

10. Derived from George S. Day and Prakash Nedungadi, "Managerial Representations of Competitive Advantage," *Journal of Marketing* (April 1994).

CHAPTER 9

1. Lagnado and Arntz were interviewed in a special edition of *Red*, Ogilvy's in-house magazine, published in 2008.

2. For more on Dove's Campaign for Real Beauty, see www.campaignforrealbeauty.com (accessed February 13, 2008).

3. From a Mintel research report, "Anti-Aging Skincare in the United States," April 2008.

4. Reinhard, chairman emeritus of the DDB ad agency, created McDonald's iconic "You deserve a break today" campaign based on his intuitive understanding of what the fast-food restaurant meant to busy parents. Similarly, "Like a good neighbor, State Farm is there," capitalized on the neighborliness of insurance company's local agents.

5. Castro-Wright was interviewed by Ann Zimmerman in "Engineering a Change at Wal-Mart," *Wall Street Journal*, August 12, 2008.

6. See Ernest Becker, *The Structure of Evil*, part 2, chap. 9, "A Brief Ontology of Love" (New York: George Braziller, 1968).

7. Benoît Heilbrunn, "Cultural Branding Between Utopia and A-topia," in *Brand Culture*, ed. Jonathan E. Schroeder and Miriam Salzer-Mörling (London, New York: Routledge, 2006).

8. CDW Research quoted in Micheline Maynard, "Say 'Hybrid' and People Will Hear 'Prius,'" *Wall Street Journal*, June 24, 2007.

9. S.M. McClure, et al., "Neural Correlates of Behavioral Preference for Culturally Familiar Drinks," *Neuron* 44 (October 14, 2004): 379–87.

10. Ibid.

11. Alan Wolfe, *The Human Difference: Animals, Computers, and the Necessity of Social Science* (Berkeley: University of California Press, 1993).

12. Lagnado explained the thinking behind the Real Beauty campaign in an article she wrote for the December 6, 2004, issue of *Advertising Age*, "Getting Real about Beauty."

13. Katherine White and Darren Dahl, "Are All Out-Groups Created Equal?" *Journal of Consumer Research* (December 2007): 525–26.

14. See Schroeder and Salzer-Morling, *Brand Culture*.

15. Gregory was quoted by Al Ehrbar in "Breakaway Brands," *Fortune*, October 31, 2005.

16. Toward the end of the last Ice Age, what is now Europe was inhabited by a people known as the Magdalenians who painted cave walls with images of large wild animals such as bison, horses, aurochs, and deer. The oldest of these paintings, in southern France, dates to 32,000 B.C. Since the caves show no signs of ongoing habitation, the paintings don't appear to have been decorations for living areas. Some experts believe they were a way of transmitting information, such as the game to be found in the area. If that's true, they would have constituted the world's first advertising. See Jean-Marie Chauvet, *Dawn of Art: The Chauvet Cave* (New York: Harry N. Abrams, 1996).

17. The CEO of Victoria's Secret was quoted by Amy Merrick in "We're Too Sexy," *Wall Street Journal*, March 3, 2008.

18. In the best seller he wrote with consultant Ram Charan, *The Game-Changer: How You Can Drive Revenue and Profit Growth with Innovation* (New York: Crown, 2008), Lafley actually calls it "abductive thinking," as opposed to inductive (based on directly observable facts) and deductive (logic and analysis, typically based on past evidence). But he also points out that abductive thinking is taught in design schools, while the other forms of analysis are the stuff of business schools. Design thinking became the shorthand in use at P&G.

CHAPTER 10

1. Bill Breen, "Who Do You Love?" *Fast Company*, May 2007.

2. Clorox's Vlahos was quoted in "Lost and Found," *The Hub*, July 1, 2008, http://www.hubmagazine.com/ (accessed August 11, 2008).

3. *Condé Nast Traveler*'s 2008 Readers Poll ranked destinations across a host of categories. Among countries, India ranked second, following New Zealand, but ahead of Italy, Thailand, and Brazil, which rounded off the top five. For more, see www.cntraveller.com/ReadersAwards/2008/Countries/.

4. Howard Schultz and Dori Jones Yang, *Pour Your Heart Into It* (New York: Hyperion, 1997), 51.

5. Rob Huffman was interviewed by Brad Reese in *Network World*, July 3, 2007, http://napps.networkworld.com/community/comment/reply/17100 (accessed August 11, 2008).

6. As reported by the Editors Weblog, a publication of the World Association of Newspapers, Zuckerberg made the comment at the World Economic Forum in January 2007 when a newspaper publisher asked him how he could build an online community. Zuckerberg's answer was concise and to the point: "You can't." See www.editorsweblog.org/news/2007/09/news_per sonalization_at_the_sun_and_tele.php (accessed November 27, 2008).

7. Wales was quoted in Neil Perkin's excellent presentation on social media, which is available on Slideshare, www.slideshare.net/neilperkin/whats-next-in-media?src=embed. Perkin's blog is also worth following: www.neilperkin .typepad.com.

8. For more on Dove's use of online media, see a working paper by Harvard Business School professors John A. Deighton and Leora Kornfeld, "Digital Interactivity: Unanticipated Consequences for Markets, Marketing, and Consumers," released in September 2007 and available at http://hbswk.hbs .edu/item/5783.html (accessed August 12, 2008).

CHAPTER 11

1. Quoted by Rana Foroohar in *Newsweek International*, "Listening to the Kids," August 25, 2003.

2. Reed Hastings was quoted by Bob Garfield in *Advertising Age*, "Your Data with Destiny," September 15, 2008.

3. Lévy was interviewed by *The Guardian* for "Tell Me the Future," May 3, 2007.

4. The survey was commissioned by Deloitte & Touche USA LLP and conducted online by an independent research company between August 28 and September 6, 2007. The survey polled a sample of 3,331 consumers over the age of sixteen.

5. "User-Generated Content," Report of the Pew Internet & American Life Project, November 6, 2006.

6. Pete Blackshaw, "The Pocket Guide to Consumer-Generated Media," June 28, 2005, http://www.clickz.com/showPage.html?page=3515576 (accessed June 24, 2008).

7. Jo Brown, Amanda J. Broderick, and Nick Lee, "Word of Mouth Communication Within Online Communities: Conceptualizing the Online Social Network," *Journal of Interactive Marketing* 21, no. 3 (2007): 2–20.

8. Robert Metcalfe, one of the inventors of Ethernet technology and a cofounder of 3Com, observed as long ago as 1980 that the value of a network is proportional to the square of the number of users of the system (n^2). It is based on the fact that the number of unique connections in a network is the number of nodes (n) times that number minus one ($n-1$), divided by two, or $n(n-1)/2$, which is n^2. George Gilder termed the observation "Metcalfe's Law" in the September 1993 issue of *Forbes ASAP*.

9. The Aberdeen Group studies businesses' use of technology. One of its analysts wrote a report that included a review of the social media practices of best-in-class companies. See Alex Jefferies, "Customer 2.0: The Business Implications of Social Media," June 2008.

10. The entire exchange is described in greater detail in Tom Vander Well's blog at http://www.qaqna.com/2006/11/service_its_not_1.html (accessed June 25, 2008).

11. According to ZDNet's "IT Facts," the Internet's total audience grew 11 percent in June 2008 while the audience for social networking sites grew 25 percent. See www.itfacts.biz/category/web-traffic (accessed September 16, 2008).

12. Garfield wrote an excellent overview of widgets in the December 1, 2008, issue of *Advertising Age*.

13. Check out Rubel's blog at www.micropersuasion.com.

14. Jeff Jarvis, "Dell Learns to Listen," *BusinessWeek*, October 17, 2007.

15. Ibid.

16. Prospectiv's survey results were described in a news release issued on January 8, 2008. It indicated that 76 percent of consumers would like to receive e-mail on savings offers and 47 percent would subscribe to an online newsletter. It also indicated that 27 percent gather product information from e-newsletter subscriptions versus 25 percent from search engines, 12 percent from newspaper and magazine sites, and 8 percent from comparison-shopping sites. Among the 86 percent of consumers who didn't use branded sites, 67 percent weren't aware of them, 17 percent said they weren't very helpful, and 16 percent just didn't trust them. See http://www.prospectiv .com/press142.jsp (accessed June 24, 2008).

17. O'Connell's posting appeared in her blog, "Generational Tension," July 9, 2008. See www.businessweek.com/business_at_work/generation_gap/ archives/2008/07/reverse_mentori.html (accessed August 15, 2008).

CHAPTER 12

1. Hugh MacLeod is a former advertising copywriter who now publishes a thoroughly entertaining blog, which consists primarily of the cartoons he draws on the back of business cards, commenting on marketing. He posted this entry on May 23, 2008: www.gapingvoid.com/Moveable_Type/archives/ 004557.html (accessed August 11, 2008).

2. Sarah Webster, "Oprah Buzz Works No Magic for Pontiac G6," *Detroit Free Press*, March 22, 2005.

3. Richard Edelman is the CEO of Wal-Mart's public relations agency. He made this comment in his blog, "6 a.m.," under the heading "A Commitment," on October 16, 2006, about a week after the story broke. See http://www.edel man.com/speak_up/blog/archives/2006/10/ (accessed August 11, 2008).

4. From the Word of Mouth Association website: www.womma.org/values/ (accessed June 12, 2008).

5. The role of opinion leaders in communications was first introduced by Paul Lazarsfeld, Bernard Berelson, and Hazel Gaudet in *The People's Choice*, a 1944 study focused on the process of decision making during a Presidential election campaign.

6. Duncan Watts, "Is Justin Timberlake a Product of Cumulative Advantage?" *New York Times*, April 15, 2007.

7. Watts was quoted in a February 2008 *Fast Company* magazine article, "Is The Tipping Post Toast?"

8. Much of what I learned about Tremor came from a presentation Knox gave at a meeting of the CMO Council in December 2007, but interested readers can learn more from the company's own website, www.business.tremor .com/index.html.

9. Knox's approach is in line with the academic literature. Ernest Dichter suggested four main motivations for word-of-mouth communications in a seminal article in the *Harvard Business Review* ("How Word of Mouth Advertising Works," November–December 1966): *positive or negative product involvement, self-involvement (i.e., the need to gain attention), other involvement (i.e., the need to help others),* and *message involvement* (genuine interest in an ad). Later studies elaborated on these motives. Knox's approach collapses these motives into two.

10. Julian Villanueva, Shijin Yoo, and Dominique Hanssens, "The Impact of Marketing-Induced Versus Word-of-Mouth Customer Acquisition on Customer Equity Growth," *Journal of Marketing* (April 2008).

11. Roper Reports (Winter 2004) indicated that nine out of ten people consider other people like themselves their best source of information on purchases. An A.C. Nielsen global survey in 2007 showed that 78 percent of people consider the recommendations of other consumers "trustworthy," compared with just 63 percent of people considering newspaper ads, the second-most-trusted medium, trustworthy. (See http://www.nielsen.com/media/2007/pr_071001.html.)

12. The study was sponsored by Jack Morton Associates and consisted of online interviews with 700 executives in the United States and the United Kingdom between March and April 2007, combined with interviews with 2,188 executives participating in Keller Fay's TalkTrack tracking study of word of mouth.

13. The Marketing 50, which was founded by a former Spencer Stuart recruiter, is by invitation only and open only to one member per industry. It's member list is strictly private, but it does maintain a website—www.w50.com—that describes its activities in a quiet and discreet manner. The CMO Club is open to any senior marketing people. For more information, see its website, http://www.thecmoclub.blogspot.com/.

14. Constellation Wine's "Project Genome" research project was conducted by Copernicus Marketing Consulting (www.copernicusmarketing.com). For more detail and a copy of the full report, see www.cbrands.com/CBI/constellationbrands/OurBusiness/Wine/ (accessed December 5, 2008).

15. David Brooks, "The Cognitive Age," *New York Times*, May 2, 2008.

CHAPTER 13

1. Stengel initially made this observation in a discussion with Geoff Colvin of *Fortune* magazine at the Time & Life Building in New York. Edited excerpts were published in the magazine on September 5, 2007. In a later discussion with me in mid-2008, he reconfirmed his belief that winning people's trust remains one of the greatest challenges facing marketers today.

2. Philip Kotler has written seven marketing textbooks, which are available in eighteen languages in fifty-eight countries. *Marketing Management* is considered his seminal work and is probably the most widely used text in MBA programs. The thirteenth edition was written with Kevin Lane Keller (Upper Saddle River, NJ: Pearson Prentice Hall, 2009). For recent, easy-to-digest summaries of Kotler's marketing wisdom, see *According to Kotler: The World's Foremost Marketing Authority Answers Your Questions* (New York: AMACOM, 2005); *Marketing Insights from A to Z* (Hoboken, NJ: John Wiley and Sons, 2003); or *Kotler on Marketing* (New York: Free Press, 1999).

3. David C. Court, Mark G. Leiter, and Mark A. Loch, "Brand Leverage," *The McKinsey Quarterly*, no. 2 (May 1999).

4. Comstock was quoted in "The Transformer: Beth Comstock," *Business Week*, August 1, 2005.

5. Ibid.

6. Jeffrey R. Immelt, "Growth as a Process," *Harvard Business Review* (June 2006): 64.

7. Claire Atkinson, "The Player: Comstock Took the PR Path to Reach Top Destination at GE," *Advertising Age*, April 14, 2003.

8. Ibid.

9. John A. Byrne, "The Fast Company Interview: Jeff Immelt," *Fast Company*, Issue 96, July 2005.

10. Amanda Griscom Little, "GE's Green Gamble," *Vanity Fair*, July 2006.

11. From an open letter to all Apple iPhone customers on September 6, 2007. See http://www.apple.com/hotnews/openiphoneletter/ (accessed August 11, 2008).

12. Mattel news releases dated August 1 and August 14, 2007. See http://www.shareholder.com/mattel/releases.cfm (accessed August 11, 2008).

13. From a September 21, 2007, BBC News Report. See http://news.bbc.co.uk/2/hi/business/7006599.stm (accessed August 11, 2008).

14. Schumer was quoted by the *New York Times* in "An Apology In China From Mattel," by Louise Story, September 22, 2007.

15. From GE's 2007 Ecomagination Report, 3. See http://ge.ecomagination.com/site/news/media/2007ecoreport.html.

CHAPTER 14

1. McKinsey's analysis is presented in an article in the *McKinsey Quarterly* by David Court, Jonathan Gordon, and Jesko Perry, "Boosting Returns on Marketing Investment," June 2005. They suggest that devoting as much as

25 percent of marketing budgets to carefully structured media and message experimentation is critical to managing risk in the current unstable media environment.

2. From the American Express 2007 10-K filing with the Securities and Exchange Commission.

3. Gary Loveman was a professor at Harvard Business School before becoming Harrah's chief operating officer in 1998. He says he borrowed many of his strategies from some of the case studies he used to teach. He became Harrah's CEO in 2003. For a fuller description of Loveman's strategy, see "Diamonds in the Data Mine," *Harvard Business Review* (May 2003).

4. Prevor was quoted by Cathryn Creno in "Wal-Mart's Sustainability Efforts Draw Praise," *The Arizona Republic*, May 26, 2008. Interestingly, the first sentence of the story paraphrased Immelt's "green is green" slogan. Creno wrote: "Being green and having the green stuff aren't mutually exclusive, according to the world's largest retailer." The article is online at www.az central.com/business/articles/2008/05/26/20080526biz-greenretailers0526-ON.html. *The Perishable Pundit* is online at www.PerishablePundit.com.

5. Ad agency margins have undoubtedly suffered as clients replaced media commissions with negotiated, cost-based fees that, on average, are probably a third lower. Still, the four largest ad agency networks had average operating margins of 12.5 percent in 2007, and that included an outlier (Interpublic) that is still recovering from a series of bad acquisitions and accounting problems. According to *Advertising Age*'s "Agency Report," published on May, 5, 2008, Interpublic's operating margin in 2007 was 5.3 percent; Omnicom's, 13.1 percent, WPP's, 15 percent; and Publicis's, 16.7 percent. Without Interpublic, the four largest ad agency holding companies would have reported operating margins of 15 percent, on a par with the 14 percent reported by management consulting firm Accenture.

AFTERWORD

1. Boorstin's *The Image* (New York: Vintage, 1968) should be required reading for all marketers, along with Walter Lippmann's *Public Opinion* (New York: Harcourt, Brace and Company, 1922). While the examples in both works are dated, their insights into human communication are timeless.

2. See Thomas E. Patterson, *Out of Order: How the Decline of Political Parties and the Growing Power of the News Media Undermine the American Way of Electing Presidents* (New York: Alfred A. Knopf, 1993), 20.

3. Sean Silverthorne, "Does Democracy Need a Marketing Manager?" *Harvard Business School Working Knowledge* (February 11, 2008), http://hbswk .hbs.edu/item/5774.html. See also John Quelch and Katherine Jocz, *Greater*

Good: How Good Marketing Makes for Better Democracy (Boston: Harvard Business School Press, 2007).

4. Cookies are bits of computer code that websites deposit on the computer hard drives of people who visit them. They allow the website to recognize returning visitors and, in some cases, even include information on their prior actions on the site.

5. The poll results were widely reported. For more, see news.yahoo.com/page/ election-2008-political-pulse-candidates.

6. "Obama Responds to Crush," *Des Moines Register,* June 19, 2007.

7. Obama's use of Twitter is another example of his team's deep understanding of Internet culture. He not only had 60,000 followers, his campaign staff ensured he appeared to be following even more Twitter users. That is, "he" subscribed to their Twitter feeds, demonstrating that he knows how the application works and that he wants communication to be two-way.

8. Jonathan Salem Baskin, "Conversations Need to Yield Actions Measured in Dollars," *Advertising Age,* July 7, 2008.

9. See Jenkins's blog entry for February 18, 2008, www.HenryJenkins.org/ 2008/02 (accessed July 23, 2008).

10. See Karl Rove, "Barack's Brilliant Ground Game," *Wall Street Journal,* July 10, 2008. To be fair, while expressing admiration for many of Obama's campaign techniques, many of which he claimed were cribbed from Bush's previous campaigns, Rove said Obama would ultimately lose to John McCain.

11. John P. Avlon is the author of *Independent Nation: How Centrists Can Change American Politics* (New York: Three Rivers Press, 2005). He served as chief speechwriter and deputy policy director for Rudy Giuliani's presidential campaign. This quote is from a piece he wrote for Politico.com on August 24, 2008, "A Generation Rises with Obama," which argues that Obama is the first Generation-X candidate. See www.politico.com/news/ stories/0808/12763_Page2.html (accessed August 25, 2008).

Index